KU-546-782

FRANCE TODAY

LANGUAGES
CENTRE

NEW

ILLUSTRATED
7th EDITION

Edited by J E Flower

Hodder & Stoughton

LONDON SYDNEY AUCKLAND

British Library Cataloguing in Publication Data

France Today.—7Rev.ed.
I. Flower, J. E.
944.083

ISBN 0-340-55752-4

First published 1993
Impression number 10 9 8 7 6 5 4 3 2 1
Year   1998 1997 1996 1995 1994 1993

Typeset by Rowland Phototypesetting Ltd,
Bury St Edmunds, Suffolk.
Printed in Great Britain for the educational publishing division of Hodder &
Stoughton Ltd, Mill Road, Dunton Green, Sevenoaks, Kent TN13 2YA by
Clays Ltd, St Ives plc, Bungay

FRANCE TODAY

Contents

Acknowledgements vi
Contributors vii
Foreword to the seventh edition ix

1 Social Structures 1
Andrée Shepherd

2 Political Parties 36
Malcolm Slater

3 Trade Unions 71
Richard McAllister

4 Immigration 99
Brian Fitzpatrick

5 Foreign Policy 126
Alan Clark and Robert Elgie

6 Education 156
Roger Duclaud-Williams

7 Religion 186
John Flower

8 The Press 207
Ray Davison

9 The Broadcasting Media 238
Geoffrey Hare

Index 271

Acknowledgements

The publishers are grateful to the following copyright holders for permission to use copyright material in this book:

Photographs:
L'Etablissement public EPAMARNE and photographer E. Morency (p 4); Zefa Picture Library (UK) Ltd (p 32); Sygma (photographer: Jacques Langevin) (p 38); Topham Picture Source (pp 83 and 213); Pierre Domenech (p 110); Hulton Deutsch Collection (p 164); A. de Anrade/Ana (p 180); J. E. Flower (p 188).

Artwork:
L'Express, distributed by *New York Times* Syndication Sales (p 116, redrawn by Taurus Graphics); Plantu (p 145); Serguei (p 152); l'Association 15 août 1989 (p 196); André Barbe (p 210).

Tables:
Ministère de l'Intérieur (pp 42, 43 and 104); *Société française d'études par sondages* (SOFRES) (p 51); *Ministère du Travail, de l'Emploie et de la Formation professionnelle* (pp 105 and 106); *Ministère des Affaires sociales et de l'Intégration* (p 106); *Office français de Protection des Refugiés et Apatrides* (p 107); *L'Express*, distributed by *New York Times* Syndication Sales (p 118); Presses universitaires de Lille (pp 158–9); *Ministère de l'Education nationale et de la Culture* (p 172); *Le Monde* (p 255, redrawn by Taurus Graphics).

Every effort has been made to trace and acknowledge ownership of copyright. The publishers will be glad to make suitable arrangements with any copyright holders whom it has not been possible to contact.

The cover photograph shows *la géode* at the *Cité des Sciences et de l'Industrie* at La Villette, Paris (Tony Stone Associates).

Contributors

ALAN CLARK, B.A., Ph.D., Senior Lecturer in French, University of Canterbury, Christchurch, New Zealand. Main interests: French literature; intellectual, social and political history of the twentieth century; ideas and policies of the French left; the history and politics of New Caledonia. Publications include *La France dans l'histoire selon Bernanos* (Lettres Modernes), an edition of Valéry Giscard d'Estaing's *La Démocratie française* (Methuen/Routledge) and of *Anthologie Mitterrand* (Methuen/Routledge). He has written numerous articles and broadcast extensively on French foreign and Pacific policy.

RAY DAVISON, B.A., M.Phil., Lecturer in French Studies at the University of Exeter. Main interests: modern French literature and thought. Publications include critical editions of Camus's *L'Etranger* (Methuen/Routledge), Simone de Beauvoir's *Une mort très douce* (Methuen/Routledge), and a contribution to *The Second World War in Fiction* (Macmillan). He has also written on Camus and Dostoevsky and made a number of tapes for Drake Educational Tapes on Sartre, Gide and Camus.

ROGER DUCLAUD-WILLIAMS, B.A., Ph.D., Lecturer in the Department of Politics and International Studies at the University of Warwick. Publications include *Politics of Housing in Britain and France* (Heinemann), and more recently articles on various aspects of French educational policy-making in *The British Journal of Political Science*, *Western European Politics* and *The European Journal of Political Research*.

ROBERT ELGIE, B.A., Ph.D., Lecturer in Politics in the Department of European Studies, Loughborough University of Technology. Main interests: contemporary French politics; political leadership in west European states. Publications include *The Role of the Prime Minister in France, 1981–91* (Macmillan); articles in *Governance*, *West European Politics*, *Modern and Contemporary France*. He has also written on Christian Democracy in France.

BRIAN FITZPATRICK, M.A., Ph.D., Lecturer in Modern European History in the University of Ulster at Jordanstown. Main interests: nineteenth-century conservative and counter-revolutionary groups in France and Spain. Publications include *Catholic Royalism in the Département du Gard, 1814–1852* (Cambridge), 'L'Ultrarealisme francès del Midi i les seves contradiccions internes' in J. M. Fradera and R. Garrabou, eds, *Carlisme i Moviments absolutistes* (Estudis Universitaris, Vic, Catalunya), 'Ultraroyalism and Legitimism in the French Midi' in J. Aggirreazkuenaga and J. R. Urquijo Goitia, eds, *150 Años del Convenio de Bergara y de La Ley del 25-X-1839* (Parlamento Vasco, Vitoria), 'The emergence of Catholic politics in the

Midi, 1830–1870' in F. Tallett and N. Atkin, eds, *Religion, Society and Politics in France since 1789* (The Hambledon Press).

JOHN FLOWER, M.A., Ph.D., Chevalier des Palmes Académiques, Professor of French, University of Exeter. Main interests: French literature and history of ideas from late nineteenth century to the present. Most recent publications include *Literature and the Left in France since the Late Nineteenth Century* (Macmillan and Methuen), *Provence* and *Lombardy and the Italian Lakes* (George Philip), *François Mauriac: Visions and Reappraisals* (with B. C. Swift) (Berg), and an edition of the correspondence between François Mauriac and Jacques Rivière. General Editor of the *Journal of European Studies*.

GEOFFREY HARE, B.A. Ph.D., Senior Lecturer in French Studies, University of Newcastle-upon-Tyne. Main interests: media studies and political communications, and methodology of language teaching. Publications include: *Alphonse Daudet: a Critical Bibliography* (Grant & Cutler), *Parlons Sciences Po* and *Parlons Sciences Po '89* (British Institute in Paris), *Media Studies in France: a Guide to Sources of Information* (with A. Chauveau) (Kingston Polytechnic), *Communicative Approaches in French in Higher Education* (with M. Bate) (AFLS), and *Le français en faculté* (with nine others) (Hodder & Stoughton); contributions to journals *Francophonie*, *French Cultural Studies* and *Modern and Contemporary France*.

RICHARD McALLISTER, M.A., Senior Lecturer in Politics, University of Edinburgh. Main interests: the politics and policies of the European Community: politics of certain west European states, notably France and Germany. Publications include the regular Annual Review of the Activities of the EC for *Journal of Common Market Studies*; contributions to several books including R. Davidson & P. White (eds) *Information and Government* (Edinburgh University Press); articles in *Common Market Law Review, Futures*, and *The New Atlantis*. Work completed on historical and political survey of the EC; and working on jointly-authored book on the EC's institutions and policies.

ANDRÉE SHEPHERD, L. ès L., Agrégée d'Anglais, Lecturer in English, University of Tours. Main interests: twentieth-century French and English sociology and politics. Publications include a study of the occupation of French factories in May 1968, *Imagination in Power* (Spokesman Books), a translation of Serge Mallet's book *The New Working Class* (Spokesman Books), and contributions to the *Encyclopédie de civilisation britannique* (Larousse) and *Littérature anglaise* (Bordas). Research in progress on New Left in Britain.

MALCOLM SLATER, M.A., B.Sc. (Econ.), LL. B., Lecturer in French, University of Bradford. Main interests: French foreign policy, European Community politics. Recent publications include *Contemporary French Politics* (Macmillan).

Foreword to the seventh edition

As winter moved into spring in France in 1993 one of the few bright spots which focused much national attention was the progress of the three football clubs – Auxerre, PSG and Olympique-Marseille – in European competitions. But Europe otherwise was not a subject to arouse unanimous enthusiasm and opposition to the Treaty of Maastricht continued to be led vociferously by politicians such as Charles Pasqua or Philippe Seguin. On the domestic front, discontent with issues like immigration, unemployment, the threats real or imagined posed by German unity or by Islam, a rising cost of living and a national currency under threat despite massive support from the German government, and the relevations of financial scandals involving government ministers, all helped to fuel a crisis of confidence. Early in 1992 it had already become apparent that desire for a change and support for the right were growing apace and that the government had few answers. Moreover, feuding and disputes within the socialist ranks and the jockeying for position as potential candidates kept their eyes on the presidential elections in 1995 did not help. As the general elections of March 1993 approached, the only matters of speculation were not whether the right would win but by how big a majority and how the new Assembly would be constituted.

For a while some supporters of the government saw a glimmer of hope in a rising ecology vote and even in some possible negotiations in the second ballot. Michel Rocard produced his theory of 'Le Big-Bang', a dissolution of traditional lines of political demarcation and a new kind of consensus politics. And only days before the first ballot Salman Rushdie was suddenly produced by Jack Lang, Minister for Culture and Education, like a rabbit out of a hat, to hold a conference with writers and intellectuals in that presidential monument the *Grande Arche* at *La Défense* – as though this could indicate to people the government's concern for real problems even in a period of crisis, and thereby persuade them to think again before casting their votes. But this was all to no avail. The results of the election give the right – predominantly the RPR and the UDF – a majority which is without precedent in the history of the Republic. There has also been a significant increase in the support for the extreme right-wing *Front national*. And a number of socialist ministers – Rocard, Dumas and Jospin – have all lost their seats. What is more, with Mitterrand still able to continue as President for a further two years (despite calls from some quarters – notably from Jacques Chirac – for his resignation), another period of 'cohabitation' is inevitable and one that is likely to be more painful than the last. But as Mitterrand continues, his impassive exterior gives little hint of what he is thinking or planning. He is even strongly rumoured to have enjoyed his customary Monday round of golf on the day after the first ballot. The next two or three years, therefore, will be critical for France in a number of ways and only time will tell whether the alarmist noises uttered by the outgoing government about such crucial matters as immigration, social benefits, medical care or education will be seen to be justified.

All the chapters of *France Today* have been substantially or completely revised so that, as far as possible, this new seventh edition gives a rounded picture of the *état actuel des choses* in the early 1990s. It is therefore the most up-to-date volume of its kind currently available. (Students and observers of modern France will no doubt be aware that another publication which had originally appeared under different titles had in its most recent edition, in 1987, adopted that of *France Today*, a decision which may cause confusion.) Those already familiar with earlier editions of this volume will note that our publishers have changed, as have several of the contributors. My personal thanks go to all concerned as well as to those who have contributed so willingly and knowledgeably to *France Today* in the past.

John Flower
Exeter, March 1993

1

Social Structures
Andrée Shepherd

Introduction

French society today can no longer be neatly divided into the traditional units of ruling class, middle class, working class and peasantry. During the last hundred years in particular, wars and social unrest, demographic change and developments in industry, science and technology, have all helped to create a kind of uniformity and standardization which makes any clear-cut divisions of this nature difficult. This trend has also been emphasized by the evolution of the more traditional institutions of society – the Church, the family, the educational system and even military service. French society has changed, and is still changing, a fact which has been recognized in social legislation and in a number of important administrative reforms, such as the breakdown of excessive centralization and the creation of twenty-two regions as increasingly autonomous units, each with an appointed head (the *préfet*), an elected regional assembly (the *Conseil régional*) and its own budget. Essential social and cultural services are now administered on a regional level. Much remains to be done, however, and the economic crisis still weighs on the future.

Population

Today, France has 56.6 million inhabitants including some 4.4 million foreigners – less than 8 per cent of the total. With low birth and death rates and with legal immigration now at a standstill, the population is still increasing but at a much slower rate. By the year 2000 it is expected to reach only 58 million. During the last fifty years French governments have been in favour of larger families – the *Code de la Famille* was first drafted in 1939 though not put into effect until after the Second World War and, more recently, there have been campaigns to encourage couples to have three rather than two children. However, in spite of government incentives (in the form of increased benefits and allowances for families with three or more children), the birth rate has fallen to 1.4 (which is below replacement level), and family-forming habits seem to have settled into a stable pattern: people marry later, divorce more (one in six marriages ends in divorce) but tend to remarry and have two rather than three children, or even fewer. Except perhaps in working-class and immigrant groups, large families are very much a thing of the past. With increasing numbers of women at work (often in low-paid, insecure and part-time jobs), there seems to be little chance of a reversal of recent trends, and the present balance between the 24.4 million economically active (out of which, in 1990, 2.2 million were unemployed, with numbers rising to almost 3 million in early 1993) and the thirty million or so dependent members of the population is unlikely to improve. Almost one in every three people is still under twenty and one in five, over sixty: with more time spent in education, earlier retirement and steadily increasing unemployment, there is bound to be a mounting burden on health, social and educational services.

A large proportion of the population lives in towns – 75 per cent in towns of over 2,000 people compared with 40 per cent in 1900 – and the migration from countryside to town continues at a faster rate than ever before. But even more significant is the fact that the population has become tripartite: 16 million in towns proper, 25 million in suburbs and *grandes banlieues*, and the remaining 16 million spread over a countryside of about 500,000 sq.km. This growing suburbia has created new challenges and new problems. The architectural horror of Sarcelles, north of Paris, for example, brought with it fresh social problems. The very existence of this kind of dormitory-suburb, catering for vast numbers of industrial and office workers, has had unexpected consequences, one of which is a growing tendency to introduce the continuous working day, which was anathema to French workers used to one or two hour lunch breaks. A solution may be to develop these distant suburbs into viable economic units. From 1956 to 1965, Sarcelles grew from 8,400 to 30,000 inhabitants, a *grand ensemble* with no life of its own. Socio-cultural facilities have gradually changed it into a proper town. Sarcelles in 1990, with its population of some 56,000 inhabitants, regional commercial centre, industrial development zone and municipal bus service, no longer relies on Paris, although it is only nine miles away. A few miles to the west the 'new town' of Cergy Pontoise is still expanding around new factories, office blocks, schools and colleges in an attempt to avoid previous mistakes, but so far, with only limited results. Together with the other eight 'new towns' in France – five of them in the Paris area – Cergy Pontoise still suffers from the rapidity of its growth rate and its close proximity to the capital. Another problem is the change in the overall plan, especially in the development of the Paris area: originally the five 'new towns' (Marne-la-Vallée, Melun-Sénart, Saint-Quentin-en-Yvelines, Evry and Cergy Pontoise) were supposed to be large autonomous units, close to, but not too dependent on, Paris. Together, they now have 600,000 inhabitants and are seen as an integral part of a restructured greater Paris with its fast suburban RER network. By the year 2000, the capital will be a megalopolis of 14 million inhabitants.

The massive exodus of French people from the land towards the expanding towns has meant a radical change in the distribution of the population between agricultural and other activities: over the last fifty years, the number of people employed in agriculture has decreased from 25 per cent to less than 6 per cent of the active population today, while the professionals and *cadres*, grew from 9 to 20 per cent. This points to a large-scale reorganization of the socio-economic structure. A direct comparison between agriculture and

SAINT-QUENTIN-EN-YVELINES
ESPACE ET MODERNITE

CERGY PONTOISE
UNE VILLE BIEN DANS SON TEMPS

MARNE-LA-VALEE
Un nouvel art de vivre

industry (still strong, with 30 per cent of the population in blue-collar jobs in 1989) leaves aside the most important sector of activity, known as the tertiary sector – transport, distribution and services. Today, this 'non-productive' sector (which accounts for almost two-thirds of the active population) is still growing apace: most of the new jobs are in non-manual occupations and are filled by an increasing proportion of women. Industrial growth is still greatly impaired by the effects of successive economic crises, with large-scale redundancies resulting from restructuring in all the major industries. A further factor is the regional imbalance between the hard-hit areas in the North and in Lorraine and the still developing regions – the Ile-de-France around Paris, the Rhônes-Alpes area and the southern regions of Provence-Alpes-Côte d'Azur. A continuation of these trends because of further technological change, mechanization and rationalization is leading to a society in which only a minority will be directly involved in production, with the majority occupied in administrative and servicing activities. The division between manual and non-manual workers has become more marked, leading to a greater proletarianization of a smaller manual working class, the increasing marginalization of the unemployed (many of them young people) and growing social unrest. With a large number of people facing redundancy, and in spite of retraining facilities, the wealth created by automation will only heighten the problem of inequality and a new class of 'unemployables' will emerge. The expression 'Fourth World' (*le Quart-Monde*) has been coined to refer to the growing social group living mostly in twilight zones surrounding the large conurbations. Around Paris, Lyon and Marseille, for example, the combination of suburban dilapidation with large-scale youth unemployment has meant that rioting has become so frequent an occurrence that the first Edith Cresson cabinet placed a minister in charge of urban development and widened the definition of the Minister of Social Affairs' task to include 'integration' of the immigrant population. Such administrative changes point to an assumption that the pressures of urban living are heightened by the presence of immigrant minorities which are often only too readily accused of being the cause of the outbursts of violence. However, the immigrant community proper does not represent a higher percentage of the total French population than it did ten years ago: many of the young *Beurs* are French-born and educated. Even though they remain identifiable as belonging to a racial minority, their integration into a youth culture which cuts across racial barriers is undeniable. The Saturday night 'rodeos' with 'borrowed' cars, and the looting incidents in suburban hypermarkets and shopping precincts in the spring of 1991 which led to violent clashes with gun-carrying guards and to police intervention, caused a number of casualties and aroused public concern. Hopefully, these events will provide the impetus for change: increased public expenditure channelled into those areas will lead to improved housing, educational and training facilities, making the suburbs 'safer' places for the whole population and preventing the development of a ghetto mentality.

Country v. town

Where have all the peasants gone?

France can no longer be described as a nation of small farmers, as the widely used phrase 'the death of the peasantry' indicates. The French farmers' lobby still carries weight in Brussels even though there are fewer farmers. This does not mean that the countryside has become a desert: moving away from agriculture has not necessarily meant moving out of the countryside. Many former farmers have only moved a short distance away to the nearest market town in search of a job, or even continue to live in their village and commute to work. Many families are now earning only part of their income from the land. The husband may, for example, remain a farmer but a supplementary (and regular) income is provided by his wife who has become a shop assistant, or by his sons and daughters who work as nurses, secretaries or factory workers. This may not be by choice, but rather out of necessity, since small family farms are no longer viable economic units. Many small farmers and agricultural workers are among the poorest in the

French community, while the regrouping of land, modernization of farming methods and judicious reconversion to intensive fruit, cereal or meat production has enabled the few (who may also draw high profits from the Common Market) to become very wealthy indeed.

Whether or not they are still deriving their income from the land, villagers can no longer be sharply distinguished from the rest of the population in their way of life. In the 1960s they became bitterly aware of the fact that, far from being protected by the welfare state, they had not joined the consumer society and were not receiving their fair share of the national income in spite of the fact that they were doing more than their fair share: harder work, longer hours, lack of cultural facilities and modern conveniences were their lot. This is no longer the case and, increasingly, village, suburb and town-dwellers alike watch television, own a car and do their Saturday shopping in a neighbouring hypermarket. They may not all yet have a bathroom or an indoor toilet, but they have a deep-freeze (well-stocked with home-produced as well as pre-packed food) and a washing-machine. In the last twenty years, country life has in fact become an attraction for former town-dwellers who are no longer weekend migrants, but have turned what was originally a weekend cottage (a *résidence secondaire*) into their permanent home and commute daily from their rural home. The farming community has become a minority on its home ground, and village life has often been transformed out of recognition by these 'neo-villagers' who have sometimes captured key positions on local councils.

Generalizations are, of course, dangerous: historians and sociologists have repeatedly demonstrated through case studies that the contrast between town and countryside within a given area is less striking than the extreme regional differences. The great plains of the Paris basin with their rich crops of wheat and intensive farming, the mixed-crop farming of Brittany and the Rhône valley, the vine-growing areas and the mountain deserts of central France present widely differing problems and prospects. The healthy areas seem to be of two kinds: the capitalist type of intensive farming, and the more traditional type of mixed farming, which by increasingly involving co-operative enterprise, fulfils the need for skilful crop rotation and the division of labour. The extension of the Common Market to include vegetable and fruit-producing Mediterranean countries has made the situation of some French farmers more difficult because of new competition. Future prospects are certainly favourable given certain conditions: namely, large farms; concentration on products in high demand like good quality wine; sufficient organization (co-operatives); and well-planned marketing. In some favoured areas like the Côte d'Or, the agricultural labour force (vineyard labour) earns salaries comparable to those of the Dijon factories nearby. In less prosperous areas, like Brittany, however, some poultry farmers are worse off than industrial labourers. A large firm may deliver day-old chicks and chicken food and impose precise planning. After nine weeks the chickens are collected for slaughtering. The farmer is a home-labourer paid to work according to conditions laid down by the firm. He may own his poultry farm, but this is probably a liability as he is usually tied down by debts and is entirely dependent on the firm employing him. Some poultry farmers have managed to organize themselves into co-operatives, but these are exceptions. For the majority of the smaller farmers, proletarianization has reached the countryside in a brutal form, and even in the richer Rhône valley there are increasing tendencies for the farmers to contract with freezing and canning firms like the American firm, Libby's. All too often, the farmers' share of the profits is a minor one, and agricultural incomes vary even more than industrial ones. Over the last decade, competition within the European Community and Community regulations have been influential in making French agriculture evolve and become a prosperous export industry deriving just under half its income from cattle and poultry farms and dairy produce, the remaining income deriving from the production of cereals, fruit and vegetable and industrial crops. France exports more than it imports, three-quarters of the exports being directed at EC countries. The average agricultural income, however, points to continuing regional inequalities – top of the league are the Champagne-Ardennes area, the Ile-de-France and Burgundy areas, which fare twice as well as Brittany, the

Franche-Comté and the Rhône-Alpes areas, and four times as well-off as the poorer Massif Central and Corsica.

In the last forty years or so, a certain amount of government planning has been introduced to improve the lot of rural communities, very often in answer to growing unrest and insistent demands by younger farmers who first began to organize themselves in the early 1950s around a Catholic youth organization, the JAC (*Jeunesse agricole chrétienne*). From Bible meetings and socials to study groups on accountancy and farming techniques, they developed a growing awareness of their lack of formal schooling and absence of cultural facilities. They soon openly entered the trade union arena, led by Michel Debatisse, who had coined the phrase 'the silent revolution of the peasants' to describe their aim. The main farmers' union, the FNSEA (*Féderation nationale des syndicats d'exploitants agricoles*) was controlled by the older, richer, conservative farmers. But its moribund youth section, the CNJA (*Centre national des jeunes agriculteurs*) could be revived. They took it over and gradually captured key posts in the trade union movement, while using their position as a platform to advocate new policies. They claim peasant unity is a myth, that there are rich and poor farmers whose interests are different. They admit that the rural exodus is normal – most of the small family farms are not economically viable – but they want it to be 'humanized' by the provision of proper training facilities. They insist on the importance of maintaining prices and act as a powerful pressure group to influence EC negotiations, but also wish to give greater importance to structural reforms (land and marketing) Finally, they question the sacred principle of property ownership and individualism: 'The fishermen do not own the sea. Why do we need to own the land?' They have started implementing their own proposals by renting rather than owning their farms, by establishing group enterprises for marketing and shared production, by introducing computerized farm management, by supporting the government agency set up for buying land and letting it in order to prevent speculation and by encouraging the regrouping of land (parcelled as a result of equal inheritance laws dating back to Napoleon). The movement has not always been peaceful, however. There were notorious riots in Brittany in 1961, for example, when ballot boxes were burned, and there are still frequent demonstrations by farmers and vine-growers disrupting car traffic on roads and motorways. Constant petitioning of the government has been effective; greater concentration and specialization has also had some benefit; agricultural schools and training have been developed, with the added concern of environmental protection in recent years, regional investments are co-ordinated and government grants are given to young farmers willing to settle in depopulated areas. Loans for equipment are now easier to obtain and the old-style co-operatives have federated into vast units and modernized their methods. There are also industries contracting out work over large areas of the countryside. This *saupoudrage industriel*, as it is called, provides regular work for women at home or winter occupation for the whole family, but this has tended to decrease in recent years as industrial restructuring affected the industries concerned: watch-making in the Jura, textiles in the Loire, footwear around Cholet and cutlery in the Lozère. Another drawback is that it frequently leads to the exploitation of cheap labour.

Finally, the extension of tourism has brought a new lease of life to areas which are often beautiful but deserted (mountainous areas in particular). But the development of the tourist potential must provide new jobs (as ski instructors or in the hotels in the mountains) if the local youth is to stay in the village and earn a proper and regular wage, while in the coastal areas those responsible for development must beware of ecological – and architectural – disasters. The growth of the tourist industry, if properly controlled by local communities rather than by capitalist sharks, may help provide extra income and facilities for country folk while answering the need of town-dwellers for open-air leisure activities and rest – thus further bridging the gap between the 'two nations'.

Paris and the French desert

And yet, it remains traditional to underline both the contrast between town and country and the divorce between Paris and the provinces – a metropolis in 'the French desert'. Taine put it in a nutshell as long ago as 1863:

> There are two peoples in France, the provinces and Paris: the former dines, sleeps, yawns, listens; the latter thinks, dares, wakes and talks; the one dragged by the other like a snail by a butterfly, now amused now worried by the capriciousness and audacity of its leader.

As the focus of national life in France, Paris is unrivalled and the Parisian has a somewhat haughty attitude towards anybody who does not belong there. This is somehow surprising to outside observers who happen to know that while one in every five Frenchmen lives in Paris or the Paris region, relatively few have been established in the capital for more than a generation, and one in five Parisians is a foreigner. In spite of the pressure of life in the capital, the constant rush and noise (one million commuters spend two or more hours travelling to and from work every day) the still desperate housing situation, and the very high cost of living, the prestige and desirability of life there were unaltered until recently. Stifled by cars which encroach even on the pavements, much of the old Paris is being demolished and replaced by tall tower blocks, or tastefully renovated at high cost, thus driving the original slum inhabitants into the distant suburbs. With the extension of the underground outwards and the creation of fast RER lines, there has been a definite move to the outskirts of the city – a phenomenon which is true of all large towns – and since 1968 the number of provincials moving into the capital has consistently been smaller than the number of Parisians moving away.

Just as it is a social centre, so, too, is Paris an intellectual one: with *grandes écoles*, specialist schools, its thirteen university campuses and its flood of students it contrasts sharply with quieter provincial university towns. But is prestige necessarily matched by excellence? Certainly it appears to be so. In a centralized and fiercely competitive system, a Paris appointment is often seen as a promotion for teachers, as indeed for most civil servants; and students compete for places in the *grandes écoles* which are still more often to be found in the Paris conurbation than outside. Paris used also to be considered the world's cultural capital. It is still a very lively but expensive centre. Many of the new films are now released in provincial towns at the same time (and often at cheaper prices) as on the Champs-Elysées or the Boulevards. The decentralization policy for the arts has enabled provincial theatre companies to survive and the increasing number of summer festivals, such as the one in Aix or Avignon, has made culture available to more provincials than ever before, though often at such a high price that many lower-paid people are effectively debarred from enjoying it.

With industry the situation is similar and, in spite of efforts to decentralize, the city is bursting at the seams. Tax rebates are awarded to industries moving outside the Paris area. Thus, between 1968 and 1975, half a million new jobs were created in provincial cities, and government incentives are still helping to create jobs in manufacturing, especially in the small and medium-sized firms (PME). Just as Paris, with its 2.2 million inhabitants, has lost out to its satellite towns, so have large provincial cities like Lyon or Lille served as poles of attraction and developed faster-growing surburban towns like Villeurbanne (117,000 inhabitants, in 1990) or Villeneuve-d'Asq (now over 65,000). Thus Marseille (1.1. million) moves from second to third place (after the Lyon complex, with almost 1.3 million) when the conurbation is taken into account, but neither can compare with the 9 million of the metropolis. With only three other cities numbering over 500,000 (Lille, Bordeaux, Toulouse) and another eleven over 300,000, this shows a lack of balance greater than in most neighbouring European countries.

Efforts to fight the growing suffocation of Paris have been extended by a policy of regionalism – a positive effort to adapt to the requirements of contemporary life and needs. It has involved the formation of viable and autonomous economic units, rather than being a negative rejection of the arbitrary division into *départements* and a resulting return to historical provinces. The ninety-five departments have thus been grouped into twenty-two economic regions, the eight largest towns have been singled out as *métropoles d'équilibre*, and the first regional councils were elected in 1986. The regions are now asserting themselves politically and administratively, and are beginning to develop their own economic policy with their advisory economic and social council. But the economic imbalance remains great, and real industrial decentralization is proving difficult. Too many Paris-based firms are setting up one or even several factories in the provinces while retaining their headquarters in Paris. As a result, decisions are often taken in Paris without enough direct knowledge of local conditions. Regional development is bound to improve as the regions develop their own identity and even establish links with other regions in the EC, helped by better road and rail communications between towns with the extension of the 'bullet train' links (like the Lille-Paris-Lyon-Marseille TGV and the *TGV Atlantique*), and by greater specialization of each industrial centre to avoid costly competition within one region. However, the *question régionale* still remains, with its political, economic and cultural undertones, because of the enormous differences in size and wealth between the richest (Ile-de-France and Rhône-Alpes) and the much poorer Limousin or Corsica. Regional cultures and languages, which the introduction of compulsory schooling and the imposition of the French language had helped to destroy, are being revived, for example in the south and Brittany. Nationalist, political or religious minorities act as pressure groups, attempting to restructure local communities. This quest for local, regional roots may be part of a search for identity in a mass society in which so many local and traditional features have been ironed out.

Young and old, men and women

In the early 1960s, the cult of youth invaded advertising, fashion and the entertainment and holiday industries. And *les jeunes* were the basis of France's faith in its political and economic future. This faith was shaken by the explosion of May 1968 when young workers and students were suddenly seen as a threat to the establishment. Until then rebellious minorities had largely been ignored by the wider public. Even pop culture was tame. It was the reign of '*les copains* walking hand in hand' and listening to Françoise Hardy and Johnny Halliday on their transistor radios – nothing resembling the wild English or American crowds. They were on the whole conforming to accepted patterns of behaviour. The more culturally aware formed the audience for Georges Brassens, Juliette Gréco and other upholders of the poetical or the political tradition of the *chansons*; the more politically minded were militant in innocuous-looking *groupuscules* torn by in-fighting.

Rebellious youth was brought to the fore in May 1968 – untamed university and secondary school students, un-organized union militants all defying the establishment. They questioned authority in all its manifestations and won some concessions. Student unrest of that magnitude has receded, but protest continues to simmer under the surface as the 1986 widespread demonstrations indicate, and this will remain the case as long as educational reforms remain inadequate. In a labour market dominated by unemployment, which neces-sarily hits hard the least-qualified youngsters, there will be youth revolts due to the crisis, especially among the suburban poor.

Today, in spite of the successive youth employment schemes, over 40 per cent of the unemployed, among whom two-thirds are women, are under twenty-five. Worse still, according to the *Agence nationale pour l'Emploi* (ANPE), 35 per cent are still unemployed after six months, the jobs they find are often temporary (*emplois intérimaires*), and unqualified school-leavers only represent a small proportion of those who gain admission to one of the government schemes – a situation which the Socialist government is still trying to remedy by reviving special training schemes and offering firms rebates for each young trainee they take on. However, a hard core of unqualified young unemployed is emerging and it is hardly surprising that suicide and criminal rates are increasing. But accusations of apathy, rejection of adult values or downright laziness are misguided for a number of reasons. These accusa-tions both ignore educational and social disparities (a univer-sity graduate has three times more chance than an unqualified school leaver of finding a first job), and fail to acknowledge the fact that most young people still share the same values as their elders. Recent opinion polls and government reports alike paint a more positive picture: most young people do not reject their own family and wish to have one of their own; they want to work and are worried about their prospects in a society which only offers them insecure and uninteresting jobs with no prospects of obtaining further qualifications. Work, there-fore, is no longer the central value in their life since it will bring them neither satisfaction nor social recognition: their questioning of traditional hierarchical models, of repetitive fragmented tasks, their demand for greater autonomy and a sense of purpose are aspirations they share with many adult workers. They did not invent the consumer society, they were born with it and want to join it – though it may be true to say that they prefer spending their money on going to concerts or buying stereo equipment rather than a colour television or a new settee. And their life styles often imply different values, rather than a rejection of all values: cohabitation before marriage is widespread and may be read as the sign of a search for marital harmony and true respect for marriage itself.

One reason for the tension between young and old may be that adults fear the approach of old age. While earlier retire-ment (at sixty) is welcomed by those for whom work has been synonymous with physical strain, repetitive tasks, noise and long hours, those who find fulfilment in their job are often loath to retire. Nevertheless, there are already signs that retirement no longer means relinquishing an active social life: pensioners have their own clubs (*clubs du troisième âge*), travel, take up university courses and enjoy leisure activities – all the more so when they receive a decent pension and have not been worn out by a life of toil. Moreover, the pensioners of today are the last pre-war generation of workers; the grandparents of tomorrow will have spent their active life in the prosperous 1950s and will probably not have the same value systems. With its aging population, French society must adapt to the new distinction between the 'younger pensioners' and the 'very old' (*le quatrième âge*) for whom isolation and health will remain the main problems.

Women, both young and old, are claiming their place in French society. Fairly recently, legislation granted them formal equality with men: joint choice of the matrimonial home (1965), freedom to work, open a bank account and own property without the need for the husband's consent (1965), equal pay (1972), protection from sex discrimination (1975), birth control (contraception and abortion Acts of 1974 and 1975), divorce reform (1975). Yet French women, who now represent over 43 per cent of the workforce, constitute a majority of unskilled industrial jobs, while in white-collar occupations (where they are mostly concentrated) they still rarely rise to a position commanding responsibility and initiative. As a result, they remain lower paid (in the proportion of two to one in the lowest wages and of one to seven for the highest), and are twice as likely to become unemployed. Such inequalities were officially recognized in 1981 with the appointment of a Minister for Women's Rights who in the early 1990s is campaigning for better protection against violence and improved living conditions.

Some observers are quick to point out that, paradoxically, women may have lost more than they gained by leaving their home for the world of work: the subordinates of men at work, they have also lost 'control' over the home since the domestic tasks are often shared – though often unequally – and they may well have the worst of both worlds. Yet most women, except perhaps the unskilled labourers, claim that having a job has meant an overall improvement in their lives, and many young mothers choose to continue working after the birth of their first child, helped by much better nursery provisions than in Britain. Thereafter, however, economic and practical difficulties may force a choice between outside employment and the birth of a second or third baby. But for over 3 of the 9 million women at work, there is little freedom of choice: they are single wage-earners, many of them with dependent children. Though still a minority in militant trade unions, political or cultural organisations, they are beginning to assert themselves. Opinion is divided as to the social consequences of these continuing trends.

Social classes

The general improvement in the standard of living, the development of hire-purchase and changing patterns of consumption in the (relatively) affluent society have caused a blurring of former class distinctions. The family car and the television set have entered working-class homes, holidays are no longer the privilege of the rich and even home ownership is spreading (55 per cent of the population), though it is still less common than in England. Could this mean a destruction of class barriers and the end of the struggle for control and power which were the hallmark of pre-war French society, with its powerful working class and strong Communist Party? The language of the class struggle may have changed; but it does not necessarily mean that a classless society is emerging.

Wealth and income

Between 1950 and 1980, the purchasing power of the average annual wage has more than trebled, but progression in the 1980s has been very slow. The introduction, in 1968, of the index-linked minimum wage – the SMIC (*salaire minimum interprofessionnel de croissance*) – has helped to reduce the gap between high salaries and low wages: a gap which is still greater in France than in any other European country except Italy. In 1981, a comparison between the top and bottom 10 per cent of the salaried workers showed a ratio of one to fifteen over 34,000 francs (about £3,000) a month for *cadres supérieurs*, less than 2,200 francs (about £200) for unskilled manual workers – a ratio which, according to the INSEE (*Institut national de la statistique et des études économiques*), was still the same in 1985. Even more serious is the fact that, since 1976, the growth of wages has hardly kept pace with the cost of living; in 1989, the improvement in the purchasing power of salaried workers was 0.1 per cent only. And for the period 1986–89, an official report recorded a stagnation for salaried workers, while the incomes derived from private enterprise and investment continued to grow (by 6.1 per cent and 7.7 per cent respectively for the year 1989). Low paid workers are among the new poor and below them, excluded from the consumer society, we find the 'submerged' – the unemployed, the old, the immigrants and the handicapped who barely survive on social security.

At the other end of the social scale, the wealthy *grande bourgeoisie* still possesses considerable power and influence, particularly in the *Chambre des députés* (the legislative assembly) and in the civil service, especially, for example, in the Foreign Office. The economic rule of this class remains undisputed, though the frequency of mergers and takeovers by foreign firms (American and Japanese in particular) caused signs of strain to appear. In the educational, social and cultural spheres, its influence is less marked. State education which is fairly democratic (but perhaps more formally than truly democratic), has almost completely escaped its grasp; but it still controls élite recruitment through private education and the prestigious *grandes écoles*. There is an ever-widening gap between the very rich and the very poor, but if we exclude the two extremes, we may agree with Peter Wiles's comment in his survey of the evolution of disposable income per household carried out for the OECD: 'France is more equal than she thinks'.

The working class

The traditional condition of the working class has changed considerably in the last fifty years. The growth of unionization, the system of social security and the increasing mechanization of industry, leading to an overall higher level of training and skill, have certainly improved the lot of the workers. However, some problems remain and still more are heightened. There is a particular sense of insecurity at a time when many industries are under threat: mining and steel, as in Britain, are declining; the car industry is shaken by regular crises; bankruptcies have caused regional disasters; even in more advanced sectors like the aircraft industry, rationalization has led to large-scale redundancies.

Class consciousness seems to have remained somewhat sharper than in Britain, in spite of the electoral decline of the Communist Party which lost half its voters in five years and now polls less than 10 per cent of the vote. A certain language or jargon and an analysis based on the class struggle are being kept alive by the labour movement, although the staunch unionists form a minority of the workers, and the commitment of workers to their unions seems to be changing: the very militant are probably becoming more politically conscious and active, while those on the fringe of union activity only snatch a limited amount of time and energy from their main commitment to a better standard of living. The search for security is a key word for the working class, who now prefer the monthly paid status to the hourly paid insecurity of the past. For many of them, more secure employment can no longer guarantee the maintenance of a newly acquired standard of living now under threat. As the shorter working week spreads, those with safe jobs will be able to satisfy their new cultural and leisure requirements, though time thus gained is too often wasted commuting to distant suburbs.

The new middle classes

The new, extended middle classes are not a purely French phenomenon. But there are some specific French characteristics: the number of minor civil servants (*petits fonctionnaires*) who often earn less than manual workers, do a repetitive and often tiring type of office work, and yet consider their position as promotion, mainly on account of the 'image' (that of a white-collar worker) and the security (no fear of redundancy and guaranteed retirement pension) which such posts offer.

It must be remembered that the French civil service represents one third of the active population and includes, besides administrative workers, other sections of the working population such as teachers, post-office workers and those working in local government and hospitals. The social status of teachers is certainly higher than in Britain, though large numbers of supply teachers (a quarter of the total number) have low pay and no security of employment. Teachers are generally held to belong to the very French category of *cadres*, which forms a new middle class largely corresponding to the growth of the service sector. The *cadres* are distinguished from managers because they are salaried workers, not employers. They may be responsible for a large section of a factory or administration (*cadres supérieurs*) or only a smaller group of workers (*cadres moyens*). In some industries, they represent 3 per cent of the salaried workers only (mining), in others 12 per cent (mechanical and chemical industries), and even 18 per cent (power) or 19 per cent (oil). They enjoy a high standard of living, due to the relative security of their jobs, but they too are increasingly suffering from unemployment. Their number has been estimated at around 1.5 million and is still rising. They mainly enjoy a better education, are more numerous in large towns and differ from the traditional bourgeoisie by their more reckless way of life with a tendency not to save but rather to consume.

Social mobility: a myth or a reality?

It is generally acknowledged that it takes three generations for the gradual change from the worker/peasant class to postgraduate or professional status to be achieved. But formal education, which plays such an important role in this, is not always attainable: scholarships and grants are scarce and in most cases insufficient to ensure reasonable chances of success. Of course, the unification of syllabuses, the *tronc commun* for all children between eleven and fifteen, and centrally organized examinations, though criticized for being overdone, are to some extent helping to standardize things. But inequalities remain, between those who are deemed capable of following the three-year *lycée* course leading to the *baccalauréat (cycle long)* and the others, who join technical schools for shorter courses of study, enter apprenticeship or drift out of school with no qualifications at all only to join the dole queue. Although all the *lycées*, in theory, cater for anybody according to ability, they do in fact have different clienteles. The best *lycées classiques* are still largely a preserve of the bourgeoisie, while the others, because of geographical distribution and lack of prestige, get more working-class and fewer brighter children. Access to the very top of the social structure remains the privilege of the very few: recruitment to the administrative élite (executive class of the French civil service) may be considered to be predominantly incestuous. However, there is considerable mobility around the middle of the occupational scale: investigation into the family background of the *cadres moyens* shows their extremely varied social origins, but this is also the case for the manual workers and the unemployed – social mobility is not always upwards.

Institutions: stability and change

In May 1968, after ten years of stable Gaullist rule, France woke up in turmoil. The country came to a standstill, the regime itself was threatened. Everything seemed to be called into question: parliament and political parties, trade union bureaucracies, the educational system, the mass media, bourgeois culture. With the breakdown of normal communications – press, radio and television – came a general release: everybody talked to everybody else in university lecture theatres and cafés and on the streets (this was of course more true of large towns than villages, of Paris rather than the provinces, of young people than of old). For a short while, there was an impression of liberation from the constraints of normal life, an awakening, for people normally held down by routine; theatre companies, journalists, writers, television personalities who visited the occupied factories and universities, were struck by the overwhelming response of their audiences. People became aware of the censorship of the government-controlled radio and television, of the cultural desert in which they were kept. But romanticizing is of no avail: the wave of excitement was followed by a Gaullist landslide victory. The staying power of institutions had proved stronger than the wind of change.

The stability of the basic institutions of the state was not at stake. And, in 1981, the electoral victory of the socialists did not mean a radical departure from the past either. The government did not attempt to change the Gaullist constitution of the Fifth Republic and was content to introduce reforms within the existing framework. Nor did it lead a frontal attack against the Church in the form of a straightforward nationalization of the private schools which are often Catholic schools, nor an attack against the army by abolishing conscription or altering defence policy. The institutions closer to economic and social life were, of course, modified, but not out of recognition. Nationalization itself was not new – cars (Renault), banks (Crédit Lyonnais), railways and cigarettes were already nationalized. The reform of the judiciary and the symbolic transfer of the guillotine to a Paris museum have not meant a radical transformation of the system: the Home

Secretary, when faced with the continuing problem of terror-
ist bomb attacks and insecurity, repeatedly asserted confidence and pride in his police force. Social and education
policy tried to reduce inequalities, but the school and the
university system were not lastingly modified, and the
survival of the family as a basic element in the social fabric
continued to be encouraged by government incentives.

And yet, consumer groups and lobbies of all kinds are
sprouting everywhere, organizing protests, putting pressure
on civil service and local authorities, on trade union and
political bureaucracies. Over the last twenty years, a new
consciousness seems to have developed, however diffuse. It is
revealed through many initiatives and practices which are
growing at local level, close to the grassroots; just as if the
French, realizing the rigidity of their institutions, were
constantly trying to find ways of bypassing bureaucracies in a
constant battle against an abstract enemy – the 'administration'. Thus, unofficial strikes and claims for workers' control
(*autogestion*) have at times been given equal weight with more
traditional wage claims, all the more so in a trade union like
the CFDT (*Confédération française et démocratique du travail*)
which is less centralized than the vertically structured CGT
(*Confédération générale du travail*). Grass-root militancy has also
developed within political parties: the socialists are often
faced with minor revolts from their rank and file, while the
right-wing parties hold regular summer schools hoping to
develop a new image among the young by extending the
activities of their local branches outside election periods.
Christian associations openly debate problems of doctrine,
young magistrates and judges criticize the judicial system,
conscripts demand new rights of association, and discipline
has been transformed beyond the wishes of many teachers and
administrators in the *lycées*. More say in decision-making is
the order of the day, even though 'participation' tends to be
quickly formalized, and therefore anaesthetized in the
process.

This may be painting too bland (or too fractious?) a picture:
activists will remain a minority in a population which is above
all trying to survive economically and snatch as many crumbs
as possible from the cake of affluence. The fabric of society is

being changed, but this does not necessarily mean a lack of continuity.

The best example is perhaps the family: its death has been prophesied. Some people deplore the loss of many of its former functions while others attack it for curbing the development of its individual members. And yet the French family is going strong. When asked about ideal family size many people say they would like to have three or more children, and yet they only have one or two. This contradiction may be partly explained by factors like poor housing and economic difficulties which bring them down to earth. Young parents are not willing to have larger families at the expense of a standard of living which has been painfully attained through the added source of income of the increasingly numerous working wives and mothers. Indeed, as a result of the number of working mothers, there are twice as many places in crèches for young children in France as in England. Young people seem to favour 'juvenile cohabitation' rather than marriage and a large-scale survey carried out by the INED (*Institut national d'études démographiques*) showed that 44 per cent of the couples who married in 1976–7 had lived together before marriage as against 17 per cent in 1968–9. At the same time, their decision to have children is usually linked with the decision to legalize the union and illegitimate births make up only 10 per cent of all births.

Close ties still exist everywhere between the small family unit (parents and children), and the extended family (grandparents, uncles, cousins and so on) – ties which have survived the move of the children to the city. Parental authority, respect and politeness are on the whole more sternly enforced than in England, though all this is being eroded in urban communities. In this respect, French society seems nearer to Irish than to English society, though just how far this is due to a common Roman Catholic tradition is difficult to ascertain. Kinship links remain important in all social groups: they are useful when you look for a job, or a home; grandparents look after children after school and during the holidays; and with the widespread search for cultural roots, they recover a role lost in most Western societies – transmitting to the younger generations the traditions and language of their own family's past, thus helping to bridge the gap between young and old, between peasant origins and urban living.

Another unifying element between social groups, conscription, is still enforced, and young men face ten months of military service (this was reduced from twelve at the end of 1991). Until the Second World War, this period *sous les drapeaux* used to create a real melting-pot, some kind of initiation rite in which young men from varying backgrounds shared. It still remains a meeting ground, but offers less social mixing. Great numbers of students used to obtain several years' delay but the law is trying to enforce early military service for all young men of eighteen, and attempting to reduce the number of exemptions from military service. However, students still tend to serve their time as teachers in ex-colonial countries or, if they serve in the armed forces, very often do so as NCOs, and in any case do not mix well because of their age and different interests. So the rift between the educated and the uneducated is no longer bridged as it once was by this common experience of army life, and conscription itself still provokes bitter controversy.

Some new or forthcoming changes must not be minimized. The most momentous is probably 'decentralization' (the Act came into force in 1982), hailed by the socialists as 'a quiet revolution' (*une révolution tranquille*), an attempt to bring decision-making closer to the people affected by these decisions – hence greater democracy. Inevitably it was denounced by their opponents as a divisive measure and a wasteful manipulation of committees and personnel, since the local and regional assemblies would need brains trusts and advisers to help them perform their new functions. The *préfet* was the eye of the Home Secretary in each *département*; he is now the local representative of the executive, and the elected Presidents of each regional council also carry a lot of weight. Time, and decisions over financing, will decide where power lies.

Decentralization may help defuse the Corsican time-bomb and may bring a new lease of life to regions like Brittany, the Jura, the Auvergne or the Dordogne, for which the distance from Paris ministries meant files sometimes 'got lost' on their way through the red-tape of administration and, in any case, suffered long delays. The results are already visible in the regional initiatives in cultural policy – a departure from the long tradition of Jacobin centralization.

Leisure and culture

For three years there were in France two ministries in charge of leisure and cultural activities. *The Ministère de la Culture* was responsible for the development of libraries and museums, music, theatre and the cinema, and the *Ministère du Temps Libre* dealt with problems connected with leisure: the timing of holidays to avoid the August mass migration and its consequences for both the tourist industry and the economy; the development of the tourist potential of the country areas to counterbalance the dominant choices of seaside or mountain holidays; the diversification of state subsidies to enable the less affluent members of the community to enjoy a holiday away from their urban or village homes; the balancing of work and leisure (*aménagement du temps de travail*). The reversal to a single *Ministère de la Culture* in 1984 implied a change of emphasis and perhaps a recognition that, for the unemployed and those on early retirement schemes, 'enforced leisure' was a burden rather than a conquest. But the concern with holidays and leisure still remains a leading issue in French society today. The pressure of urban living, longer life expectancy and earlier retirement, rising unemployment (hence the slogan '*travailler moins pour travailler tous*' – shorter hours mean jobs for all) combined with the return of a socialist government committed to fulfilling the task started by the Popular Front in 1936 which was for a shorter working week (forty hours, now reduced to thirty-nine with the aim being a thirty-five hour week) and an annual paid holiday for all (increased from four to five weeks).

Holidays

The French seem obsessively to live for *les vacances* – eleven months of noise, work and stress, of scrimping and saving for an annual spending spree. Two-thirds of the population regularly migrate south and west in the summer while farmers account for nearly half of those who remain behind. Half the holiday makers rush to the seaside and the sun. The spectacular success of such institutions as the *Club Méditerranée*, with its thatched-hut villages built around the Mediterranean as well as in more exotic places like Tahiti, Mexico or China, is a witness to this trend. But the majority of holiday makers either stay with friends or relatives (35 per cent), go camping (23 per cent) or rent a flat or a cottage (*gîtes ruraux*). Among the less affluent, schoolchildren often go away without their parents, staying with grandparents or in *colonies de vacances* (holiday camps) – the social security system partly footing the bill. Underprivileged children from the towns and suburbs frequently have only the streets and some adventure playgrounds for their holidays, and confrontation with the police for their excitement – a problem which, after the long hot summer of 1981 (with all the headlines reporting 'rodeos' being carried out with stolen cars in a Lyon suburb), the

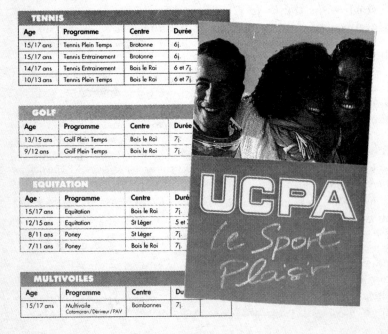

TENNIS

Age	Programme	Centre	Durée
15/17 ans	Tennis Plein Temps	Brotonne	6j.
15/17 ans	Tennis Entrainement	Brotonne	6j.
14/17 ans	Tennis Entrainement	Bois le Roi	6 et 7j.
10/13 ans	Tennis Plein Temps	Bois le Roi	6 et 7j.

GOLF

Age	Programme	Centre	Durée
13/15 ans	Golf Plein Temps	Bois le Roi	7j.
9/12 ans	Golf Plein Temps	Bois le Roi	7j.

EQUITATION

Age	Programme	Centre	Duré
15/17 ans	Equitation	Bois le Roi	7j.
12/15 ans	Equitation	St Léger	5 et
8/11 ans	Poney	St Léger	7j.
7/11 ans	Poney	Bois le Roi	7j.

MULTIVOILES

Age	Programme	Centre	Du
15/17 ans	Multivoile Catamaran/Dériveur/PAV	Bombannes	7j.

government tried to tackle by providing special holiday camps and day outings.

When they can afford it, families go away together with organizations like *Villages-Vacances-Familles*, *Les Maisons familiales*, *Vacances-Loisirs-Familles* and so on, which offer family accommodation, communal catering and leisure activities for all ages. A more recent trend is the distribution of holidays over a (longer) summer period and a (shorter) winter period. Even skiing holidays, still a preserve of the urban upper-middle class (only 8 per cent of the population can afford them), are in a minor way open to the underprivileged. This is through the system of *classes de neige* whereby primary schools from town areas can in turn send one or more classes to the mountains for a month, complete with teacher and skiing equipment, to combine normal teaching in the morning with outdoor activity in the afternoon. This is still far too sporadic to be effective in any general way, and too expensive for all children concerned to be able to go, but it does point to a future when what used to be the privilege of the better off may be available to many more.

Pastimes and leisure

Besides holidays proper, leisure activities of many kinds develop in all social groups – the advent of a 'civilization of leisure' has even been prophesied. People often say they would prefer a longer weekend to a bigger pay packet: time is too often 'wasted' in the mad rush to earn a living (*'on perd sa vie à la gagner'*) and increasingly, the French insist on choosing how to divide their life between work-orientated and leisure activities (*le temps choisi*), or increasing the amount of time to be devoted to leisure (*le temps libéré*).

Pastimes vary greatly depending on social class and education. Gardening has become a national pastime for rich and poor alike; one Frenchman in three now mows his lawn, grows vegetables or flowers, and may even decorate his garden with plastic gnomes or reproduction nymphs. Radio, television and newspapers are part of most people's daily lives, though they were only mentioned by a tiny minority as being among their 'favourite pastimes' in a recent IFOP (*Institut français d'opinion publique*) survey, while reading and sports vied for the lead followed by music, needlework, do-it-yourself (*bricolage*) and gardening. 'Sports', of course, holds a different meaning for teenagers and adults, for workers and professionals. Football and cycling are the most popular sports and are more often watched than actively practised, with the ritual Tour de France taking over from cup matches in July on television. Elite sports like tennis, golf, horse-riding, sailing and wind-surfing are becoming accessible to increasing numbers of young people through the multiplication of municipal clubs and investments. However, cultural activities outside the home remain largely the preserve of the middle and upper classes: few people frequently attend concerts (7 per cent) or go to the theatre (12 per cent), though one person in five still goes out to the cinema at least once a week – the highest percentages being among the *cadres* and Parisians. More films are watched on the family television than on the screen, however, and the number of films hired from video clubs doubled between 1983 and 1985.

There is certainly greater demand for cultural activities now than ten or twenty years ago, as the success of classes for classical or modern ballet dancing, learning languages, pottery, playing the guitar and other instruments has demonstrated. However, the dream of a popular culture bridging class differences remains, at present, a pious dream. The gap between the cultured and the deprived (rural communities, the working class) seems likely to continue for quite a long time. Formal education is still insufficient, and adult education sadly underdeveloped. Industrial workers may be alienated for a number of reasons: working with machines, closed community living, lack of time and facilities, or the poor quality of the mass media, for example. This alienation causes a reversion to what one such workers calls 'illiteracy' when he compares the reading and writing abilities of adult factory workers to that of their children still in junior schools. But the role of associations of all kinds in developing an awareness of cultural needs has led to initiatives – both private and public – for extending cultural activities to an ever-growing audience, and the dominance of Paris is beginning to be challenged by provincial initiatives.

Decentralization of culture

There are 1,200 *Maisons des jeunes* and *Maisons de la Culture* (youth and arts centres) in France, with some 600,000 members (half workers, half schoolchildren and students). They are subsidized partly by the state, partly by local and regional councils, and each centre is administered by a permanent head (who nearly always has experience outside the educational profession) and by a House council elected by the young members themselves. Very often, the centre is the only meeting-place for young people in a small town, apart from the local café, and is used for amateur dramatics, film shows, lectures, concerts, dances, and other indoor leisure activities; it also serves as a base from which to organize outings, holidays and so on. A high proportion of the worker members of the *Maisons des jeunes* are active trade unionists, and their members in general are among the most literate young people apart from students. Over the last ten years, they have been under attack for being hotbeds of politicization of youth, and for wasting public money through bad administration. Not surprisingly both charges have been denied, but action has been taken against them. Under the pretext of decentralization, state subsidies have been reduced by 13 per cent, and more financial responsibility has been placed on local councils who thus became direct employers of the staff. The consequences of this are tighter control over cultural policy by local councils (generally right of centre) and the tendency to demand that what is supposed to be a public service should also be economically viable. A new source of finance is the regional councils which sometimes seek to develop cultural activities in order to boost the reputation of their region. But budgets are too limited for this to mean a large-scale extension of activities.

The *Maisons de la Culture* were created by André Malraux. The idea was to give a single home to all the arts, where culture would be represented with its many facets, and where various types of audience could meet under one roof. The fifteen *Maisons de la Culture* created since 1961 in provincial cities (except for Créteil and Nanterre near Paris) have helped the development of a variety of cultural projects and practices.

They have three principal aims. The first is creativity (*création*), the presentation of new high-quality productions often undertaken by permanent theatre or ballet companies (Grenoble and La Rochelle), by teams of film makers (Le Havre) or musicians (Amiens) and sometimes with the collaboration of specially invited and well-known artists. The second is cultural dissemination (*diffusion*) and outside companies, itinerant exhibitions and orchestras are welcomed. The third is cultural animation, an encouragement for all forms of cultural activity, especially those which favour confrontations and exchanges between actors, designers, musicians, painters and their public, thereby encouraging cross-fertilization and experiment. Though the *Maisons de la Culture* have developed into lively arts centres transforming life in their city, they are plagued by a shortage of funds and often have to curtail their own most adventurous projects and instead invite in well-known companies on tour to boost their bookings. Unfortunately the development of a real cultural policy is bound to be inhibited by the need to make a profit. The decentralization policy may be a source of new subsidies because of the competition between regions for artistic as well as economic dominance over other regions (regional councils have their cultural department and budget). The impact so far has been the opening of provincial museums to contemporary art (in Lyon, Marseille, Bordeaux) or even the creation of new museums of modern art (Saint-Etienne) or additional buildings (Strasbourg, Grenoble). The Regional Collections of Contemporary Art (FRAC: *Fonds régionaux d'art contemporain*) are funded by equal state and regional subsidies.

The *Maisons de la Culture* regularly welcome the regional theatre companies, themselves formed as a result of the decentralization policy for the arts and also fighting for survival. When Jean Vilar's *Théâtre national populaire* in Paris (founded in 1951) was forced to close down through lack of government subsidy in 1972, Roger Planchon (who had gathered together his company in Lyon during the early fifties) inherited the title of national theatre for his *Théâtre de Villeurbanne*. This may have been a victory for decentralization but it also meant the disappearance of the stronghold of popular theatre in élitist Paris. In the provinces, nineteen

Centres dramatiques sprung up, with financial support from both government and local councils: the *Comédie de l'Est* (Strasbourg) . . . *de l'Ouest* (Rennes), . . . *du Centre* (Bourges) and so on. Their policy is to serve both the town where they are based and the surrounding rural community by regular tours, and their 'consecration' comes when they are invited to Paris for a season. Their aim is obviously to reach out to a working-class audience and they partly succeed: some 30 per cent of the audience of Planchon's *Théâtre de Villeurbanne* is *populaire*. But the public reached is mainly skilled workers, foremen and the like – perhaps because the ordinary workers have fewer contacts with the trade union bureaucracy that handles the bookings. There is now an increasing realization that the theatre must go out to people in their normal surroundings; the general difficulties then are how to combine artistic quality with mobility, and to ascertain what degree of effort can be demanded of the audience. Much more specific is the financial problem. It is much easier to organize a summer festival every year to catch the tourist audiences than to create a base for regular artistic life in the regions and support permanent structures.

In 1981, only 0.5 per cent of the national budget went to support the arts. In 1977, state help to the centres dramatiques increased by only 7 per cent, even though a 25 per cent increase had been written into the contracts. The same year, the prestigious *Centre Beaubourg* opened, absorbing in running costs almost half the state budget allotted to the arts. Mitterrand's choice of a well-known personality of the arts, Jack Lang, as his Minister of Culture, and his government's commitment to a larger share of the national budget undoubtedly helped make culture available to all. Subsidies are distributed very widely, even though the money available is never enough and the *Conseils régionaux* are increasingly asked to supplement state grants. Whether this is a democratic phenomenon or a new form of twentieth-century bourgeois patronage remains to be seen, however. Debates on what exactly is meant by 'the explosion of culture' have been revived in the wake of the spectacular success of the *Centre Beaubourg* whose futuristic and metal architecture in the historic heart of the city attracts millions of visitors from all countries and backgrounds

(8 million visitors a year). Provincials and foreigners discover Paris from the top of the escalators encased in glass across the west façade; Parisians, young and old, visit the Public Information Library, the Cinémathèque, the Museum of Modern Art's permanent collection, one of the many temporary exhibitions, the Centre of Industrial Creation or the Experimental Music Department (IRCAM) directed by Pierre Boulez. Everything cultural is under one roof, with permanent fairground activities outside. Is it culture made available to the masses, a catalyst for artistic development, or a kind of supermarket of culture? In any case the *Centre Beaubourg* has become a leading landmark on the tourist route from the Eiffel Tower to Notre-Dame.

The *Centre Beaubourg* remains attached to the name of President Pompidou to whom it is dedicated. The Mitterrand era will be remembered by such architectural landmarks as the new Museum of Science and Technology at La Villette in northern Paris, with its futuristic, many faceted *géode*, the renovation of the Louvre museum preparing for the twenty-first century with the glass pyramid designed by the Japanese architect Pei, the new prestigious arch built at La Défense – all reflecting the Paris sky with their glass structures. They will remain a lasting testimony to an audacious policy for the arts which also included the large-scale development of theatre and music festivals in the provinces, and the controversial new *Opéra Bastille* which has already attracted motley crowds

The *fontaine Stravinsky* outside the *Centre Beaubourg*.

of spectators. The festival marking the two-hundredth anniversary of the French Revolution which attracted millions of visitors and viewers was the most publicized – and costly – of Jack Lang's initiatives. Less publicized developments, like the opening to the public of the reconstructed Lascaux prehistoric caves and the renovation of many old city centres with new pedestrian precincts also testify to the determination of successive national and local administrations to preserve the country's historical heritage.

Bibliography

Bauer, G. and Roux, J. M., *La Rurbanisation ou la ville éparpillée*. Paris, Le Seuil, 1976. On the invasion of rural areas by the urban overspill which thus creates the new 'rurban' phenomenon.

Biraben, J. N. and Dupaquier, J., *Les Berceaux vides de Marianne*. Paris, Le Seuil, 1981. Analyses the failure of the government incentives to increase the French birth rate.

Chenu, A., *L'Archipel des employés*. Paris, INSEE, 1990. On the white-collar workers and civil servants.

Chombart de Lauwe, M. J. and P. H. *et al.*, *La Femme dans la société, son image dans les différents milieux sociaux*. Paris. Editions du CNRS, 1977. A comprehensive survey: women at home, at work, at university; the evolution over the last fifty years.

Données sociales. INSEE (Institut national de la Statistique et des études économiques), Paris, 1986. Statistical information on all aspects of social life, with an analysis of the main trends and reports on social surveys and consumer studies.

Dossiers et documents. Paris, *Le Monde*, ten issues per year. A supplement to the well-known daily newspaper, gathering together recent articles concerning social, political and economic problems. A very useful tool for the student who wants to keep up to date with the evolution of French society. Recent issues include 'La Ville et ses banlieues' (Feb. 1991), 'Le Dernier Etat de la France' (May 1991).

Dupeux, J., *La Société française, 1789–1970*. Paris, Colin, 1972, and London, Methuen, 1976. See its analysis of the population structure and migrations in particular.

Le Roy Ladurie, E. and Vigne, D., *Inventaire des campagnes*, Paris, J. C. Lattès, 1980. The first part traces the history of the 'peasantry', the second presents the *paysans* in a series of live interviews. Both informative and enjoyable reading.

Mallet S., *La Nouvelle Classe ouvrière*. Paris, Seuil, 1963 and Nottingham, Spokesman Books, 1976. A classic on the changes in working-class life and consciousness.

Mendras, H. *et al.*, *La Sagesse et le Désordre: France 1980*. An excellent collection of articles including social and institutional aspects of contemporary France.

Nicolas, J. P., *La Pauvreté intolérable*. Paris, Erès, 1985. The life of a family on public assistance.

Potel, J. Y., *L'Etat de la France et de ses habitants*. Paris, La Découverte, 1985. A wide-ranging survey covering society, politics, the economy and the geography of France and including maps and statistics.

Reynaud, J. D. and Grafmeyer, Y. (eds), *Français, qui êtes-vous?* Paris, La Documentation française, 1981. A collection of articles on social classes, the industrial world, the institutions and intellectual life, with useful statistics. Most informative.

Roudy, Y., *A cause d'elles*. Paris, Albin Michel, 1985. The socialist Minister for Women's Rights presenting her work.

SOFRES, *Opinion publique 1986*. Paris, Gallimard, 1986.

Sue, R., *Vers une société du temps libre*. Paris, PUF, 1982. The changing patterns of leisure.

Syndicat de la Magistrature, *Justice sous influence*. Paris, Maspero, 1981. An examination of the judicial system by judges who analyse its evolution and discuss the balance between social control and individual liberty.

Vaughan, M., Kolinsky, M. and Sherif, P., *Social Change in France*. London, Martin Robertson, 1978.

A very comprehensive collection of government reports was published in 1982, the result of surveys carried out by commissions appointed to study the state of the country at the time of the Socialist return to power in 1981. Well-informed, comprehensive, programmatic as well as analytical, they are all published by La Documentation française, together with many other books and reviews, among which are *Les Cahiers français*. There are five issues per year, each devoted to a particular subject: for example 'La Fonction publique', nos 194 & 197; 'Le Monde urbain', no. 203; 'la Décentralisation', no. 204. These publications are available from La Documentation française, 29–31 Quai Voltaire, Paris, which also houses a well-stocked documentation library.

2

Political parties
Malcolm Slater

Introduction

The basic outline of political parties in France is, from left to right on the political spectrum:

> PCF   PS   UDF   RPR   FN

PCF – *Parti communiste français* (communists)
PS   – *Parti socialiste* (socialists)
UDF – *Union pour la Démocratie française* (Giscardians)
RPR – *Rassemblement pour la République* (Gaullists)
FN   – *Front national* (extreme right).

The background to this outline is: firstly, in 1981 the socialists captured the presidency when François Mitterrand narrowly beat Valéry Giscard d'Estaing in the second round run-off; a few weeks later the nation confirmed this choice by electing a new National Assembly with a socialist majority which for nearly five years supported the policies and guaranteed the survival of governments consisting overwhelmingly of socialists. Secondly, although Mitterrand's term of office was for seven years, the end of the five-year parliament in 1986 led to the replacement of the socialist majority in the National Assembly by a right-wing majority supporting a new government under Jacques Chirac which had to 'cohabit' with President Mitterrand. Thirdly, Mitterrand was re-elected

President in 1988, beating Chirac in the second round run-off; as in 1981, he dissolved the right-wing dominated National Assembly, and enough socialists and supporters were then elected to support a minority government under Michel Rocard, then Edith Cresson, then Pierre Bérégovoy, which was in danger of being overthrown only if the communists and the right-wing opposition united to pass a vote of censure. Fourthly, the March 1993 elections gave the 'parliamentary right' (RPR and UDF) an overwhelming proportion of the 577 National Assembly seats; this victory led to a second period of 'cohabitation' between President Mitterrand and a right-wing government, with Edouard Balladur as Prime Minister and Jacques Chirac as the real power behind the scenes.

Policy programmes

What policies did the parties put to the electorate in March 1993, after five years of socialist government? Clearly, it is at election times that the parties are at their most salient, and the average voter has the best chance to be aware of the difference, not just between right and left, but also between individual parties, large and small. Electoral choice is a complex process, often with a high degree of irrationality, but obviously the established parties play an important part in this process, by dominating the institution which makes the choice necessary (parliament), by having a virtual monopoly of candidate selection, and by indulging in political marketing.

French political parties in the run-up to the June 1988 elections had tried to differentiate themselves from their rivals in the major policy spheres. The socialists, having lost popularity in the second half of their 1981–6 period of office with their policy of economic austerity (*rigueur*), were campaigning on the coat-tails of Mitterrand's presidential victory. Mitterrand's campaign in May was based on his image as a paternal *rassembleur*; his victory was attributable to his appeal both to former voters of the declining Communist Party and to centrist voters (that is, supporters of Raymond Barre, and those on the left of the UDF) who rejected Chirac's hard line

President Mitterrand with Prime Minister Jacques Chirac and Finance Minister Edouard Balladur in 1987 during the first period of *cohabitation*. The second, more tense, period of *cohabitation*, with a much stronger right from 1993, saw Balladur as Prime Minister and Chirac preparing a third presidential bid.

on immigrants and law and order. The Socialist Party in the June 1988 National Assembly elections also pursued a strategy of *ouverture*. They picked up communist votes on the second round by showing a general commitment to the reduction of inequalities and the creation of jobs (and a specific promise to introduce a wealth tax). They also appealed to centrists with a cautious economic policy (later expressed as '*ni privatisation, ni nationalisation*', though 1991 saw a partial sell-off of state assets), full commitment to the post-1992 European Single Market, and the prospect of peaceful decolonization by negotiated settlement of the New Caledonia question.

In fact, the 1988 election campaign was relatively lifeless and devoid of salient issues. The right-left divide had been significantly reduced by the Socialist Party's move to social democracy, and to some extent by the 1986–8 period of *cohabitation* which had confirmed a national consensus on foreign affairs and defence. Both factors coincided with, and to a large extent provoked, a decline in partisan attachment and a 'recentring' of attitudes, so that by the end of the 1980s electoral choice was more volatile and abstention rates higher.

The Gaullist RPR and the UDF (nominally Giscardian, but in reality a fragmented collection of political groups rather than a party) campaigned under the *ad hoc* umbrella organization of the URC (*Union du rassemblement et du centre*), which ensured a single right-wing candidate in most constituencies in the first round. The right's weakness however was that both its leaders (Chirac and Giscard) were losing presidential candidates, and Chirac's failure as Prime Minister between 1986 and 1988 in important areas (education and reform of the nationality laws) meant a lack of dynamic electoral programme to put to the electors. Moreover, there was continuing internal disagreement about how far to co-operate with the *Front national* – most leaders were opposed to this, but a majority of right-wing electors was in favour. The *Front national* was weak at grass-roots level except in Marseille and other parts of the Mediterranean coast; it tried to exploit fears by attributing economic ills to the presence of immigrants, but its basic lack of legitimacy and the reversion to the two-round electoral system led to the loss of all but one seat in the National Assembly elections of 1988.

To a large extent, the 1993 election focussed on personalities, rather than differences over issues and ideology. Specific issues such as unemployment, immigration, Europe (the subject of the September 1992 referendum), and law and order appeared less important for voters than the basic fact of disenchantment with twelve years of socialist power which had increasingly put economic efficiency above political appeal. Corruption tainted politicians of all parts of the political spectrum and heightened voters' perception of the increasing moral bankruptcy of successive governments.

The socialists were in disarray, with Mitterrand trying to distract attention by Constitutional reform proposals and Michel Rocard calling for a 'big bang' aligning social democrats, ecologists, communist reformers and centrists. The Socialist Party campaigned on its record of 'economiic recovery, and social and democratic modernization', stressing their commitment to closer European co-operation and a new world order of development, disarmament and defence of human rights and the environment; but even Pierre

Bérégovoy said, '*Je sais que ce bilan n'apparaît pas toujours comme positif aux Français.*'

The RPR–UDF coalition offered tax reforms and government spending cuts, together with a rather less radical privatization programme than that of the 1986–8 Chirac government, when Balladur was Finance Minister. The right promised a job-creation drive, with cuts in social security and other charges to firms offering more jobs and training; they rejected the left's plans for job-sharing – an issue which raised much heated argument.

The right tried to run a closely-knit campaign ('*une campagne de proximité*'), but was reluctant to make clear promises in areas of policy disagreement within the coalition – membership of the ERM, role of the state, defence, former Yugoslavia, regulation of broadcasting, Europe (there was a strong anti-Maastricht element in the RPR), and even immigration.

The *Front national* continued its campaign for 'French people' to have priority on jobs, for no welfare rights for foreigners, expulsion of foreigners convicted of crime, stronger police powers, reintroduction of capital punishment, and greater recourse to national and local referenda; in 1993 they added denunciation of the Maastricht Treaty, abolition of the EC Commission and a tougher defence stance. However, their electoral influence was in decline in 1992 regional and cantonal elections after Le Pen's high point of 14.4% in the 1988 presidential elections.

Green issues took on greater significance in the 1993 election because of a determined, though unsuccessful, attempt at electoral breakthrough by an alliance of *Les Verts* and the more recently established *Génération écologie*. However, there were major differences between the alliance partners. The Greens' commitment to ·scrapping nuclear power conflicted with their partners' more modest aim of tougher rules on the environment.

An analysis of the main parties' programmes on major issues was published in *Le Monde* on 16 March 1993.

Proliferation of parties

The scheme of political parties in France is complicated by the existence of many minor parties. The 1988 law on state financial aid to political parties introduced the concept of an official list of parties which qualified for such aid by having at least one parliamentarian (*député* or senator) as a member. This had the odd effect of giving official status to what was in effect a party of non-party members (the *Union des sénateurs non-inscrits* – see Table 1 on page 42), but more importantly was another indication of party proliferation – twenty-nine were registered in 1990, though fourteen of these, many from the overseas territories and *départements*, had only one parliamentarian member. The 1992 count was forty-one and twenty-two respectively.

The one-off experiment of a single-round proportional system in the 1986 election did not reduce the incidence of minor parties which are usually eliminated on the first round of a two-round system. It simply meant that they were presented to the electorate either as no-hope lists, sometimes of minor parties in combination, or as adjuncts of the major parties trying to extend the range of their appeal.

In the March 1986 legislative and – for the first time – direct regional elections, voters had a wide range of electoral lists from which to make their choice, giving another indication of the proliferation of French political parties. As an example, Table 2 shows the range of choice available to voters in Paris (the *département* of the Seine) and the success of each list of twenty-three names, including two 'stand-in' candidates (*suppléants*).

Of course, the generic name 'party' is not always helpful in definitional terms. Of the five main parties in the early 1990s only two were called '*parti*'. Sometimes a word with more rousing connotations is preferred such as 'Front *national*', '*Nouvelle* action *royaliste*', 'Lutte *ouvrière*', or 'Initiative *86*'. Similarly, the Gaullist party in its various guises has always been an *union* or a *rassemblement*. Use of the term *mouvement* may foster the impression that there is a wider basis of sympathy for political aims waiting to be mobilized, as in *Mouvement des radicaux de gauche*, *Mouvement solidarité-participation*, the extreme

Table 1

Official list of political parties and groups qualifying for state financial aid in 1990

Party or political group	Number of parliamentarians
Parti socialiste	323
Rassemblement pour la République	218
Parti républicain	90
Union centriste *(senators only)*	57
Centre des démocrates sociaux	49
Parti communiste français	41
Association de gestion des adhérents directs de l'Union pour la Démocratie française	25
Mouvement des radicaux de gauche	14
Parti radical	11
Clubs perspectives et réalité	9
Union pour la Démocratie française	9
Parti social-démocrate	6
Centre national des indépendants et paysans	6
Union des sénateurs non-inscrits	5
Parti progressiste martiniquais	3
AIA-API	1
Association des démocrates	1
Convention libérale européenne et sociale	1
Développement et avenir de la Réunion	1
Fédération des indépendants	1
Groupe d'action économique et sociale	1
Groupement France-Réunion	1
Parti communiste gaudeloupéen	1
Parti communiste réunionnais	1
Parti socialiste guyanais	1
Parti Te-Tiarama	1
Rassemblement pour la Guyane dans la République	1
Union départementale des élus socialistes et républicains des Hautes-Pyrénées	1
Union pour le renouveau de Sainte-Marie	1

right-wing *Mouvement nationaliste révolutionnaire*, or the Trotsky-ist *Mouvement pour un parti des travailleurs* (though this was the *Parti communiste internationaliste* from 1981 to 1985 and became the *Parti des travailleurs* in 1991). Moreover, *parti* can refer to what are clearly groups limited in membership, in appeal

Table 2

Parties and groups with candidates in the 1993 legislative elections (first round, metropolitan France only)

Association des démocrates
Alliance des Français pour le progrès
Alternative démocratie socialisme
Association des usagers de l'administration et des services publics
Accolta naziunale corsa
Alliance populaire
Alliance rouge et verte
Corsica Nazione
Centre des démocrates sociaux
Centre national des indépendants
Chasse, pêche, nature et tradition
Clubs perspectives et réalités
Démocratie chrétienne française
Entente des écologistes
Front national
France plus
France unie
Génération écologie
Ligue communiste révolutionnaire
Lutte ouvrière
Mouvement des démocrates
Mouvement des citoyens
Mouvement des réformateurs

Mouvement pour l'autodétermination
Mouvement des radicaux de gauche
Nouvelle action royaliste
Nouveaux écologistes
Nouvelle solidarité
Parti communiste
Parti des forces nouvelles
Parti humaniste
Parti de la loi naturelle
Parti ouvrier européen
Parti radical
Parti républicain
Parti socialiste
Parti social-démocrate
Parti des travailleurs
Ras le bol
Rassemblement des démocrates et républicains de progrès
Rassemblement pour la République
Solidarité écologie gauche alternative
Union démocratique bretonne
Union pour la démocratie française
Union des indépendants
Union écologie démocratie
Union pour la France
Verts

(*Parti humaniste* – see Table 2 above), or in territorial concern (*Union démocratique bretonne*).

Parties and pseudo-parties can often spring up at the whim of a single person. Examples are:

1988 – *Convention libérale européenne et sociale* (Raymond Barre)
1988 – *Association des démocrates* (Michel Durafour)
1990 – *Forum républicain* (Alain Carignon)
1990 – *Convention pour la Ve République* (Jean Charbonnel)
1990 – *Génération écologie* (Brice Lalonde)
1990 – *Démocratie 2000* (Jacques Delors, in preparation for a return to French politics from the EC presidency)
1991 – *Société civile* (Bernard Kouchner)
1991 – *Union des indépendants* (Général Lacaze)
1992 – *Mouvement des citoyens* (Jean-Pierre Chevènement)
1993 – *Nouveaux écologistes* (Bernard Manovelli)
1993 – *Union écologie et démocratie* (François Donzel)

A 1982 count identified some seventy-five parties, clubs and movements across the whole political spectrum, but small groups often disappear by amalgamation. In May 1985, the *Parti démocrate*, *Clubs avenir centre gauche*, *Europe environnement*, *Rassemblement fédéraliste européen*, and several members of the *Parti démocrate français* went to make up the '*Union républicaine et démocrate – Parti réformiste*'. In 1990, the declining *Parti socialiste unifié* (PSU), which was Michel Rocard's political home in the period 1960–74, and the even smaller *Nouvelle gauche* dissolved themselves and threw in their lot with the Greens. Parties can also disappear on being dissolved by the authorities; this happened in forty-four cases between 1958 and 1982, sixteen on the extreme right, thirteen on the extreme left, and fifteen separatist or 'liberation' movements.

The 1988 National Assembly elections saw the reinstatement of the electoral system in operation during 1958 to 1981 – a single-member two-round system (*scrutin uninominal majoritaire à deux tours*), though with redrawn constituency boundaries. In listing the results of this and the 1993 elections, *Le Monde* adopted the Ministry of the Interior's traditional ploy of describing candidates from minor and insignificant parties as '*extrême gauche*', '*extrême droite*', or more dismissively, '*divers gauche*' and '*divers droite*'.

Party identity

Even if the plethora of minor groups is ignored, the student of French politics will meet an abundance of initials created by two common phenomena of French political parties; firstly their tendency to change their names much more frequently than is the case in Britain or the USA, usually to emphasize to the public that they have a new image. The Socialist Party was called *Section française de l'Internationale ouvrière* (SFIO) from 1905 to 1969 and the *Parti socialiste* (PS) from 1971. During the 1969–71 hiatus, it was referred to as the '*Nouveau parti socialiste*' which was a description rather than a title. The PCF was originally (1920–36) called *Section française de l'Internationale communiste*. The Gaullist Party has assumed various titles:

1946	*Union gaulliste.*
1947–53	*Rassemblement du peuple français* (RPF) (during 1953–8, after the dissolution of the RPF, Gaullists in Parliament called themselves *Républicains sociaux*).
1958	*Union pour la Nouvelle République* (UNR).
1967	*Union des démocrates pour la Ve République* (UDV^e).
1968	*Union pour la défense de la République*, then *Union des démocrates pour la République* (UDR).
1976	*Rassemblement pour la République* (RPR).

Secondly, parties and groups frequently co-operate just for election periods under umbrella titles established only weeks before. Examples have been in the elections of:

1993	*Entente des écologistes*, linking *Les Verts* and *Génération écologie*.
1993	*Solidarité écologie gauche alternative* (SEGA), co-ordinating *Alternative rouge et verte* and *Alternative démocratie socialisme*.
1993	*Union pour la France* (UPF), co-ordinating the RPR and the UDF.
1988	*Union du rassemblement et du centre*, co-ordinating the RPR and the UDF.
1986	*Alternative 86*, comprising the *Parti socialiste unifié* (PSU), *Ligue communiste révolutionnaire*, *Parti pour une alternative*

communiste, *Fédération de la gauche alternative*, and assorted ecologists, regionalists and trade unionists.

1981 *Union pour la nouvelle majorité* linking the RPR and UDF.

1978 *Union pour la Démocratie française* (UDF) mainly comprising the *Parti républicain* (PR), *Centre des démocrates sociaux* (CDS), and *Parti radical*. This co-operative venture of course survived the election for which it was originally intended.

1973 *Union de la gauche socialiste et démocrate* linking the PS and *Mouvement des radicaux de gauche* (MRG); these two parties co-operated closely in all subsequent elections.

1973 *Union des républicains de progrès* (URP) comprising UDR, *Républicains indépendants* (RI) and some centrists.

In June 1990 the establishment of the *Union pour la France* (UPF) linking Jacques Chirac's RPR and Valéry Giscard d'Estaing's UDF was conceived by its founders as 'the first stage towards a united Opposition', rather than just an umbrella group in anticipation of cantonal and regional elections in 1992 and National Assembly elections in 1993.

Development of parties and political groups

It must not be forgotten that parties, in the sense of permanent and centralized organizations, did not appear on the French political scene until the beginning of the twentieth century, whereas a durable parliamentary Republic was established in 1875 and universal masculine suffrage in 1848. But a very limited suffrage before then meant that 'parties' (in the sense of loose groups) in parliament had no incentive to organize or appeal to the electorate, as was the case in Great Britain; political activity outside the *pays légal*, as Guizot called it, was restricted to clubs, often existing clandestinely. This fact, together with the massacre or exile of thousands of insurgents who had taken part in the Paris Commune of 1870–1, meant that even after the establishment of the Third Republic in the 1870s, socialists in France were divided over aims and methods, and a Socialist Party (the SFIO) was not founded until 1905.

In other parts of the political spectrum, parliamentary politics was traditionally organized through loose groups of local worthies (*notables*) whose electoral clientele was limited to their own constituency and who felt little need of a national party organization, with the constraints which this implied. Thus it was not until 1901 that the radicals created a *Parti républicain radical et radical-socialiste*; it survived in the 1980s as a shadow of its former self under the new official name of *Parti radical-socialiste*, though people always referred to it simply as the *Parti radical*. This phenomenon of a loosely organized group with minimal parliamentary discipline and electoral co-ordination was still evident until the 1960s. In 1962, Valéry Giscard d'Estaing formed a pro-de Gaulle group of *députés* of the *Centre national des indépendants et paysans* (CNIP) into the *Républicains indépendants* (RI), but it was not until 1966 that he decided to organize it as a party in the sense of a nation-wide organization dedicated to disseminating a doctrine, recruiting members and maximizing electoral support. It became the *Parti républicain* (PR) in May 1977.

In fact, as late as the 1960s, the French political party scene reflected almost perfectly Maurice Duverger's analysis of the distinction between the old established *parti de cadres* (such as the ones described above) and the newer phenomenon of the *parti de masse* such as the SFIO and PCF. These were more suited to parliamentary democracy in the second half of the twentieth century because of their higher membership, tighter organization, clear policy alternatives based on a distinct doctrine, and their high level of political activity outside election periods. But this analysis needed to be refined in the light of the emergence of a Gaullist Party in the 1960s and a new *Parti socialiste* in the 1970s which perceived their functions in a different light and could best be called a *parti d'électeurs*, that is, a party which tried to appeal to the widest possible electorate. The consequences of this development were, firstly, a more even geographical spread of the electoral support for a specific party (though some 'bastions' survive) and, secondly, a reduction in the extent to which party programmes were inspired by ideologies, which provided a source of slogans used to mobilize support, justify allegiance and attack adversaries. In the run-up to the 1986 National Assembly elections, one of the PS's themes was to try to strike horror in voters' minds by slogans such as *'Au secours, la droite revient'*, and *'Dis-moi, jolie droite, pourquoi as-tu de si grandes dents?'*. Presidential campaigns, however, relied on more emollient phrases such as Mitterrand's *'La force tranquille'* (1981), *'La France unie'*, *'Génération Mitterrand'* (both 1988), and Barre's *'Du sérieux, du solide, du vrai'* (1988).

Party appeal

All parties now have to appeal to a wider circle than their 'natural' or traditional supporters. Aware of its waning support, the PCF adopted less ideologically specific slogans calling for an *'Union du peuple de France'* (at its 22nd Congress in 1976) and a *'Rassemblement populaire majoritaire'* (25th Congress, 1985). Conscious of the mobilizing force of the word 'socialism', the RPR-UDF was led in the mid-1980s to use 'liberalism' as a counter, even though this created problems of interpretation in such a wide-based coalition before and after the March 1986 elections. Moreover, the distinction must be made between the anti-interventionist emphasis of continental liberal tradition and the preference for state-sponsored social reform characteristic of British liberalism.

In more concrete terms, political parties in France can hope to enlarge their appeal through the press and television, but by publishing political manifestos and sometimes 'blueprints for society' (*projets de société*) in paperback they have also exploited the relatively high propensity of the French people to buy easily digestable reading material. Early examples were the Radical Party's *Ciel et terre* in 1970 (the most comprehensive electoral promise of all time?), *Changer de cap* (PCF, 1971), *Changer la vie* (PS, 1972), *L'Enjeu* (UDR, 1975), *Des hommes, des femmes responsables dans une France terre de libertés* (CNIP, 1978). In the mid-1980s appeared *Libres et responsables* (RPR, 1984), *Réflexions pour demain* (Raymond Barre, 1984) and *Pour la France* (FN, 1985). By the end of the 1980s, however, the paperback book format tended to give way, on the grounds of cost, to mere booklets such as *La France citoyenne* (*Parti radical*, 1987), *Propositions pour la France* (PS, 1988) and *Le Pacte UDF pour la France* (UDF, 1988).

Opinion polls confirm the suspicion that television is the main influence on electoral behaviour, followed by news-papers, radio, magazines, and meetings, leaflets and posters. But 'conversations' and opinion polls themselves, over which the parties legally have no control, also figure on the list.

Party organization

The major political parties in France tend to have remarkably similar organizational structure. The basic geographical framework of party organization, as in so many aspects of French administrative life, is at the level of the *département*, and usually called a *fédération*; these normally have at least some full-time staff and co-ordinate groups at the local level, whether *comités de base* (Rad.) or *cellules* (PCF) grouped into *sections* (PCF and most other parties). The focus of member-ship activity in organizational terms is the national delegate conference held typically every two years, and called *congrès* (PCF, CDS, UDF, Rad., FN), *congrès national* (PS, *Fédération anarchiste*), *assemblée générale* (*Les Verts*), or *assises nationales* (RPR, *Génération écologie*). Parties can of course call special conferences when necessary, and they sometimes hold mini-conferences on matters of the moment in the intervals between full party conferences.

The conference elects (or rubberstamps the appointment of) a consultative body, sometimes referred to in the press as the 'parliament' of a party, called *conseil national* (RPR, PR, UDF, *Génération écologie*, CDS), *comité central* (PCF, FN), *comité directeur* (PS, CNI, MRG), or *conseil statutaire* (*Les Verts*), above which is the central policy-making group, the 'government' of the party. This is variously called the *bureau national* (Rad., PSD, MRG, CDS, *Génération écologie*), *bureau politique* (PCF, Rad., PR, UDF, RPR, UPF, FN), *commission exécutive* (CNI), *bureau exécutif* (PS) or *collège exécutif* (*Les Verts*), sometimes with a smaller core of leaders, a *secrétariat* (PCF, PR) or *commission exécutive* (RPR). The party leader, with whom of course the party will be associated in the minds of the public, is a *président* (RPR, UDF, CDS, Rad.), or *premier secrétaire* (PS); a *secrétaire général* can be the leader (PCF) or the number two to a president.

Party membership

Membership of French political parties is always difficult to assess with accuracy, since parties tend to inflate figures to prove their own popularity. In 1991, party claims were: PSU 500 (before it dissolved itself), PCF 600,000 (at the 27th Congress 1990), PS nearly 180,000 (though the 1990 Rennes Party Conference led to many non-renewals of membership), Radicals 6,000, CDS 30,000, PR 100,000, UDF 'direct members' 20,000, FN 100,000, RPR 800,000 (though 234,812 paid-up members was the figure deducible from the 'member subscription' part of their 1990 accounts). The sum of these figures, in fact, is in contradiction with the more objective estimate of academic commentators who put the total membership of French political parties at less than one million. Accuracy concerning party membership used to be possible only in relation to increasing or decreasing trends over, say, five-year periods, but the 1990 law requiring publication of accounts by those parties receiving state grants sheds more light on the matter. The major problem, of course, is to determine what constitutes membership. Parties which emphasize the possession of a membership card tend to ignore the concomitant requirement of a valid contribution payment record throughout the year, and their claims may rely too much on the number of cards sold, or given away, at mobilizing events such as the long-established *Fête de l'Humanité* (PCF, annually on the second weekend in September), the more recent *Fête de la Rose* (PS) or *Fête des bleus-blancs-rouges* (FN). In fact, even among French people who identify positively with one particular party, that is, whose interest goes potentially beyond merely voting reasonably consistently for a party, the desire to join or financially support that party is not strong, as Table 3 shows (the figures add up to more than 100 because of multiple replies).

Table 3
Question: *Parmi les choses suivantes, quelles sont celles que vous seriez prêt à faire pour le parti politique auquel vont vos préférences?*

Parler de son programme autour de vous	32
Assister à une réunion organisée par ce parti	33
Adhérer à ce parti	16
Participer à une manifestation organisée par ce parti	11
Lui donner de l'argent	6
Distribuer des tracts ou vendre des journaux de ce parti	6
Aucune de celles-ci	29
Sans opinion	7

Source: SOFRES, December 1983

Party youth movements

Youth movements are an obvious way in which parties can influence the political education of young people, as well as mobilize their energies at election times. Thus there is the *Mouvement de la Jeunesse communiste* (PCF) of which the *Union des étudiants communistes* is a part, *Mouvement de la Jeunesse socialiste* (PS), *Mouvement des jeunes radicaux de gauche* (MRG), *Mouvement des jeunes démocrates-sociaux* (CDS), *Mouvement des jeunes giscardiens* (PR, but obviously hitched to the political fortunes of Valéry Giscard d'Estaing) and the *Front national des jeunes* (FN). Even party factions have youth wings: *Mouvement des jeunes pour le changement* (*Socialisme et république*, a PS faction). Some parties however have no separate youth organization as such: the *Parti radical* has none because it is too small and not very youth-oriented, neither has the RPR because of its predecessor's experiences with its youth movement, the *Union des jeunes pour le progrès* (UJP), which caused problems. The latter could not decide whether it was a force for dynamic independent thought or a breeding ground for future party leaders; it could not stomach Chirac's alleged distortion of 'pure' Gaullism, and survived into the 1980s only as a minuscule isolated group.

Mobilization of the party faithful can take the form of

periodic meetings of the leaders of the *fédération* in each of the ninety-six *départements* in metropolitan France (though not all parties have an organization in every *département*). Alternatively, parliamentarians may meet together for *journées parlementaires* before the October and April National Assembly sessions, or sitting members and candidates, actual or potential, may gather in *université de printemps* or *université d'été*; these tend to be held in a salubrious part of Southern France (in Beaune in 1991, for example), though in the early 1990s, the *Front national* was denied a meeting place in many towns and cities.

Parliamentary candidature

Candidature in parliamentary elections is open to every citizen fulfilling certain legal conditions, but was progressively monopolized by political parties between 1958 and 1981, and after 1988, when a single-member constituency system operated. Moreover this tendency was compounded in 1986 by the system of proportional representation requiring a list of at least four people, which presupposed some coincidence of viewpoint and led to a reduction of the number of candidates not readily identifiable by party.

The typical candidate will emerge directly from the party, regarding candidature as a further step in commitment or in a political career. This is particularly so on the left, where PS candidates must have three years' party membership behind them, and about one-third of PCF candidates will be full-time party members – which explains why the proportion of 'new' candidates tends to be smaller for the PCF than for any other party. But a strongly entrenched 'independent' local politician is sometimes able (frequently on the right, very occasionally on the left) to negotiate, or tactically oblige, endorsement by a party with which he or she has the closest political affinities. Party central leaderships have played an increasingly important part in the Fifth Republic in approving candidatures arising at local constituency (or, in 1986, *département*) level, sometimes by mediating between rival personalities and their supporters, for example between a local contender and a total outsider indulging in what is called *parachutage*.

Financial aid

The question of the financial support which parties need for their activities, particularly at election times, has caused considerable problems. Parties receive contributions from members, but the level is far from adequate: it is supplemented by the handing over by *députés* of some of their salaries. In 1991, a *député* received, as well as free research and secretarial help, official postage and telephone expenses, rail and internal air travel, 29,113 francs monthly. Of this, UDF *députés* gave 2,000 francs to their party, and those of the RPR, 1,500 francs. PCF *députés* gave 15,000 francs, and the contribution of PS *députés* was means tested, working out at between 7,500 and 16,500 francs a month.

At present, if a parliamentary election candidate receives 5 per cent of votes cast, the state repays costs incurred in printing ballot papers, the propaganda sheets which are sent to voters with ballot papers, and the posters put on official hoardings outside polling stations. The money involved is not insignificant, but proposals to give state financial aid to the parties themselves to cover adequately the whole range of their activities have always run into difficulties. Giscard in his reforming mood raised the question in 1974 and again in 1978, but recognized the problems. For example, which 'parties' would qualify? Would there have to be a stricter legal framework, including of course a definition of a political party? On what basis would money be distributed – should it be on the percentage of votes received at parliamentary elections? The parties themselves, as one would expect, were generally in favour of official funding, but doubts about the destination of money given to the PCF was a problem; and sceptics pointed to the Italian and German examples, where a system of state financial aid did not put a stop to secret funding.

A 1988 law, instigated by the parties themselves (except for the PCF) in defiance of public opinion, established a system of state finance for parties. A sum was to be given:

– partly according to the proportion of total votes received in the previous National Assembly election (as a proviso there was to be a candidate in at least fifty constituencies; but no threshold percentage of votes was laid down)

– partly according to the number of *députés* and senators declaring themselves as belonging to a registered party (see Table 1 on page 42).

A total of 260 million francs was granted in 1991 under this heading: 95.5 million of this went to the *Parti socialiste* alone.

The 1988 law was complemented by another in January 1990 to enforce openness (*transparence*) of political party accounts, bringing them into the public domain. Thus *Parti socialiste* total receipts for 1990 consisted of 95.5 million francs state grant, 53 million in dues from ordinary members and elected members at all levels, and 25 million in donations and fund-raising channelled through national and local party organizations – the legal upper limit for donations was 50,000 francs for individuals and 500,000 francs for companies.

For the *Rassemblement pour la République* (RPR), total receipts in 1990 were 135.7 million francs, including 64.5 million state grant, 24 million in dues, 7.4 million local fund-raising mainly from businesses, and 39 million from mailshots and subscription dinners.

A 1991 National Assembly commission of inquiry nevertheless found that the new legislation had not eliminated shady financial practices in political parties. The *Front national*, which is funded largely from the personal fortunes of its leaders, collections at meetings, local councillors' allowances, and donations from business, nobility and former members of the armed forces, gives explicit hints on evading the legal constraints on political funding in its *Guide du candidat du Front national*.

Intra-party relations

The organizational structure of parties can lead to significant variations in the degree of internal democracy. The constitution (*statuts*) of the new PS in 1971 was based on a determined effort to move away from the 1945–69 period which allowed domination of the former SFIO by a small group under the leadership of Guy Mollet. The composition of the *comité directeur* is a direct reflection of the proportion of support at the party conference for general policy motions proposed by different factions (*courants*) within the party. On the other hand, delegates to the 1984 Grenoble Conference of the RPR merely confirmed Chirac's decision rather than debate a proposal to change the party's organizational structure. In the PCF, in keeping with the doctrine of 'democratic central-ism' (which survived an attempt at abolition at its 27th Congress in December 1990), the party conference elects the *comité central*, but there is only a single list of candidates already drawn up by the *bureau politique*.

Moreover, internal democracy in the PS of the kind described stops at the *comité directeur*. When this body comes to elect the smaller *bureau exécutif*, it does this by voting for lists, and the new leadership is composed of those names on the list which receive the most votes: in this way, a faction can be *majoritaire* (in the sense that it participates in the highest decision-making body of the party) or simply be excluded. For example, the faction called *Centre d'études, de recherche et d'éduca-tion socialistes* (CERES), a left-wing ginger group within the party, allied in 1971 with the faction around Mitterrand, to give the latter the leadership. But CERES was not happy with the increased importance within the PS from 1974 of a 'modernist' faction led by Michel Rocard. Rocardism repres-ented a technocratic approach to socialism, rejecting explicit doctrinal references, especially Marxist ones. The Mitterran-dists followed the pragmatic line of '*le socialisme du possible*'.

The PS in power after 1981 tried to minimize the centrifugal tendencies of the factions in an effort to present a united front. The factions continued to put forward their own motions on party strategy and self-image to party conferences, but com-posite motions (*motions de synthèse*) were hammered out and usually carried overwhelmingly, though difficulties did occur occasionally, such as at the Rennes Conference in March 1990. Issues sometimes cut across factions, for example, the schools question of 1983–84. Also some PS *députés*, feeling that existing factions were insufficiently attuned to changing cir-cumstances, created a new forward-looking *transcourant* group in 1985, though the suspicion was that this was a vehicle for the political ambitions of Laurent Fabius. Pulling in the opposite direction, a small extreme left faction, *Socialisme maintenu*, appeared in 1984–5, opposed to any move of the PS towards a social democratic position. CERES, always a vigorous PS faction, also attacked the '*social-libéralisme*' represented by Michel Rocard, but then in April 1986 adopted a milder stance and the new name of *Socialisme et république*, though still led by Jean-Pierre Chevènement, later a controversial Defence Minister (1988–91).

An examination of individual French political parties shows that they are not monolithic blocs, any more than parties in other countries, and that the extent of intra-party strife is quite significant. In 1972 the Radical Party split and its left wing broke away, soon afterwards taking the name of *Mouvement des radicaux de gauche* (MRG). In the 1980s the MRG was wracked by the dilemma of whether to revert to the search for a united Radical 'family', or whether to convert close electoral co-operation with the PS into outright amalgamation. In an effort to strengthen his right flank, Mitterrand in 1990 instigated *France unie*, a closer grouping, under Jean-Pierre Soisson and Michel Durafour, of the MRG, the *Association des démocrates* (i.e. non-PS government ministers) and vestigal left-wing Gaullists calling themselves *Convention de la Ve République*.

Even the Gaullist Party (RPR) officially recognized factions in 1988 and institutionalised them in 1989, in an effort to contain a revolt of younger *rénovateurs* against the Chirac-led old guard. Factions formed around Chirac and Alain Juppé as a mainstream; the 'odd couple' Charles Pasqua and Philippe Seguin, who set up an organization called *Demain la France* in 1991; Richard Cazenave who took over a social justice oriented faction called *Vie* when Alain Carignon was suspended in 1990; and Michel Noir and Michèle Barzac who left the party in 1990 and fought by-elections against official candidates.

Party leaderships are often in acute conflict with local branches: in 1986 FN dissidents in the *département* of Bouches-du-Rhône accused the local leadership of operating an old-boy network (*politique du copinage*), and left to create a *Front d'opposition nationale*; and the whole Radical Party membership (about 200) of the *département* of Puy-de-Dôme resigned from the party on the grounds that its incorporation into the UDF had taken it inexorably to the right. The composition of party lists for the March 1986 elections provoked much local ill-temper: the FN national leadership was accused of authoritarianism, and PS members did not like the inclusion of individual candidates and groups to its right, at the expense of its traditional working-class base. Earlier, the proposal to change to proportional representation for the 1986 elections caused strong resentment in those PS federations whose parliamentary representation would be reduced.

The most dramatic manifestation of intra-party conflict in the 1980s and 1990s was in the PCF. In an effort to emerge from the long period of opposition which had begun in 1947 (usually referred to as a 'political ghetto') the PCF in the 1960s and 1970s adopted a less uncompromising stance and showed signs of ideological flexibility. But the close co-operation with the PS which produced a joint policy programme to be applied when the left came to power was abruptly halted in 1977. This heralded a period of internal dissension hardly muted by the 1981–84 participation in a left-wing government. Factions representing differing strategies appeared:

1987 – *rénovateurs*, at first led by Pierre Juquin, who was soon expelled, stood as an independent left-wing presidential candidate in 1988, and in 1991 joined the Greens.

1987 – *reconstructeurs*, led by Marcel Rigout, who remained members but were stripped of leadership positions. They formed the *Association de recherche et d'initiatives pour l'autogestion et le socialisme*.

1989 – *refondateurs*, led by the four former PCF ministers of 1981–4, whose strategy was to reform the party from within. In 1990 Charles Fiterman founded the group *Refondations*.

By December 1990, the last two factions represented 25 per cent of the party, in terms of votes at the 27th Congress. The natural concomitant of this fission was a further decline in electoral support; the PCF presidential candidate's showing in 1988 was less than 7 per cent, the lowest since 1945.

Inter-party relations

Relations between parties in France are focused on the need in a multi-party system to maximize chances of electoral success, however slim these may be in reality, by co-operation with other parties. The Greens (*Les Verts*) try to apply the maxim '*ni gauche, ni droite*', but local factors often force them to ally with the left, or with the smaller *Génération écologie*, which claims to be more 'realistic'. Even parties which have been dominant at a given time – the Gaullist party in the 1960s, the PS in the 1980s – cannot ignore the fact that the circumstances which gave them this advantage (principally disarray in the opposing camp) may not endure in the longer term.

The post-war party system in France is best seen as a concretization in party terms of six main 'political families'. This term implies a tradition of shared memories, attitudes and beliefs which may pre-date the parties themselves: thus there was a body of thought and doctrine appearing at different points in history for communism, socialism, radicalism, Christian democracy, liberalism, and (more recently, of course) Gaullism, before the existence of the respective parties PCF; SFIO then PS; *Parti radical*; MRP then CDS; CNI/RI then PR and later UDF; the successive Gaullist parties (see page 45).

Inter-party relations during the Fifth Republic can be understood by reference to a 'snapshot' of the party system at three representative times:

A	Nov 1962	PCF	SFIO		Rad. MRP RI		UNR	
B	Mar 1977	PCF	PS+MRG		Rad. CDS PR		RPR	
C	May 1993	PCF	PS	ecologists	UDF		RPR	FN

Elections in 1958 to the new Fifth Republic parliament had continued the post-war pattern of a National Assembly in which the six political families mentioned above were represented by a party. But even though this six-party configuration was preserved after the election in November 1962 of a second parliament, a new phenomenon also appeared which has profoundly affected inter-party relations since that date. This was *le fait majoritaire*, that is, the existence in the National Assembly of a majority group of *députés* willing to give support to the government's policies. This group could be a government party, or closely co-operating group of parties, owing its majority position to the fact that voters were impressed by the past record of the President and the government appointed by him or, on the other hand, that voters preferred, as in 1981, 1986 and 1993, opposition policies. This *alternance* (peaceful transfer of power) made parties more 'respectable' in that an election could now mean a change of party or coalition of parties in power and not just a reshuffle of the previous governing coalition; but it took a long time to materialize. The majority in 1962 comprised the UNR and the RI led by Giscard; the Christian Democrat MRP was also very briefly associated, until de Gaulle alienated them by his anti-European utterances. The existence of this right-wing majority obliged the remaining parties to reassess their position. The MRP dissolved itself in 1966 to become the *Centre des démocrates sociaux* (CDS), dropping explicit allegiance to reformist Catholicism, but preserving its pro-European leanings and hoping to keep alive a separate centrist identity at a time of increasing bipolarization of the party system between right and left.

Bipolarization was fostered by the new method of electing the President, first applied in 1965. This was a two-round system where only the two best placed candidates went through to the second round. It was required from 1966 that a candidate in the first round of National Assembly elections must receive a number of votes equal to 10 per cent of registered voters in order to be permitted to stand again in the second round. This requirement was raised to 12.5 per cent in 1976.

It was particularly necessary for the left to adjust to the new reality of a majority in Parliament, if it was itself to constitute a majority of its own, but changes were slow to appear. The PS and PCF found it easy to continue with electoral co-operation, begun tentatively in 1962, whereby the candidate with fewer first round votes withdrew and urged his or her supporters to back the other party's candidate (*désistement réciproque*). This rational tactic allowed both parties to maximize their parliamentary representation in elections between 1967 and 1981, (and it applied informally in some constituencies in 1993) but co-operation on actual policy was a different matter. The strategy which eventually bore fruit in 1981 was begun in embryonic form by Mitterrand's presidential bid as the candidate of all the left and the 1965 elections. It was Mitterrand who realized that the left must accept that:

– the new Fifth Republic regime was entrenched in public opinion;

– the presidency was the locus of power in this regime;

– a majority in sociological terms could be converted into a parliamentary majority only if the non-communist left first united, and then acted in close political, and not just electoral, conjunction with the PCF.

To try to unite the non-communist left, Mitterrand in 1965 linked the SFIO, his own group of political clubs (CIR) and the Radical Party, but this attempt foundered in the aftermath of the 'events' of May–June 1968. The Radical Party then pursued its own course, and split in two in 1972. It was not until 1971 that the non-communist left was effectively united in the new *Parti socialiste*. Relations between socialists and the PCF, which had been characterized during the 1960s by 'two steps forward, one step back', took a major step forward in 1972 when the Joint Programme for Government was signed by the PS, the PCF and soon afterwards the MRG, and the *Union de la gauche* began actually to mean something. This development, together with the progressive incorporation between 1969 and 1974 of the centre (CDS) and the rump of the Radical Party into the governing right-wing majority, gave the party system a distinct bipolar appearance in the mid-1970s – in line B in the chart on p.58 the division between the two 'poles' of right and left would come between MRG and the Radical Party.

However, perfect bipolarization was impossible so long as left and right were not solid coalitions. Not only was the Giscardian wing of the right loosely structured and lacking a coherent policy – and the establishment of the UDF in 1978 did nothing to change this – but its relations with the Gaullists were far from harmonious during Giscard's presidency. This was especially true after 1976 when Chirac decided he could no longer continue as Prime Minister, and transformed the Gaullist Party into the RPR as a vehicle for his presidential ambitions. Chirac refused to let the RPR be 'giscardized'; and when Paris was finally allowed to have a mayor in 1977 he soundly beat Giscard's candidate in the election for the post.

On the left, the *Union de la gauche* suffered a setback in 1977 in failing to update the 1972 Joint Programme, and the PCF, unwilling to accommodate a shift in the centre of gravity (*rééquilibrage*) within the left, resumed hardline criticism of its socialist partners. When, in 1981, the dimension of joint participation in government became available, it should have marked the supreme achievement of the left's objectives, but instead it merely served to underline the divergent perceptions and strategies within the union. The PCF indulged in *participation sans soutien*, and this only until 1984. In any case the PS parliamentary landslide in June 1981 allowed it to constitute a majority on its own without having to rely on communist votes. The *Union de la gauche* appeared dead and buried by 1986 in national terms though there was some degree of electoral co-operation in the 1989 municipal elections, and some talk of the *Union* in anticipation of 1993 National Assembly elections. The *Union* had, since 1962, taken the form of joint opposition and joint government, but had never been put to the supreme test of joint parliamentary majority – a test which the right passed with difficulty in 1976–81 and again between 1986 and 1988.

The fact that Jacques Chirac failed to convert his two years as Prime Minister into a successful presidential bid in 1988 was a bitter blow to the parties of the right; moreover, in the

1988 parliament they could overturn the minority left-wing government on a motion of censure only if the communists voted with them. In the late 1980s, moves to closer co-operation between the RPR and the UDF were painfully slow in anticipation of the 1993 National Assembly elections, even though co-operation had been central to Giscard's strategy since 1983. Disagreement in 1989 over whether the co-ordinating organization should be called an *union* or an *alliance* was symptomatic of the way in which constraints on RPR-UDF co-operation remained strong. With a history of significantly divergent political culture and approaches to Europe and economic intervention, and with two long-established politicians and several younger aspirants in leadership contention, all that initially united the *Union pour la France* (UPF), set up in June 1990, was a determination not to countenance electoral co-operation with the *Front national*; the small CNI, which favoured co-operation, was therefore excluded from the UPF. Moreover, the UDF brought to the UPF not a dynamic mass organization strong at grass-roots level, but merely a loose amalgam of smaller groups with separate identities – CDS, PR, *Parti radical*, *Clubs perspectives et réalités*, *Parti social-démocrate* (PSD), and 'direct members' who asserted their identity by holding 'forums'. Of these groups, the PR contemplated a separate direct participation in the UPF, rather than through the UDF; and the CDS, in an effort to reassert centrism as a political force, had formed an autonomous parliamentary group, the *Union démocratique du centre* (UDC) in 1988. The RPR–UDF held single-issue conferences (*états généraux*) in 1990–1 in parallel with the establishment of the *Union pour la France*, but the latter was seen by opponents as little more than a device for future electoral co-operation by the selection of single right-wing candidatures, like the URC in 1988; Le Pen more harshly called it '*une combine pour la survie de l'Opposition*'.

The political fortunes of the extreme right in France were at a low ebb after 1945, but decolonization and especially the Algerian war (1954–62) gave a boost to virulent anti-system (which from 1958 meant anti-de Gaulle) nationalism; however, Jean-Marie Le Pen, as the leader of one of the extreme right factions – among which fusion and fission were rife – received only 0.76 per cent of the votes in his 1974 presidential bid. In 1981 he was unable to collect the 500 signatures legally required for a presidential candidature (raised from 100 in 1976) and the FN received only 0.18 per cent of the total vote in the National Assembly elections. But by making race and immigration an electoral issue – or as Le Pen would have it, by 'saying out loud what everybody thought in their hearts' – support climbed to 11 per cent in the 1984 European elections, and 14.4 per cent for Le Pen's 1988 presidential candidacy, before falling back again in 1993.

The post-1988 party system, therefore, revealed elements of bipolarization, in that an inchoate coalition on the right faced a party on the left – the PS – which had dominated the 1980s and which held, in the presidency, the trump card to deal with any future period of cohabitation. There were also elements of a multi-party system: two parties – the PCF and the FN – were excluded from the major 'poles' and this reinforced their anti-system tendencies.

Limits to party influence

In fulfilling their traditional function of 'intermediaries' between governors and governed, political parties in France, as elsewhere, aggregate interests, channel demands and draw up policies. Much political action, however, takes place out-side political parties or involves them only marginally. Some elements of this exclusion arise from factors specific to France:

– the particular circumstances of the first decades of the Third Republic, proclaimed in 1870, militated against the formation of a broad party representing labour interests. Political action in defence of the economic interests of labour has been undertaken as much by trade unions as by the parliamentary left.

– groups in the French second chamber pre-dated the foun-dation of political parties, and there are still groups in the Fifth Republic Senate not identifiable with a party (see Table 1 on page 42).

- during the nineteenth century, political clubs kept alive republican humanism associated with the 1789 Revolution. They still undertake political education and, especially in opposition, doctrinal renewal – functions which are not always performed well by the parties themselves.

- the phenomenon, not exclusively French, of broad-based nationalist movements has also militated against political parties – Bonapartism, particularly in its plebiscitary phase under the Second Empire, and in more recent times Petainism (1940–4) and pre-1969 Gaullism.

In his bid to re-establish the authority of the state, de Gaulle made a deliberate attempt to reduce the role of political parties in the new Fifth Republic regime: the President of the Republic was to be elected not by the two Chambers of parliament as before, but by a much larger *collège* (since 1965, of course, by the whole people); single-member constituencies were to reduce the salience of parties in electoral choice; the upper Chamber, peopled by largely non-party *notables*, was renamed the Senate and its role increased.

Moreover, political parties which played a crucial role in France, if not in establishing representative democracy, at least in defending it under the Third and Fourth Republics, have not always found it easy to come to terms with participatory democracy in the second half of the twentieth century. The *participation* which was a central element of de Gaulle's political thought has always occupied a minor place in the policy programme of the Gaullist Party, though it occasionally resurfaces. Advocacy of the self-management (*autogestion*) of units of economic – and by implication political and cultural – activity was half-heartedly undertaken by the left in the 1970s, particularly in the Rocardian faction of the PS. By the early 1990s, however, after the PSU dissolved itself, *autogestion* was reduced to a strand of left-wing Green thinking. Directly elected regional councils and a measure of administrative decentralization had to wait until the 1980s.

Parties would also be bypassed if, on presidential initiative, large issues of public concern were opened up to direct consultation of the people by referendum. De Gaulle did this successfully in 1962 and tried it unsuccessfully in 1969, but the notion is far from dead. The FN would want it on the question of capital punishment for terrorists and international drug dealers; Mitterrand briefly toyed with the idea in 1984 in the aftermath of the schools reform fiasco, and in 1991 suggested a referendum on reducing the presidential term of office to five years (a *quinquennat*).

A further measure of how political parties are far from all-pervading is that politicians, particularly on the left, are at pains to show awareness of a *société civile*, which is best understood as those non-state economic, social and cultural forces which give life to a society through their own initiative, outside spheres where the state has monopoly action or maintains a bureaucracy. Commentators have suggested that located within, or arising from, this civil society are counter-vailing forces (*contre-pouvoirs*), including the expanding phenomenon of *associations*, not all of which are explicitly political, which serve to limit the power of the state. Political parties in France may find it increasingly difficult to reconcile their desire to foster or exploit or supplant these forces, with their close involvement in the institutions of the state.

The role of parties in the system

It was this close involvement which, as the Fifth Republic developed, allowed political parties to recover the influence of which the framers of the 1958 constitution tried to deprive them. It was accepted that parties, as traditional defenders of representative democracy, would dominate the National Assembly – which was why the latter's powers were signifi-cantly curtailed; but parties came into their own again in three ways: firstly, the unforeseen emergence after 1962 of a parliamentary majority, and the coincidence of this with a presidential majority, if necessary by dissolving the National Assembly and holding new elections as in 1981 and 1988; secondly, the growth of bipolarization which made electoral choice between policy programmes or presidential candidates the determinant of political decisions; and, thirdly, the close relationship between political parties and the presidency.

While it is true that the original Gaullian concept of a

non-party President lingers (some people in 1965 thought somebody like Albert Schweitzer could take over from de Gaulle, and the equivalent line of thought in the 1980s produced names like Bernard Tapie or Yves Montand), the parties have become indissociable from political power by offering what they did before 1958, namely a path to the highest political office. Because this office is the directly elected presidency, every party in France has to be in the basic sense a *parti d'électeurs*. The phenomenon can be looked at in two ways.

Firstly, one can speak of the 'presidentialization' of political parties. Public acceptance in the 1962 referendum of a directly elected presidency meant that politicians who were recognized as serious potential candidates (*présidentiable*) gained in stature within their party, and parties began to discard ideological baggage and detach themselves from too specific class clienteles. The formal structure of parties, or at least the leadership composition and role of grass-roots members, tended to be modified (e.g. UDR in 1967, PS gradually during the 1970s) to give support to any member who appears to be *présidentiable* and, more importantly, to increase his or her general popularity; the obvious reason was that, to win a second round run-off, candidates need much wider support than the traditional electorate of a single party. Thus Pompidou needed the support of some centrists in 1969, Giscard of some Gaullists led by Chirac (rewarded with the office of Prime Minister) in 1974, and Mitterrand of communists in 1981 and centrists in 1988. A party needs a candidate of stature in the eyes of the electorate, but a serious candidate needs more than a party. Moreover, having more than one candidate who is *présidentiable* can be a source of weakness for a party, for example Mitterrand and Rocard in the PS in 1981, and in the mid-1990s Rocard, Fabius, Chevènement and Delors on the left, and Giscard, Chirac, Léotard and Carignon on the right.

The second aspect of the close association of a political party with the presidency is when a presidential strategy is successful and a party's candidate becomes President. Already under the Giscard presidency (1974–81) the decisive role of the parties in government composition and presidential action was being felt – the President needed the Gaullist Party and ministers were in the government as representatives of their party; also, party nepotism and administrative clientelism began to take root. So it might have been thought, when the 1981 and 1988 elections produced a socialist President and a PS majority in the National Assembly (actual in 1981, virtual in 1988), that the Socialist Party would be in a position to determine the major orientations of policy. But while it is true that there could be hard bargaining before the party gave its support to the government (for example the 1990 recasting of the social welfare contribution scheme as a *contribution sociale généralisée*), the *Parti socialiste* was never allowed to impose its will on the President or the government. The party leadership was not allowed to assume a mediating function between the post-1981 and post-1988 governments and the PS parliamentary group; and there was acrimony in 1985 when both Jospin as party leader and Fabius as head of the government claimed to be in charge of the socialists' campaign for the forthcoming elections.

In the final analysis, the PS in power was subject to the institutional logic of the Fifth Republic. Mitterrand used presidential powers to reduce party influence in Chirac's 1986 government by rejecting party leaders as Defence and Foreign Affairs ministers, and imposing non-party ministers. Even Chirac himself had to call Francois Léotard to order for putting his party role as PR leader before his ministerial functions.

Mitterrand's electoral triumph in 1981 and 1988 was based on a programme worked out by his own team, not by the party leadership, though obviously there was cross-membership. When people spoke of a 'PS State' in 1981–6, as they had of a 'UDR State' in the late 1960s, they were saying no more than that there was a dominant political party which had successfully adjusted to a novel situation. French political parties have largely recovered from the subordinate position to which the Fifth Republic regime, as initially conceived in 1958, had consigned them. However, in a decade when French people speak of a 'crisis in politics', of 'democracy in danger' and of the need for a 'renewal of politics', the role, perceived function and mutual relations of political parties in the France of the mid-1990s are far from settled.

Bibliography

Chapsal, J., *La vie politique sous la Ve République*. Paris, PUF, vol.
1: 1958–74 (1987); vol. 2: 1974–87 (1989). Provides a
historical narrative on Fifth Republic politics from an
institutional perspective.

Duhamel, A., *La République giscardienne*. Paris, Grasset, 1980;
and *La République de Monsieur Mitterrand*. Paris, Grasset,
1982. Provide a readable account of the political background between 1974 and late 1981, and could be supplemented by the more recent: July, S., *Les Années Mitterrand*.
Paris, Grasset, 1986; and Giesbert, F.-O., *Le Président*.
Paris, Seuil, 1991.

In English, the following introductory books are suggested:

Slater, M., *Contemporary French Politics*. London, Macmillan,
1985. Description and analysis are accompanied by texts in
French and linguistic exercises.

Stevens, A., *The Government and Politics of France*. London,
Macmillan, 1992.

Wright, V., *The Government and Politics of France*. London,
Hutchinson, 1989.

Books which are relatively easy to read and digest from the
point of view of content are:

Adereth, M., *The French Communist Party: a critical history 1920–
84*. Manchester, MUP, 1984.

Bell, D. S. and Criddle, B., *The French Socialist Party: the
emergence of a party of government*. Oxford, Clarendon Press,
1988.

Bennahmias, J.-L. and Roche, A., *Des Verts de toutes les couleurs
– histoire et sociologie du mouvement écolo*. Paris, Albin Michel,
1992.

Borella, F., *Les partis politiques dans la France d'aujourd'hui*. Paris,
Seuil, 1990.

Charlot, J., *The Political Parties in France*. A fifty-six page
booklet published by the Ministry of Foreign Affairs in 1986
and available from embassies.

Dupin, E., *L'Après-Mitterrand: le Parti socialiste à la dérive*. Paris, Calmann-Levy, 1991.

Frears, J., *Parties and Voters in France*. London, Hurst, 1990.

Lancelot, A., *Les élections sous la Vᵉ République*. Paris PUF, 1988.

Petitfils, J.-C., *L'Extrême-droite en France*. Paris, PUF, 1988.

Sainteny, G., *Les Verts*. Paris, PUF, 1991.

Tartakowsky, D., *Une histoire du PCF*. Paris, PUF, 1982.

Ysmal, C., *Les Partis politiques sous la Vᵉ République*. Paris, Monchrestien, 1989.

Books which are useful, but which may be of greater conceptual difficulty are:

Avril, P., *Essais sur les partis politiques*. Paris, Payot, 1991. Not all on France.

Bergounioux, A. and Grunberg, G., *Le long remords du pouvoir – le Parti socialiste français 1905–92*. Paris, Fayard, 1992.

Bourseiller, C., *Extrême-droite: l'enquête*. Paris, F. Bourin, 1991.

Juquin, P., *Autocritiques*. Paris, Grasset, 1985. By a former member of the PCF bureau politique.

Kergoat, J., *Le Parti socialiste*. Paris, Le Sycomore, 1983.

Nay, C., *Le Noir et le rouge*. Paris, Grasset, 1984. On Mitterrand's political career.

Petitfils, J.-C., *La Démocratie giscardienne*. Paris, PUF, 1981.

Philippe, A. and Hubscher, D., *Enquête à l'intérieur du parti socialiste*. Paris, A. Michel, 1991.

Robrieux, P., *La Secte*. Paris, Stock, 1985. On the PCF.

Roucaute, Y., *Le Parti socialiste*. Paris, Huisman, 1983.

Roussel, E., *Le Cas Le Pen – les nouvelles droites en France*. Paris, J. C. Lattes, 1985.

Todd, E., *The Making of Modern France: ideology, politics and culture*. Oxford, Basil Blackwell, 1991; translation of *La Nouvelle France*. Paris, Seuil, 1987.

Touchard, J., *La Gauche en France depuis 1900*. Paris, Le Seuil, 1981.

The following are useful journal articles:

Pouvoirs, no. 1, 3ᵉ édition (1984): 'L'Alternance'.

Pouvoirs, no. 20 (1982): 'La Gauche au pouvoir'.
Pouvoirs, no. 28 (1984): 'Le RPR'.
Pouvoirs, no. 41 (1987): 'Le Président'.
Pouvoirs, no. 49 (1989): 'La Vᵉ République'.

Revue française de science politique: vol. 36 no. 1 (Feb. 1986) includes articles on French political parties; vol. 40 no. 6 (Dec. 1990) deals with the classical right.

L'Etat de l'opinion, published annually by Seuil, has SOFRES opinion polls, but also essays by prestigious analysts on political parties and politics in general.

Other media

French-speaking radio stations can usually be received adequately on long wave and are a source of information on the current political scene (all times quoted are local times in France).

France-Inter
(1,852m): the early morning weekday news has a guest, though not always a politician, at 8.20 a.m., and a review of the press at 8.30 a.m. Twenty minutes or so into the 1 p.m. news there is a five-minute interview, often with a politician, on a topical issue. At 7.20 p.m. on weekdays except Fridays (when there is a political interview called 'Objections') a phone-in programme is the long-established pattern.

Europe 1
(1,639m): the early morning weekday political coverage is at 7.24 and 7.43 a.m., with an interview at 8.26 a.m. On Mondays at 7.00 p.m. is the well-tried formula of 'Club de la presse' where a politician is interviewed by a panel of journalists. On Saturdays, short political comment is at 8.37 a.m.; on Sundays at 8.46 a.m.

R.T.L.
(1,271m): the hour-long 'Grand jury', interviewing a politician is at 6.30 p.m. on Sundays.

3

Trade unions
Richard McAllister

Introduction

Most observers are struck by the basic continuity and similarity of the economic policies pursued by successive French governments, whether notionally of the right or left, since about 1982. These policies, including 'rigour' and austerity, have often been defended as a necessary, perhaps an inevitable, result of several developments. These have included: globalization of markets (including financial markets); the whole move towards a single market within the European Community; and the continuous pressure exercized on French manufacturing and traded goods sectors especially via the country's membership of the Exchange Rate Mechanism (ERM) of the European Monetary System (EMS).

Such conditions have not been propitious for French trade unions. A report by the national statistical institute INSEE in late 1991 suggested that the industrial share of total employment in France dropped, from about 24 per cent in 1970 to 18 per cent in 1990; that French industry had seen the loss of about one million jobs in that period; and that the steel and textiles sectors had lost more than half their workforces in that time. During the 1980s, French industrial growth had been several percentage points below the EC average.

It is true that many of these conditions applied, *mutatis*

mutandis, to trade unions in other west European states. It is also true that unions in other European states as well as France have seen their membership figures slide downwards during this period. But alongside these shared trends and common experiences, there are a number of features which are specific to the French situation. Unions in France have suffered from at least five kinds of weakness: numerical weakness; ideological divisions and difficulties in relationships among the various confederations; difficult relationships between leaderships and rank and file; between all confederations and the *patronat*; and with government and the political parties. This chapter will explore each of these. Although there have been some signs of change and some attempts at accommodation in recent years, yet many of these difficulties are of long standing, their roots going far back into French history.

Yet they continue to be influential: and this was clearly shown, amongst other occasions, in October 1991. Then, certain French trade unions promised a socialist-led government that they would create, in the words of one of their leaders, 'economic death for twenty-four hours' via a general strike. In the event, the response was poor, and for many people, the strike passed almost unnoticed.

This episode illustrates several of the weaknesses just mentioned. First, the position of the unions in general, frail a decade ago, had weakened considerably further by this time. Second, although early in the dispute several union confederations had managed a measure of agreement, there remained important elements of disunity and disagreement. Third, even the Cresson government, weak though it was, was, like its predecessors of a different political hue, adept at exploiting these differences. Fourth, most of the action, such as it was, centred on the public rather than the private sector, highlighting the long-standing dichotomy of the fortune of French trade unions. Fifth, though the unions threatened much, their bark was (as often) worse than their bite, even when faced by a government of rare unpopularity. The episode of October 1991 illustrates both the long-term and the more recent difficulties of trades unions in France. It is with the more endemic problems that we begin.

Background

When Giscard was elected President in 1974, one of his first moves was to commission a report on reform of enterprises, the Sudreau Report. It traced the origins of the 'crisis of confidence between the social partners' back to the d'Allarde decree and the *loi le Chapelier* of 1791. The latter, in particular, had prohibited members of any trade or profession from combining on the basis of their 'supposed common interests'. Reform of this situation was a long time coming, grudgingly given and limited: the recognition of unions (significantly, *syndicats*) by the law of 1884 did not give them the freedom to operate within individual plants, and most public services (including the railways) were prohibited initially from unionizing. The right to organize union sections in the workplace was not finally established until a law was passed in December 1968, in the wake of 'the Events'.

Divisions were apparent almost immediately after the passing of the 1884 law. Indeed, despite changes of name and on occasion of stance, it is remarkable how closely the original lines of division match those of much later times: revolutionary and reformist; 'confessional' and secular. Right from the start, the divisions between the main strands of socialism in France found their echo in the industrial organizations. The strategy of political action – the need to conquer the machinery of state to better the workers' lot – was represented by the Marxist *Fédération nationale des syndicats*, founded in 1886. A different approach, seeking originally to 'domesticate' the labour movement, the 'self-help' and self-improvement strategy, was represented by the *Bourses du travail*, combining employment-exchange with educational and friendly society functions. These formed a national federation in 1892. The *Confédération générale du travail* (CGT), founded in 1895, was to become the most important national organization. It preached industrial action; but, although it commanded the loyalties of the majority of the militant working class in the period up to the First World War, it has never succeeded in uniting all the main unions. Almost as if following the Leninist precept ('split, split and split again!') it has itself split three times – in 1921, 1939 and again in 1948. Yet another contrasting strain was 'social-Catholic' in origin, pre-dating, in the *Cercles ouvriers* of the 1870s, the actual legalization of unions; but given a powerful push by the Papal Encyclical *Rerum Novarum* of 1891. This urged Catholics to become actively involved in the problems of workers.

At various points during the last century, a greater degree of unity in the trade union movement has seemed possible; but at each point it has been overwhelmed by the forces making for disunity. Lack of unity was no surprise in the swirling tides of the generation that followed the Paris Commune. But it seemed that, when the different strands of French socialism came together in 1905 to form the *Section française de l'Internationale ouvrière* (SFIO), this might lead in turn to greater unity in the trade union movement. It did not do so because the CGT at that time was dominated by revolutionary syndicalists who believed that a revolutionary general strike was essential and despised those who became embroiled in parliamentary charades. The other principal occasion when unity seemed possible was the electoral victory of the coalition of the left, the Popular Front, in 1936. For three years, indeed, the CGT was reunited: but the 'Muscovite' allegiance of its leading communists was clear (not for the first or last time) in their support of the Nazi-Soviet pact in 1939, and again a split occurred.

The Second World War brought great repression and suffering to all trade unionists, and this, together with the important part played by a number in the Resistance, helped to recreate a sense of solidarity. Once again, it proved short-lived. The Fourth Republic was only a couple of years old when 'cold war' tensions once again caused a split which has so far proved enduring.

The main divisions in the French trade union movement date from this period. Since then, there have been three large confederations, as well as two other important bodies and a host of minor ones. The biggest (though its dominance has never again reached the same heights as at the time of the Liberation) was, and continues to be, the CGT. Its two main rivals were the *Confédération générale du travail – force ouvrière* (CGT-FO) and the *Confédération française des travailleurs chrétiens* (CFTC). The CGT has been, throughout its post-War history, very closely allied indeed to the French Communist Party (PCF). It has always retained token non-communists in certain positions, but the key offices are nowadays virtually monopolized by PCF Members: even now when the Party is so enfeebled. It was precisely to counter this obedience to the PCF line – and behind it, it was usually thought, the Moscow line – that the CGT-FO was set up in 1948. It was mildly socialist, and reformist in outlook and tactics. The CFTC was much older: its roots were in the social-Catholic tradition of the nineteenth century already mentioned; but it was actually set up in 1919. Although both Catholics and Protestants could be members, it was of course predominantly Catholic. As time went by, it generally became more radical; in doing so, it exchanged the earlier suspicion felt towards it by other unions that it was 'yellow', a creature of the *patronat*, for the suspicion of many Church leaders (that it was a tool of communist and socialist revolution – even if an unwitting one). As this strain grew, it gradually lost its Church links, and these ended finally in 1964. It then split; the great majority marking the shift by a change of name to that which it bears today: *Confédération française démocratique du travail* (CFDT). Only about a tenth opted to retain the 'Christian' formula and the old name CFTC, thus creating another, minor, breakaway confederation.

In addition to the 'big three', certain other organizations should be mentioned. Next largest is a trade union federation which is specific to a particular sector, and thus not affiliated to a confederation: the *Fédération de l'éducation nationale* (FEN), which has grown rapidly in line with the expansion of education since 1945. Next in importance is the *Confédération française de l'encadrement* (CFE-CGC). The original CGC was founded in 1944, representing those *cadres* – managerial, technical and scientific personnel – who disliked the political affiliations of the other confederations and wished to defend their status and income differentials. There are other minor groups as well: the *Confédération des syndicats indépendants*; the *Confédération des syndicats autonomes*; the distinctly 'mild' and non-striking *Confédération français du travail* (CFT), and so on.

The fragmentation and division of the French trade union

movement is both cause and effect of its ineffectuality – which is examined in greater detail below. This sort of fragmentation is not uncommon in western Europe. There are united trade union movements in Britain and West Germany for example; but in Belgium, Holland, Italy, Spain and Switzerland, the situation is more like that in France.

In general, such division is but one aspect of deep political cleavages that may be based on social, ideological, or geographical factors, or a combination of all three. In such a situation, the political left is almost always split too (though this is less true of Holland), and this holds whether or not there are close organizational links between parties and unions. In France, a number of factors in the general environment of the trade unions has tended to heighten divisions between them. The most important appear to be: the revolutionary tradition; the religious factor, and the pattern of economic development of the country over the last century and a half.

The tradition of seeking fundamental change through revolution is well known. In both the late eighteenth and the nineteenth centuries, the lessons to be derived from seeking social change by revolutionary means have been much contested in France. This was no less true of the blood-bath of the 1871 Paris Commune than of earlier episodes, and sharpened the divide within the working class between reformists and revolutionaries. Likewise with the religious question: despite the existence of 'progressive' Catholicism, religion was regarded as fundamentally reactionary by much of the left. In France, religious practice has for long been regionally differentiated; and has been strong in, amongst other places, several parts of the north and east which have also become main industrial centres. The religious question dominated political debate in the first years of the present century, and since then has helped to sustain a major division within the trade union movement.

The pattern of economic development in France has also enhanced division within the trade union movement. Although rapid economic change occurred only patchily in most countries, it was particularly patchy in France, and the places most affected by the new developments – including the development of an industrial working class – were often physically far removed from each other. Local conditions, too, were very diverse: again, not conducive to the growth of a unified and powerful mass movement with a sense of common cause underpinned by similarity of experience and relative ease of communication. The main industrial concentrations were around Paris, and in the north and east; there were patches (for example in mining areas) elsewhere. The result was a ghetto mentality: the industrial working class was aware of being in a minority; and in addition, often worked in relatively small plants and factories harder to organize than large units; and local conditions, including wage-rates most notably, differed strikingly until quite recently.

Recent economic changes have been numerous, but their effects somewhat ambiguous. By the mid-1970s, it was clear that twenty-five years of rapid economic growth were coming to an end. During that period, France had become a much more industrial country, and in some ways, more of a mass society than ever before. By the late 1970s, however, the talk was of de-industrialization. The high growth period was itself marked by one major explosion, in the tradition of the *drame révolutionnaire* – the Events of May–June 1968. This produced quite considerable changes in industrial attitudes – on both sides of industry. The period also saw the growth to a dominant position in the economy of a number of large firms: some already nationalized, such as Renault; some originally not, but nationalized under Mitterrand (such as Rhône-Poulenc); and some remaining in the private sector (Peugeot-Citroën). Questions not merely of ownership, but of how firms should be run, came more to the fore. France from this period has become much more urbanized, and has experienced a very large growth of salaried employees. Despite this, in general the number of trade unionists has declined; French trade unionism remains numerically weak as well as organizationally divided. And despite the many changes under the Fifth Republic, the influence of the more distant past continues to weigh heavily.

The trade unions and ideology

The influences of ideological differences upon the French trade union movement appear to be many and varied, but are in practice hard to evaluate. Two points stand out. The first is that it is not always the *same* beliefs or ideologies which have been prominent. The second is that there has always been an element of ideological competition, a tendency for some groups to indulge in leap-frogging with others in the escalation of demands (a phenomenon not limited to the unions), and for other groups to distance themselves deliberately from this process. An interesting question, but a hard one to answer is whether ideology has had any 'independent' effect on members or non-members of trade unions in France, whether it can be said to have attracted or repelled them, or to have shaped their perceptions of the world and how they relate to it.

The ideologies that have had prominence have changed; or a particular trade union grouping has sometimes changed its ideological attachment. Revolutionary syndicalism – the belief in a great general strike to bring about massive societal change – though it remains present, is now advocated by few (though often influential) people. It was the original credo of the CGT at the end of the nineteenth century, and it was especially influential around 1900–10. It was not a single, self-consistent doctrine but rather a reflection of an attitude and a mood. Thus its most famous expression, the Charter of Amiens adopted by the CGT Congress of 1906, talked about improving the workers' lot in essentially reformist ways, but added that complete emancipation required the expropriation of the capitalist class; this would be brought about by a general strike which would establish the *syndicats* no longer as mere 'resisters' but as the basis of the new social order. Revolutionary utopianism was therefore very much part of the credo too.

These years were perhaps the high watermark of revolutionary syndicalism. But in 1908, a sharp increase in unemployment was followed by severe repression by the authorities of the syndicalist movement. In the very next year, 1909, the CGT leadership was taken over by one of the hardiest perennials ever of the French trade union movement, Léon

Jouhaux. He remained its general secretary from 1909 to 1947, when, logically for one of his views, he transferred his allegiance to the CGT-FO. It was he who converted the CGT to a much more reformist approach.

This approach, however, had been directly challenged by the Russian Revolution of 1917 and events immediately following it. A growing body of opinion looked to the Soviet model of a successful revolution; others favoured continuing along a parliamentary road to socialism. This divide showed itself first in the political parties, leading to the setting up of the PCF at the Tours Conference in 1920. But its effects did not stop there, for Leninists of the PCF believed that the trade unions required the lead of a revolutionary political party with a high degree of class consciousness. They also maintained that the unions should be subordinate to the party which should infiltrate and control them, since, left to their own devices, they would concentrate only on the narrow sectional interests of their members and could achieve little. This view was totally opposed to that of the social democrats and reformists: the conflict came to a head in the violent 1921 Lille Conference which culminated in the expulsion of the communists. At this point the communists were in the minority, and set up their own organization, the CGTU (*Confédération générale du travail unitaire*).

This episode left a deep legacy of hatred between communists and non-communists, within both parties and the unions. Only on certain occasions since were the PCF and CGTU willing or able to associate closely with non-communists on the left, notably during the 1930s when the Soviet Union, alarmed at the rise of fascism and national socialism, was prepared to back the Popular Front. But the events, first of the 1930s – deep economic depression, and the fight against fascism – and then of the Second World War, served to increase the appeal of the communists. Their excellent organization helped them in the Resistance: in turn, their excellent Resistance record gave them a dominant position in the immediately post-war trade union movement. At the CGT 1946 Conference, the communists could count on about 80 per cent of the vote.

For a short while all seemed workable: Jean Monnet's

proposals for planning looked to trade union involvement; even De Gaulle's Bayeux speech had looked to increased functional representation. It did not last long. The tensions of the 'cold war' period reached very directly into French politics: after the expulsion of the communist members of government in 1947, the CGT called a wave of strikes which were widely described as 'insurrectionary' and certainly seemed aimed at bringing government and the economy to its knees. Non-communists within the CGT became more and more alarmed; an unease increased by the Prague coup of February 1948 which confirmed the worst fears of many about Moscow-inspired methods. Once again there was a split; but this time, with the communists firmly in the majority, it was most of the non-communists who left CGT to set up the CGT-FO in 1948. The bitterness of this period marked relations between the two groupings for a long time thereafter, even though the seriousness of subsequent conflicts was generally not as great. The new union, CGT-FO, sought to distinguish itself from the CGT by concentrating directly on issues of 'relevance' to its membership, rather than honing them for the wider political struggle, or, indeed, as CGT did, taking up cudgels on behalf of the non-unionized in an effort to widen its constituency. In its turn, CGT-FO was also very much a child of the 'cold war'; it was widely reported to have not only the (domestic) support of SFIO, but that of US Unions and the CIA as well.

The third main confederation had, as we have seen, a very curious history. CFTC drew much of its membership from the lower middle classes and from women; it was rather despised by other confederations, yet its membership was greater than that of GCT-FO for much of the time. Post-war, its original ideological position may be described as 'liberal-Catholic'. As with other French trade unions, however, it claimed for itself independence of all political parties, and, with the shift to the right of the Christian democratic MRP and of economic policy, CFTC took its distance. The final victory of its Reconstruction group led to the split and formation of CFDT in 1964. From that point on, as we shall see, events (and the Events) took over: the CFDT went through an 'ultra-radical' phase, before swinging rather more recently towards trying to find a middle-way between social democracy and Marxism. Its successes during the 1970s and 1980s owe not a little to the influential General Secretary of the period, Edmond Maire, to whom we shall return.

The fact that a number of different ideologies and perspectives are catered for in the unions might be thought conducive to overall numerical strength. The opposite is the case. France is virtually at the bottom of the European league in the proportion of the workforce that is unionized. In Switzerland, that proportion is about 90 per cent; the EC average is some 40 per cent, with West Germany, Italy and the UK all near the 40 per cent level. In France the figure has been falling steadily: equally significant, there are serious disagreements about just what the membership figures actually are, both overall and for individual confederations. It is certain that the overall figure is far below 20 per cent; several estimates put it around 13 per cent and one as low as 9 per cent. Thus, despite the range of ideology, there is a real problem about the 'representativeness' of trade unions in France which, when added to the hostile instincts of the *patronat*, especially at plant level, has made for prickly and difficult relations between the two sides.

Organization and record

The picture that emerges then, is one of underdevelopment and weakness. French trade unions have had an uphill struggle to be taken seriously by the *patronat*, by government and by the mass of workers. There have been surges in their numerical strength – after the First World War, after the Popular Front victory of 1936; following the Second World War, and following the Events of 1968 – but there have also been relapses.

The unions have usually been regarded by employers as unreliable partners: as unable to make a settlement stick with the shop-floor and even as unable to control strike action. The Sudreau Report commented on the tendency of the grassroots to 'spontaneous' action. The trade unions as such have generally been seen as only one of a number of channels for contact, negotiation and management of industrial relations and, depending upon the situation in the particular factory or plant, have by no means always been the preferred one. There are also the *délégués du personnel*, finally confirmed in law in 1936. In addition, there are the *comités d'entreprise* (or works councils) set up after the Second World War in all undertakings with a staff of fifty or more. The *délégués* have generally been the more effective 'grievance' channel. The *comités* (chosen by the staff from among candidates usually nominated by the unions), which deal with welfare and social activities, and are supposed also to act as a channel for information and advice between management and workers, have usually been less effective. Unions have also had to vie with each other to obtain the status of 'most representative' union. This status confers important rights (of negotiation and representation), is bestowed by the state, and may be – and has been – challenged in the administrative courts.

The organization of trade union activity in France is both territorial and functional. Most main bodies are confederations, with a decentralized and usually rather weak structure. The CGT, for example, has both a geographical structure (*unions locales, unions départementales*) and a professional (or occupational) structure (*sections syndicales d'entreprise, syndicats, fédérations nationales*) together making up the *confédération*. The total membership of French trade unions is small, almost certainly below 3 million. All confederations have habitually claimed more adherents than their paid-up membership. The CGT probably has well under a million paid-up members and the numbers have fallen in most of the last fifteen years, mainly in response to the perceived 'wrecking tactics' of the communists over the 'united-left' negotiations and the 1978 legislative elections. One recent estimate has put CGT's paid-up membership as low as 600,000. A 1984 estimate put CFDT's membership at between 800,000 and 900,000; the lowest recent estimate has been 400,000. It had grown substantially following its radical stance in the Events of 1968. The membership of CGT-FO is also disputed: the lowest recent estimate is 400,000; it is unlikely to be above 800,000. It also grew for a while, partly as its 'moderate' stance of co-operation with management found some echoes among the

Demonstration
by members
of the CGT.

more reformist and innovative sections of the *patronat* during the 1970s. FEN probably had about 0.5 million members in 1984 and may have fallen to little more than 200,000; and CGC between 300,000 and 500,000. It is striking first, that the estimates vary so widely; second, that everyone agrees that numbers have fallen steadily, and that the traditional union weaknesses in the private sector have now spread to the public sector also.

All the organizations suffer from limited financial resources and consequently limited numbers of paid headquarters staff. At 'confederal' level, CGT and CFDT each have head-quarters staffs of only between one and two hundred: FO has well below a hundred. Constituent organizations, with small budgets of their own, also support very small staffs. There is heavy reliance upon unpaid 'militants' at local level, which in turn decreases the control between the various levels. Nor do the confederations have substantial strike-funds to support a prolonged strike, and one result is a marked preference for token one-day stoppages, work-to-rule, go-slow and rotating lightning-strikes, affecting one plant after another unpredictably. Action at the plant level is very often unsuccessful, even if spectacular (e.g. occupation of sites, locking-in of management and so on). Negotiations frequently have to be referred to much higher, and usually national level if they are to succeed.

Such has been the tradition. There is also evidence of change; but the changes have not been in a constant direction. Certain changes of a 'modernizing' kind seemed to be set in train by the famous Events of 1968; others, including the steady haemorrhaging of membership, have been the result rather of the changed conditions of the 1980s and 1990s.

The Events and their aftermath

It is generally agreed that the Events took most people, and certainly much of the union leadership, by surprise. The CGT was especially alarmed at the outbreak of 'spontaneity' (demands for a transformation of work-relations and so on) and sought to alter and limit demands and to channel them into the traditional mould – rates of pay and hours, benefits and so on. Although they succeeded in doing this to some extent, in other ways the Events did signal a long period of reflection and reconsideration, on all sides, of the role of trade unions and their relationships both with employers and with the activities of the state.

From the point of view of the union leaderships, the grievances that had appeared at the time of the Events were not new. They felt left out in the cold by government economic policy; victims of a 'reform' of the social security system in 1967 in which they had not been involved and which appeared to combine higher contributions with unchanged or diminished benefits. Unemployment was rising, and real wages were held down in the name of 'competitiveness' and the wider 'financial rigour' by which France in the late 1960s sought to build a substantial balance of payments surplus which could be turned – literally – into gold; transported to the vaults of the Bank of France, hence forcing the 'Anglo-Saxon profligates' – the United States and Britain – to mend their ways. The protests began at the grass-roots; they were not directed by union leaderships. They were aimed, most of all, at antiquated social relationships, rigid and outdated attitudes especially of management. Much of what happened, too, was in imitation of the students – the occupation of factories in particular – even though no united front between students and workers was established.

At the time, it was claimed that the general strike peaked with some 9 million involved. Though this was almost certainly an exaggeration, the government was badly shaken and at one time looked as if it might fall. But the longer the chaos continued, the stronger the reaction to it became, as the massive Gaullist victory in the election a month later proved.

The main forces involved differed sharply in their reactions at the time, and in their attitudes afterwards. The CGT, along with the PCF, declared that a revolutionary situation 'did not exist'. Regardless of the ability of the government to 'defend the Republic' by military means (de Gaulle was absent, endeavouring to reassure himself on this point, at the height of the crisis) it was fairly clear that there could be no 'revolution-ary situation' if the CGT and PCF declared that there was none. The CGT settled for accommodation in the Grenelle agreements – mainly involving an across-the-board 10 per cent pay increase and a one-third rise in the minimum wage (then known as SMIG, later rechristened SMIC – *Salaire minimum interprofessionnel de croissance*), which also served to reduce differentials. They had no intention of seeking 'trans-formations' of work-relationships which might take the edge off class antagonism and alienation. Yet Georges Séguy, then General Secretary of CGT, was heckled and booed for his acceptance of the Grenelle agreements; militant workers, many of them not unionized, were seeking – realistically or not – much wider changes of outlook and regarded Grenelle as a betrayal.

This was truest in the CFDT, which was quite deeply affected by the Events, confirmed in the more radical course announced by the 1964 split. At its 1970 Congress, the CFDT linked the call for collectivization of the means of production and exchange to more novel demands which distinguished the CFDT from the other confederations. These were calls for democratic planning (as opposed to merely 'technocratic') and *autogestion* (workers' self-management). It was in the years immediately following the Events that the CFDT seemed most hostile to the existing order. Under Edmond Maire, its General Secretary from 1971, it returned to the pursuit of immediate benefits, but without dropping calls for long-term and radical change. Although its membership has grown, it is clear that this membership does not necessarily share the more radical visions of some of its leaders.

The response of FO was distinctly confused, but in general it emerged even more 'moderate', anti-communist and anti-*gauchiste* than before. Despite its animosity to the CGT and PCF, the FO under General Secretary André Bergeron, was a crucial backer of the Grenelle agreements, thus helping to ensure that 'reform', mild at that, would be the outcome.

Promises and sounds of sweeping change were fairly rapidly diminished. The 'wilder' schemes of René Capitant (briefly Couve de Murville's Minister of Justice, charged with preparing a new labour code) expired, stifled by the combined hostility of CGT and *patronat*. Although participation was severely limited, a number of changes were made. Profit sharing, introduced in very modest degree in 1967 and opposed by the unions, was given some boost; and the role of the *comités d'entreprise* was modestly strengthened. Most significant was the recognition, at long last, of union rights to organize and operate within the plant. There were more diffuse and less concrete changes of attitude and mood. For a period (1969–72) the government (under Chaban-Delmas) talked of *politique contractuelle*, the involvement of representatives of labour in a fuller and more organized way at national level in economic decisions – a process of tripartite consultations which, if it fell far short of corporatism, yet seemed to move in that direction. Union membership rose, modestly; the number of *sections d'entreprise* grew much more rapidly, on the back of the 1968

law. There began a process which, with varying success,
continued through the 1970s, and early 1980s – of the more
active involvement of workers in the organization of work-
patterns and practices, and active consultation of them, much
favoured by the FO. The glacial attitude of the *patronat*, too,
showed signs of change, especially when François Ceyrac
became its President in 1973. Between them, Ceyrac and
Edmond Maire may be taken as talismen of the new mood.

Union relationships

Relations with each other

Enough has been said to show that the main confederations
differ amongst themselves not merely over economic strategy
and issues, but over political issues also, and over the relationships between the political struggle and pursuit of economic
aims. FO takes a basically non-political approach, in the
sense of distancing itself from all the parties, and stressing
the independence and separation of political action from the
'rightful' aims of trade unions. CGT believes both in the
political role of trade unions (or at any rate of itself as
the largest, generally in support of the PCF though it occasionally takes a tactical and tactful distance), and also in the
'Statist' tradition, placing main emphasis upon the role of the
state in intervening, and of state ownership along traditional
lines. CFDT, although generally sympathetic to the PS, is by
no means so close to it organizationally as CGT to the
communists, and tends to favour economic changes which
rely far less exclusively upon the state. It is hardly surprising,
therefore, that even in terms of general policy and orientation,
relationships between them are strained.

But there are at least three other sources of difficulty. The
first concerns personalities and styles. The second is that,
broadly, the three have rather different characteristic
'constituencies', with different areas of strength and weakness
both in terms of economic sectors and regions. Third, and
notwithstanding this second factor, the three are ultimately in

competition, not just to poach members from each other (which happens on a small scale) but rather to obtain the allegiance of some substantial part of the great majority of French workers, who are non-unionized. To do this, they believe they need to maintain a degree of 'product-differentiation', to appear distinctive and different from the others.

Georges Séguy was for a long time General Secretary of CGT, until replaced in June 1982 by Henri Krasucki. Séguy was very much a tough, if on occasion genial, worker who saw the CGT through a number of important shifts of policy in the 1970s. In the days of the common programme of the left after 1972, the CGT generally showed its 'liberal' face; later, it obediently followed the PCF in making a united left victory in 1978 virtually impossible. There were those who, after that, hoped the CGT could be opened up, and its tight control by PCF activists and its role as recruiting sergeant for the party loosened. In the event, exactly the opposite happened. Henri Krasucki is regarded by most as very much a Stalinist amongst the party faithful. By contrast, Edmond Maire, CFDT General Secretary from 1971 until replaced by Jean Kaspar in the late 1980s, proved an influential and reflective individual, his manner quiet and rather shy, combining realism about what was immediately achievable with longer-range idealism or, in some eyes, utopianism. Though himself a PS member, he proved one of the most influential critics of the 1981–6 governments, asserting that it was a duty of trade unionists to speak truths which the parties did not dare, concerning the government's policies and the country's economic options. CFDT had also proved ready to enter a 'real dialogue' earlier, with the Giscard-Barre government from about 1978 to 1981, and it positioned itself to retain the ear of the Chirac government of 1986–8.

The CGT's great strength lies in heavy industry, in public sector industrial activities, and in such areas as the auto-motive sector. That of FO has been in the lower and middling echelons of the public service, (including white-collar) and also frequently in establishments where the *patronat* made clear its disapproval of the other confederations. The CFDT's strength is spread more evenly throughout activities and industries, but without a heartland of support of the kind that both CGT and FO have. It has attempted to attack CGT strongholds, especially where the CGT's attitudes have alienated immigrant workers.

Competition for the allegiance of the non-unionized seems to fly in the face of what evidence there is about the preferences of most workers themselves. Surveys suggest that a majority believe the existence of several confederations damages workers' interests and weakens the movement. In general, relations between the main confederations have grown worse since the late 1970s, and, unlike the parties of government, few formal arrangements for co-operation bind them together. For example, when in October 1991 the FO called for a general strike, and met with CFDT, this was described as an 'historic encounter', the first official meeting of its kind for twenty years: but it remains uncertain how far this heralds a far-reaching change toward greater co-operation. Until 1970, FO and CFDT had enjoyed official relations; these were broken off in 1972 when the chemical branch of FO rejoined CFDT. Subsequently, at least twice – in 1979 and 1980 – FO refused to meet CFDT.

Relations with the political parties

The trade union confederations are almost always at pains to assert their independence from all political parties. They are just as regularly accused by the bulk of French workers of having too close affiliations with one or other party. The CGT-FO goes farthest in avoiding partisan party allegiance, not surprisingly since a significant minority of its members are supporters of parties of the right and centre.

At the other end of the scale stands the CGT, practising the Leninist principle of overlapping membership, with party membership as the determinant of suitability for a union job. Almost all secretaries of CGT *unions départementales* are said to be PCF members, as well as about 90 per cent of heads of the CGT's industrial federations. The CFDT rides a little uneasily between these two situations, and has felt it of great importance not to be seen to be the spokesman of the PS.

The closeness of the CGT-PCF link was apparent throughout the period of left governments from 1981–86. The level and nature of its criticisms followed those of the Party throughout: muted at first; more strident once the 'U-turn' in economic policy became apparent in 1982–83 and until the PCF ministerial participation came to an end in 1984; moving to the 'day of action' in October 1985 in protest at the government's policies. The general verdict on this 'great day', as the CGT leadership called it, was that it had been a flop. *Le Monde* opined that most wage-earners had been 'spectators'; that even the heartland of the public sector had been far from fully supportive. It was a good bench-mark of 'united action' and 'fraternal solidarity': André Bergeron spoke of the 'predictable failure' which had 'tarnished the image of the union movement'; Louis Viannet of the CGT accused FO, CFDT and CGC of being 'passive' and only acting 'against' the CGT's initiative.

As the 1986 legislative elections approached, it was commented that seldom had the CGT been more tightly bound to the Party; and that, given the declining popular appeal of each, this was a risky strategy. To date, it has proved to be so for both. Nevertheless, those elections produced a notable 'first' in French political life: none of the main trade union confederations gave explicit instructions to its members on how to vote.

Nor did CFDT find itself in a much easier position. Maire persuaded his colleagues in the leadership not to advocate officially support for the left; but several grass-roots revolts occurred. Having established his credentials for constructive dialogue, Maire warned Chirac that if the government could not control its more extreme elements, then it was putting at risk the development of orderly and structured relations with the unions. He criticized in particular the government's proposals to make redundancies easier, which were enacted in June 1986.

At FO, Bergeron was able to follow the 'traditional' line of 'no instructions' on voting; but was aware that he could not let himself be outflanked by CFDT and CGT, or accused of inaction. His known excellent personal relationship with Chirac was in this respect something of a two-edged weapon, and it was clear that he would have to be careful not to be seen as the government's 'poodle'.

The return of a PS-led government without an overall majority in 1988 did not appear to herald major change. For one thing, this time there was no governmental talk of 'break with capitalism'; rather, only very mild changes of emphasis or policy, as over the wealth tax or (presentationally but not actually) over privatization. For another, unemployment remained stubbornly high. Large demonstrations against government policy in both 1988 and 1989 led neither to a general surge in union popularity nor to the fall of the government, which, under Rocard at least, could claim some success for its economic policy. The decline of union membership in the 1980s in France occurred without the kind of trade union legislation that took place in the UK. It seems rather to have reflected the unions' outdated organizational structure; their lack of adaptation to changed circumstances, new technologies and work patterns; the legacy of the unpopular strategies they had pursued in the 1970s; and the shrinking numbers from whom they could hope to recruit, as many industries continued to contract and unemployment stayed high.

What of the link between union membership and political allegiance or preference for the ordinary rank-and-file union member? The trends which appear are hardly startling, and the direction of causation difficult to identify, but we may note two in particular. First is family background: it appears that workers from left-voting backgrounds are considerably more likely to join the CGT than are others. Second, the question of level of political commitment: whilst fairly apathetic right- or centre-leaning workers may be prepared to join CGT, those more politically interested are much less likely to do so; also political interest among left-wing workers seems still to incline people strongly to joining the CGT.

Relations with government

From the unions' point of view, relations with government have not depended merely upon what particular governments were trying to do, important though this has been. A good deal has depended on how they have felt themselves to be received and regarded by the various organs of the state and the administration. Traditionally, they have not been held in high esteem most of the time. Initial attempts to involve them in the planning process were at best only a slight success. The CFDT showed itself the most willing to be involved for the longest time, but finally it too felt it should indicate displeasure at not being able to influence inputs and priorities in time to have much impact. The importance attributed to 'planning' has in any case been highly variable: the left made somewhat hesitant attempts to restore it from 1981–6; the apparent commitment of much of the right post-1986 to economic 'liberalism' and deregulation appeared to leave little room for it; yet it survives with modest ambitions into the 1990s.

In general, the unions are aware that the administration, in framing legislation or in seeking advice or sounding out opinion, distinguishes rather sharply between what it sees as professional associations, who are carefully cultivated and listened to, and mere lobbies or interest groups, who are usually not thought able to contribute much (apart from requests or demands) to the process of policy-formulation or implementation. For most of the Fifth Republic, trade unions have been uncomfortably aware of being labelled as the latter. They have, indeed, an even longer history of regarding the doings of government with suspicion, and the tradition remains hard to overcome.

Under the left governments from 1981, the unions saw several of their leading figures co-opted into governmental positions: for instance, André Henri of FEN was made Minister for Leisure; Michel Roland of CFDT was put in charge of the Energy Control Agency. Yet most trade unionists (especially the rank and file) remained suspicious of the 'intellectuals and technocrats' of the government. This was evident, for example, at the time of the 1982 wage-and-price freeze, whose introduction coincided with the CGT Congress at Lille. Whilst union leaders gave a mixed response to the economic policy of a government containing PCF members, the grass-roots response was distinctly chilly.

If such was the pattern under the left, there seemed little

reason to expect greater 'incorporation' or co-optation under the right after the 1986 legislative elections. To be sure, such appointments as those of E. Balladur as Minister of Economy, Finance and Privatization, and of P. Séguin at Social Affairs, were widely interpreted as signalling Chirac's concern to avoid provoking labour unrest. Yet the Chirac government was speedily warned not to pursue policies 'without wage-earners, let alone against them'.

This raises a very central issue for government-trade union relations in any country: namely, how far do the unions wish, and does the government encourage them, to be 'incorporated' into the structures of decision-making? In the French case, the answer from most quarters most of the time has been – not very much. In the early 1980s, communist ministers in the Mauroy government made plain that they felt trade unionists retained a right and freedom to attack policy which they themselves did not have. Yet non-communists fretted that the PCF, in conjunction with the CGT, would operate through the nationalization programme and the Auroux reforms to establish a much wider bridgehead of 'workers' power', as they claimed had happened back in the 'cold war' days of 1947–8.

But perhaps one of the most telling episodes regarding the ability of unions to 'dictate' policy, even to a left government, occurred over the Savary education Bill. The 1981–6 period was, after all, dubbed '*la République des professeurs*'; the teaching professions were extraordinarily heavily represented amongst Deputies and Ministers. Yet it proved to be the case that the wide control enjoyed by unions over 'personnel' and 'internal' professional matters did not extend to an ability to dictate terms over national education policy at the level of 'high politics', the shaping of the system, even under the 'ideal' conditions of 1981–6.

Relations of union leaderships with the rank and file

It is well known that French workers express greater resentment and a general sense of grievance and social injustice than, for example, similarly placed British workers. Why this is so is a more difficult issue. It is sometimes suggested that the unions themselves are the most important agents shaping the attitudes of the working class. But in France, where union membership is so low, it appears that the direct effect of the unions may be limited. It seems, rather, that the unions have played a major part in reinforcing a climate of antagonism and division inside French factories, and that this may be as much the result of their sense of weakness and inability to influence decisions as it is the result of conscious policy on their part. The resentment about their position, and about social inequality in general, seems to be a consequence of the climate of French industrial relations in most factories (at least until very recently) combined with the acknowledged high degree of inequality of income and wealth in France – higher than in almost all other west European countries.

Further, it appears that there is not any very strong correlation between the opinions of leaders of any particular union organization, and the opinions of that organization's rank and file. For example, on *autogestion*, a main hallmark of the CFDT leadership in recent years, the rank and file were less in favour of it than rank and file FO or CGT members. Further, it has not seemed to matter a great deal whether individuals were unionized or not: all French workers, unionized or not, appeared to have a greater sense of resentment and grievance than comparable groups in several other countries.

The legitimacy accorded to the union organizations by most workers appears low. A SOFRES (*Société française d'enquêtes par sondage*) survey in October 1979 indicated that whilst in general terms it was thought to be useful to be a union member, there was much more scepticism about unions' efficiency in defending their members' interests. Low membership figures are only one indicator of low legitimacy. The CGT in particular has recently seemed out of step: it suffered substantial loss of membership between 1978 and 1985. In addition, in 1979, CGT members in the steel industry accepted redundancy terms which the confederation, negotiating for them, had rejected.

Relations with management

French management has been characterized as 'at best pater-nalistic and at worst thoroughly autocratic'. This situation has been to a large degree sustained by both union and management attitudes and circumstances. Many major milestones of union rights and recognition have either been reached very late, or have still to be reached. Yet in certain respects the opposite has been true: labour practice is quite evolved, and legislation was strong on the protection of workers – over dismissal and compensation, retraining, maternity and other leave. Alongside this, however, has been a situation where, in many plants, the idea of regular bargain-ing and consultation is a real novelty. The unions have often found that they were only consulted in times of crisis – be it the 'global' one of the Events of 1968, or an acute sectoral crisis such as that in steel from 1979.

A main purpose of the proposals which Jean Auroux, as Minister of Labour, introduced in 1982, was to achieve a major update of the labour code by revising about a third of it. The proposals showed that much that was already supposed to be in operation – notably in the field of *délégués du personnel* and *comités d'entreprise* – had simply not up to that time been applied. For the large employers of the *Confédération nationale du patronat français* (CNPF), Yvon Gattaz appeared ready to enter into a dialogue with the government. In many respects, however, it was in smaller firms that basic workers' rights seemed farthest from realization; and here it was not the writ of CNPF which ran, but that of the increasingly militant SNPMI (*Syndicat national de la petite et moyenne industrie*), whose 'neo-Poujadist' guerilla warfare, under its leader Georges Deuil, seemed intended to sabotage the Auroux reforms. Nor was SNPMI any longer a tiny and insignificant minority. From the unions' point of view, the future direction of man-agement attitudes under the Chirac government appeared highly uncertain: within the CNPF leadership, disagreements that had been apparent for some time led to the resignation of Vice-President Chotard; but it was not clear how far these really indicated disagreement over policy. CNPF and govern-ment appeared to have moved swiftly to make dismissals easier, thus getting relations between them and the unions off to a tense start.

Conclusion

The present position and prospects

In 1986, both the political context and the economic context appeared very unfavourable from the point of view of trade unions in France. Government and the parliamentary majority appeared more wedded to 'liberal' economic policies, including privatization and the reduction of the role of the state, than any French government for a long time. The speed with which this programme was carried out, and its extent, were clearly influenced by electoral considerations and the demands of *cohabitation*, but also by the stock market crash of 1987.

The response of the unions, after a period of *morosité*, was to promise a hot autumn of strikes and disruption. Whilst the policies of the Chirac government might seem to give their militancy some edge, they continued to promise 'hot autumns' to socialist-led governments in 1988, 1989 and 1991, without conspicuous success. Their numerical strength and morale have been sapped considerably in recent years and seem unlikely to recover swiftly.

Any estimation of the position has to take account of the relations between the leading confederations. Whilst in several respects relations between the CFDT and CGT have improved over the last twenty or so years, ambiguities remain. The CGT still appears to be hitching itself firmly to a star which has been falling rather than rising – that of the PCF. The CGT still finds certain truths hard to face: not until after the 1986 election, so disastrous for the PCF, did CGT Secretary Warcholak admit that the membership losses suffered had been worse than those presented to the 42nd Congress only the previous November. CGT and CFDT still represent almost what have been described as two 'separate sub-cultures' within French working-class life.

In the autumn of 1991 four groupings – CFDT, CFTC,

FEN and CGC – managed to join together in a single delegation to talk to the government about its economic policy and about selective budgetary stimulus to the economy in particular. They had a cool reception. For the government, Bérégovoy spoke rather of 'competitive dis-inflation', and this was not the language they wished to hear. We have already noted the disarray that attended their other attempts at 'unity of action' at this time.

For the unions in general, the picture appears to be of considerable continuity with their past attitudes and traditions. They have become numerically weaker, and the likely economic evolution of France does not encourage belief that this trend is about to be rapidly reversed. 'United action' appears in most fields as elusive as ever. They were not sucked very far into a 'corporatist' dialogue with the left governments of 1981–6; nor have they been since, under governments of any colour.

At the time of the 1986 elections, there was a good deal of slightly airy talk about an 'emerging consensus' in French political life. One quite good indicator of how true such prognostications are will be found in those areas of life which touch trade unions most closely. It did not come to much, and this writer, for one, doubts how deep are the roots of any 'consensus'. So far, there is little indication that governments, whether centre-right or socialist, are prepared to have dealings with the unions of a more consensual kind; or that they are in a position to attract greater consensus with any new initiatives they might propose.

Bibliography

Adam, G., *Le Pouvoir syndical*. Paris, Dunod, 1983.

Adam, P., Bon, F., Capdevielle, J. and Mouriaux, R., *L'Ouvrier français en 1970*. Paris, Colin, 1970. An opinion and attitude survey of over a thousand workers.

Andrieux, A., and Lignon, J., *Le Militant syndicalist d'aujourd'hui*. Paris, Denoël, 1973. A survey of the motivations and attitudes of trade union militants.

Ardagh, J., *France Today*. London, Penguin, 1987. See in

particular Part 2: 'The economy, modernized but menaced'.

Johnson, R. W., *The Long March of the French Left*. London, Macmillan, 1981.

Lefranc, G., *Le Mouvement syndical de la libération aux événements de mai-juin 1968*. Paris, Payot, 1969. An excellent history of the trade union movement in this period.

Nugent, N., and Lowe, D., *The Left in France*, London, Macmillan, 1982.

Reynaud, J. D., *Les syndicats en France*, 2 vols. Paris, Colin, 2ᵉ édition, 1975. A comprehensive introduction with documents and bibiography.

Rosanvallon, P., *La Question syndicale*. Paris, Calmann-Levy, 1988.

Ross, G., *Workers and Communists in France*. University of California Press, 1982.

Sudreau Report. *Rapport du comité d'étude pour la réforme de l'entreprise* (Presidé par Pierre Sudreau) Paris, La Documentation française, 1975.

Touraine, A., *Le Mouvement ouvrier*. Paris, Fayard, 1986.

West European Politics vol. 3 no. 1 (Jan. 1980). Special issue on trade unions and politics in western Europe, ed. J. Hayward. See in particular the section on France by D. Gallie.

4

Immigrants
Brian Fitzpatrick

France now has between 3.5 and 4 million foreigners living within its frontiers. It is impossible to give precise figures because many foreigners are in the country illegally and remain undocumented, but there is every reason to suppose that the foreign population has remained relatively stable for some time. Proportionally, foreigners constitute nearly 7 per cent of the total population compared with 6.8 per cent in 1982 and 6.5 per cent in 1975. Indeed, in spite of the waves of immigration which have taken place since the 1940s, foreigners are proportionally no more numerous now than they were in the 1930s. By way of comparison, in the United Kingdom, foreign and Commonwealth citizens make up around 3 per cent of the population; in the former West Germany, they were about 7 per cent; in Sweden foreigners account for nearly 6 per cent of the population; and in Switzerland almost 15 per cent.

However, there are foreigners and foreigners. Racial tension and xenophobia so evident in French society in the 1990s is incomparably greater than the occasional bouts of hostility directed towards foreigners in the 1930s. Even the most cursory reading of the French press reveals that scarcely a week passes without the occurrence of serious incidents, including in recent years, large scale urban riots, involving immigrants or their children, commonly known as *Beurs* (from the *verlan* for *Arabe*). '*Le problème des immigrés*' has figured prominently on the French political agenda since the late

1970s, and has not yet been resolved satisfactorily. It is largely, if not wholly, responsible for the emergence of support for the right-wing *Front national* since the early 1980s. However, 'the problem' does not refer to Europeans living and working in France, not even to those, like the Portuguese, who began to arrive *en masse* in the 1960s and who have, with few exceptions, integrated into French society, nor even to those groups from the south-eastern confines of Europe – Yugoslavs, Romanians (the *Front national* leader, Jean-Marie Le Pen, failed utterly to score a point when, in a television debate, he suggested that the Minister of State, Lionel Stoléru, had no appreciation of true French values because he was himself *'un Français de fraîche date'*. While most ethnic minorities have faced incomprehension, hostility and a certain degree of contempt – *'ma Portugaise'* is a not uncommon term for the 'charlady', and Jews have long been targets of nationalist and right-wing prejudices – it is the black Africans, north Africans and Asians (including Turks) who are the principal object of debate, hostility and fear in contemporary France.

This racial hostility reflects the considerable differences which distinguish non-French Europeans from most immigrants from Africa and Asia who have sought to establish themselves in France. Unlike, say, the Francophile Britons who purchase secondary residences in the country, most non-European immigrants have come to France to escape poverty in their native land. They have little spending power, often very low educational attainment, and little understanding of European customs and culture. All of these factors tend to isolate them in a country which has failed to come to terms with the overwhelmingly black African, north African and Asian character of immigration since the Second World War.

The presence of large numbers and concentrations of non-European peoples in France is the consequence both of its colonial legacy and of its manpower requirements in the post-war decades. The present tensions concerning immigrants are largely the product of economic recession, poverty and relatively high unemployment since the late 1970s, and of the growth of Islamic fundamentalism since the Iranian revolution of 1979. These economic and cultural factors have proved powerful in fuelling debate and conflict in the 1980s and 1990s, and they have raised questions of citizenship, national identity rights and obligations in very down-to-earth ways 200 years after the French Revolution and the idealistic Declaration of the Rights of Man. Official policy on immigration and political asylum is under constant scrutiny, and while it has evolved to take account of both changing circumstances and changes in public opinion, it continues to be a political and ideological football.

The colonial legacy

France is an old colonial power. Having lost many of its possessions during the French revolutionary wars, in the nineteenth century, it reconstituted an empire which encompassed much of Africa north of the equator, Madagascar south of the equator, and a number of Pacific islands, as well as a considerable part of the Far East. In common with other European colonial powers like Britain and Portugal, France lost its possessions, often painfully, as in the cases of Indochina (Vietnam) and Algeria, in the decades after the Second World War. Nevertheless, generations of French occupation (Algeria was first colonized in 1830; there had been a French presence in Indochina since the seventeenth century, long before formal colonization began in the 1860s) and the systematic imposition of French culture, however basic, made France an automatic choice for many people seeking to leave the colonies and, later, the new, independent states. Moreover, France sought to create explicit and privileged links between the overseas possessions and the *métropole*. In the heady early period of the Fourth Republic, a law of 7 May 1946 declared optimistically that from 1 June 1946, 'all subjects of overseas territories, including Algeria, possess the quality of citizens with the same rights as French citizens in the *métropole* and in the overseas territories'. Equal rights, in theory at least, were complemented by freedom of movement within the entity called the *Union française*.

The major work of decolonization took place in the early

years of the Fifth Republic, and the new constitution replaced the unsuccessful *Union française* by the *Communauté* which sought to reconcile aspirations of self-government with the maintenance of close ties between France and the former possessions based on a common currency, the franc, on common economic policies and on a common citizenship. Although the original idea of the *Communauté* had to be modified to meet the desire for sovereignty expressed by its African members, its existence encouraged the development of economic and technical co-operation based increasingly on bilateral agreements which included the acceptance of annual quotas of students and workers from the member states. In the case of Algeria, whose independence was achieved after a bloody and emotionally charged struggle, the 1962 Evian Agreement preserved privileged access to France for its citizens. Through such relationships France continued to be the obvious focus for emigration in the minds of many ex-colonials long after their own countries achieved independence and, for some small groups, independence itself posed a threat: for example, the *Harkis*, the Algerian troops who fought for the French against the FLN, or the Vietnamese whose economic interests and cultural outlook left them with a bleak future after the French defeat in 1954.

The economic aspect of immigration

France has always been a prosperous country, but one which has had a chronic problem of underpopulation, aggravated in the twentieth century by the two world wars. Immigration has been a traditional means by which the demographic deficit has been supplemented. Immigration accounted for 74 per cent of the population growth in the period 1921–31; for 30 per cent in the period 1968–75; and for 14 per cent in the years 1975–82. For centuries, seasonal work in the countryside attracted migrant workers from the Iberian peninsula and from Italy. From the middle of the nineteenth century, industrial development, much of which took place near the frontiers, attracted new waves of immigrants from France's neighbours – mainly Spaniards and Piedmontese in the south, while in the north of the country, Belgians and Poles swelled the ranks of France's growing industrial working class. Their integration was relatively easy because of the European Catholic culture they shared with the French. Their children assimilated. A cursory glance at the telephone directory of virtually any French town will reveal a proportion of the population with Italian, Polish and Spanish names. These are not by any means all recent immigrants, but are families and individuals who have been French for three generations and more. In more recent times, since the 1960s in particular, the Portuguese have carried on this tradition of European immigration. Portuguese immigrants now make up the largest single national minority, some 25 per cent of all foreign nationals in France. They are also the best integrated of the new immigrants, again largely because of their European, Catholic cultural background, and they are most evident in building and agriculture. But these Europeans are not the immigrants who have been at the centre of the steadily growing controversy concerning the alleged foreign invasion of France.

Post-war economic recovery and growth were projected on the ability to attract large quantities of immigrant labour. It was hoped by the planners in the late 1940s that Europeans would be recruited to rebuild the depleted population and the shattered economy. For a variety of reasons the recruitment of Europeans was less than successful – North and South America, Australia and even West Germany which, for political reasons, enjoyed massive American economic aid and experienced the rapid growth known as the *Wirtschaftswunder*, proved more attractive. Contrary to all projections and expectations, it was Algerians – at the time French citizens with complete freedom of movement – who filled the vacuum and established a pattern for massive immigration from non-European sources which has given rise to the present racial discord. In the 1950s, Moroccans and Tunisians migrated to France as well and, by the early 1980s, 1.5 million *Maghrebins* accounted for 44 per cent of the foreign population of France.

The post-war French economy has been developed by means of five-year plans involving a partnership between government, the private sector and the large public sector.

Planning permitted a steady rate of economic growth in the industrial and manufacturing sectors followed by a 'boom' at the end of the 1950s and into the 1960s: in 1963, output was 26 per cent higher than it had been in 1957, while consumption increased by 19 per cent. At the same time, the primary and secondary economic sectors (agriculture, fishing, mining, heavy industry, construction) continued to retain a large proportion of the working population: 59 per cent in 1962 against 41 per cent in the tertiary sector (distribution, services, commerce, transport); and 56 per cent in 1968 against 44 per cent in the tertiary sector. The need for immigrant labour, formally recognized by the *Commissariat au Plan*, persisted through the 1960s and into the 1970s. In the early 1960s France entered into bilateral agreements with black African countries and with Turkey to supplement her existing sources of foreign labour.

Table 4
Origins of immigrants in France, 1987

Country of origin	Numbers in France*	% of all foreigners
Portugal	844,338	24.8
Italy	370,363	10.8
Spain	342,202	10.0
Other EC	195,206	5.7
Yugoslavia	66,455	1.95
Poland	58,771	1.7
Algeria	710,193	20.8
Morocco	575,386	16.9
Tunisia	230,073	6.7
Turkey	158,511	4.6
Francophone Africa	174,628	5.1
S.E. Asia	24,670	0.72
Indian subcontinent	22,062	0.64
Total	3,402,495	

*NB. These figures give only officially recorded, legal immigrants. They undoubtedly fall short of the real numbers of foreigners in France.

At the same time, employers were aware of the economic advantages involved in hiring immigrant labour. In the early 1970s, when 40 per cent of the labour employed in the building trade was immigrant, one builder, who wished to remain anonymous, spoke for many French employers when he said: '*Si j'avais des Français à la place des étrangers, je devrais verser des salaires supérieurs de 20 pour cent.*' Some large firms undertook their own recruitment campaigns in Turkey, Yugoslavia and a number of African states, so anxious were they to obtain manpower at low cost. In 1974, shortly after the oil-producing countries demonstrated their ability to cause havoc in the industrial world by witholding supplies and increasing prices dramatically, French employers feared that labour exporting countries might do the same: '*Nous serions bien embêtés si l'Algérie rapatriait du jour au lendemain ses 1200 ressortissants qui travaillent chez nous*', observed the managing director of Berliet trucks.

Necessity and avarice combined with the fact that immigrants were prepared to do the jobs that Frenchmen turned down as dirty or demeaning – at least until the recession of the 1980s. Even now it is relatively rare to see Frenchmen wielding the roadsweeper's broom, cleaning the bus shelters and underground stations or manning France's dustcarts. Ten years ago it would have been unthinkable. By the same token. unemployment has, until very recently, been much more acute among immigrants than among the French working population.

Table 5
Immigrants' contribution to main economic sectors

Year	Industry	Building	Services	Overall
1982	8.8	23.4	6.2	9.2
1985	7.7	23.0	6.2	8.4
1988	6.4	21.0	6.7	7.3

Source: Ministère du Travail, de l'Emploi et de la Formation professionnelle

Table 6
Immigrants by professional qualifications

Year	Labourers	Office, shop assistants	Qualified technical staff	Executives	Total
1982	84.9	9.8	3.0	2.3	100
1985	79.5	13.2	4.0	3.3	100
1988	78.8	13.3	4.2	3.7	100

Source: Ministère du Travail, de l'Emploi et de la Formation professionnelle

Table 7
Percentage changes in unemployment levels in France

Background of unemployed	1988	1989	1990	1991
French:	−1.5	−3.2	+0.6	+12.5
EC nationals:	−6.4	−6.5	−0.5	+ 9.3
Non EC:	+3.9	+7.9	+4.4	+ 6.1
Total:	−1.15	−2.3	+1.0	+11.8

Source: Ministère des Affaires sociales et de l'Intégration

Refugees

France has traditionally been *une terre d'asile* for foreigners forced to leave their own countries for political or religious reasons. Until recently, these have generally been relatively few in number and sufficiently equipped culturally to survive, even to flourish without provoking ill-feeling (a notable exception was the influx of east European Jews in the last quarter of the nineteenth century; the Dreyfus affair at the turn of the century demonstrated that anti-semitism had become widespread and vicious). One thinks of the Polish patriots of the nineteenth century, of the 'whites' in the aftermath of the Russian Revolution, of the Republicans after the nationalist victory in Spain in 1938–39. More recently, Chilean and Argentinian democrats and socialists were welcomed, and even the Ayatollah Khomeini found asylum in the land of the rights of man. The number of requests for asylum increases (from 28,809 in 1985 to 61,372 in 1989, plus 79 per cent between 1988 and 1989 alone), and latterly, requests have come increasingly from citizens of Asian and African countries.

Table 8
Principal sources of requests for political asylum in France

Continent & country:	1987	1988	1989
Europe	**1,419**	**2,180**	**3,259**
Poland	534	1,040	1,205
Romania	470	658	1,198
Africa	**10,478**	**14,725**	**23,456**
Angola	1,201	1,876	2,773
Ghana	1,081	1,240	1,409
Guinee Konakry	695	988	1,570
Mali	802	2,706	3,807
Senegal	201	447	1,388
Zaire	3,494	4,255	7,417
Americas	**1,247**	**2,236**	**3,352**
Chile	275	376	324
Haiti	648	1,451	2,240
Asia	**14,424**	**15,112**	**31,305**
China	1,320	175	1,052
India	343	466	1,110
Pakistan	594	814	1,865
Sri Lanka	1,356	1,498	3,236
Turkey	5,490	6,735	17,355
Cambodia, Laos, Vietnam	4,222	4,463	4,909
Total	**27,568**	**34,253**	**61,372**

Source: Office français de Protection des Réfugiés et Apatrides, 1990.

While the proportion of refusals increases too (from just under 35 per cent in 1985 to 72 per cent in 1989), there is growing concern at the annual increase in applications and at the procedure for examining these. It can take up to three years to adjudicate on an application and during that time the applicant enjoys full medical benefits, receives an initial grant of 2,000 francs, a work permit (until 1991) and, if unable to find work, a monthly allowance of 1,300 francs. Thousands of doubtful applicants are then said to 'disappear' into the immigrant community where they swell the ranks of the illegal immigrants.

The growing refugee question has elicited strong comments from both left and right. For conservative opinion, the right to asylum has become '*la face masquée de l'immigration*'; merely another means to gain entry to France. The *Front national* accuses Africans, Asians and *Maghrébins* of exploiting France's tradition of granting asylum in order to 'get a foot in the door', and of abusing the conditions attached to their residence. The Front's leader, Jean-Marie Le Pen, denounces hunger strikes undertaken by applicants for asylum as nothing more than an attempt at blackmail. But the right is not alone in its protests. Prime Minister Michel Rocard observed in the spring of 1991 that France could not '*héberger toute la misère du monde*', while his successor, France's first woman Prime Minister, Edith Cresson, promised that illegal immigrants and refugees would face expulsion. These attitudes have not softened.

It should be noted that the refugee problem is increasingly a 'European' problem. Italy and Spain are equally prey to the smuggling of north Africans seeking a better life in Europe and, in 1991, Italy faced an invasion of Albanians fleeing the crumbling communist regime in their home country. The United Kingdom recorded a tenfold increase in the number of applications for asylum between the late 1980s and the early 1990s when some 1,000 applications were being made each week.

French immigration policy

We have seen that France consciously set out to encourage immigration after 1945 for demographic and economic reasons. The collapse of Nazi Germany and Fascist Italy, and the Soviet occupation of much of eastern and central Europe appeared to promise a sufficient number of refugees, stateless and displaced persons to meet the criteria laid down by the *Haut Comité de la Population* established in 1945. The criteria were racial and economic: Nordic types were to make up 50 per cent of the new population, Latins and Slavs 20 per cent each, while the number of immigrants was to be determined by the needs of the planners. The state assumed responsibility for immigration through the establishment of an *Office national de l'Immigration*. We have seen, too, that these objectives were foiled by the reluctance of the desired racial groups to settle in France, and by the availability of non-Europeans to take their place. As so many of these were Algerians with a statutory right to enter France, the ONI's selection functions were thwarted too.

Because of economic pressures, immigration was virtually unchecked until the 1970s. Immigrants were given residence and work permits of one, five or ten years' duration, the latter accorded normally to those who had clearly 'settled' in France. Immediate family members were permitted to join immigrants who had found employment and whose situation was legal. It was quite easy for illegal immigrants to regularize their situation. Subsequently, measures have been taken, with more or less effect, to prevent the arrival of new immigrants, to reduce the numbers of immigrants in France, and to integrate those who appear to have settled permanently. Many observers would question whether these measures constitute a 'policy', and would rather view them as *ad hoc* or pragmatic attempts to resolve a problem that has become increasingly political.

In the early 1970s, even before the economic disruption caused by the main oil producing countries in the wake of the Yom Kippur war, the French government had concluded that immigration needed to be controlled more tightly. Employers, however, conscious of the cost effectiveness of immigrant

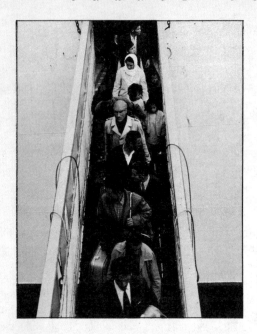

Algerian immigrant workers disembark at Marseille in 1971. *(Photo: Pierre Domenech)*

labour, resisted interference, and public opinion was not yet sensitive to an immigrant problem. It was in the summer of 1974, under Giscard d'Estaing's presidency with Jacques Chirac as Prime Minister, that the first concerted measures were taken. Immigration was stopped, including that of members of immigrant workers' families. Illegal workers were pursued and financial assistance was offered to encourage unemployed immigrants to return to their countries of origin. Moreover, higher costs associated with the 1973 oil embargo began to affect public opinion: demonstrations against foreign workers began to occur, some of which were singularly violent, so much so that the Algerian government suspended its annual quota of migrants to France.

At the same time that it instituted controls, the Secretariat of State for Immigrant Workers proposed a series of measures intended to ameliorate the frequently dreadful living conditions of legal immigrant workers, and to settle them and their families into French society. These social measures were largely thwarted by the competing budgetary demands of other ministries involved in public expenditure. For the time being, the immigrant question was not given high spending priority. The government did, however, implement measures which were designed to ensure that immigrants and their children did not lose contact with the culture of their country of origin. Arabic classes were provided in many schools frequented by immigrants' children, and the Paris Mosque was placed under the control of the Algerian government. It could be argued that these measures represented an insurance policy: if immigrants and their children were kept in contact with their native culture, eventual repatriation might not seem so threatening. In 1975, the immigration of workers' families was permitted once more.

Three years later, after Raymond Barre had replaced Jacques Chirac as Prime Minister, the cabinet attempted to attack the immigrant problem more vigorously by renewing the ban on family immigration and by seeking to introduce a scheme to repatriate forcibly some 500,000 foreigners over a period of five years by refusing to renew residence permits and by targeting the unemployed. In spite of growing concern at unemployment in France, this policy of forced repatriation failed to secure a parliamentary majority, and repatriation remained voluntary and aided. In the ten years following the introduction of the repatriation scheme, no more than 100,000 foreigners took advantage of the 10,000 francs resettlement grant.

In 1981, the election of a socialist President, François Mitterrand, and a socialist government led to a move away from the earlier preoccupation with repatriating immigrants. Many immigrants who had been in France for some time, and whose employment was secure, became immune from expulsion as did their children. Family immigration was authorized once more; and the assisted repatriation scheme was dropped. Until 1983, an amnesty was offered to illegal immigrants who were encouraged to legalize their situation. Official figures indicate that some 130,000 illegal immigrants took advantage of the amnesty. No new immigration was permitted.

The debate on immigrants took a new turn, however. Conservative opinion, disconcerted at the guarantees given to immigrants, turned dramatically to Jean-Marie Le Pen whose *Front national* made immigrants, or rather their removal, its central theme. Meanwhile, immigrant spokesmen and groups concerned with the immigrants' situation began to demand political rights for legal immigrants, notably the right to vote in local elections. The cabinet was in favour of this measure – it was most improbable that immigrants would vote for candidates of the right (in the 1988 presidential election, François Mitterrand won 80 per cent of the votes of the 'first generation' French voters) – but the constitutional council and public opinion raised obstacles which the government considered imprudent to tackle. Public attitudes to giving immigrants the vote have changed little. SOFRES polls indicate that 74 per cent of the sample questioned in 1984 were opposed to votes for immigrants, and 72 per cent in 1990.

Indeed, immigrants and their rights had become a burning issue by the spring of 1983, and the second Mauroy cabinet began to backpedal in an attempt to placate public opinion and to deprive the parties of the right of powerful political ammunition. Thus, repatriation grants were reintroduced; entry permits for immigrants' family members were made more difficult to obtain; and more effort was directed towards detecting and expelling illegal immigrants. At the same time, the system of residence and work permits was simplified. A combined residence and work permit, valid for ten years was introduced, so clarifying the position of the majority of immigrant workers in the country.

In the two years from March 1986 to May 1988, when the right regained control of the National Assembly, stricter measures were introduced by the Chirac cabinet to regulate the movement of foreigners. Family immigration was restricted further and the *loi Pasqua* of 9 September 1986 empowered the authorities to deport all foreigners illegally residing in France, and prompt action was taken in a number of cases (12,364 expulsions in 1986). The scope of the law was far-reaching: the adolescent who forgot to take out his or her papers within a week of reaching sixteen years became illegal, as did the spouse of a French citizen who did not bother to register his or her change in status. The rise in international terrorism and three Paris bombing incidents associated with it led the government to make entry visas compulsory for all non-EC citizens.

In the same period, the debate focused on the question of

citizenship or nationality. This concerned immigrants who married a French citizen, but particularly the *Beurs*, the children of immigrant parents. Under French law, according to the principle of the *jus soli*, they qualified automatically for French citizenship. Concern at the chronic unemployment and the crime rate among young immigrants – they were responsible for 17 per cent of crimes in the mid 1980s, while foreigners made up 23 per cent of the country's prison population – led sections of public opinion to demand a tightening of the *Code de la Nationalité*. In a poll carried out immediately after the March 1986 general election, 57 per cent of those questioned wanted to withhold the automatic right to citizenship which the *Beurs* enjoyed, and the new government turned its attention to ways of making citizenship less automatic. In the summer of 1987 a *commission de sages* was set up to investigate the matter.

This initiative enlarged the debate considerably. Broadly speaking, the left, including pressure groups like the *Ligue des Droits de l'Homme*, *SOS Racisme*, *Mouvement contre le racisme et pour l'amitié entre les peuples*, *Ligue internationale contre le racisme et l'antisémitisme* (LICRA) adopted a position which sought to admit that France had become a multi-ethnic society, and that the only tenable policy was one of admitting immigrants and their children to full civil rights, including citizenship and electoral participation. The main churches, too, denounced the ensemble of the government's policies concerning immigrants as punitive and unjust. The right, on the other hand, argued that the kind of immigration France had experienced, black African and Moslem Arab, precluded integration in any way comparable to the degree to which the old Europeans had assimilated, and that it was evident that not many immigrants felt much sympathy with or loyalty to French values and norms. To take a criterion dear to the heart of many Frenchmen, only one eligible *Beur* in four actually did his military service; the others found ways of avoiding it or opted to do it in the Algerian army. Right-wing opinion wanted to put the onus on individuals who would be required to take an oath of allegiance before obtaining French citizenship. '*Être Français, ça se mérite*' proclaims the *Front national*.

The Chirac government's initiative on nationality petered

out and French policy continues to admit the children of immigrants automatically. This is in line with the recommendations of the *commission de sages* which reported to the government in January 1988, and with what appears to be the majority opinion in France: a SOFRES poll taken in 1990 indicated that 72 per cent of those questioned considered that citizenship should be automatic for immigrants' children born and raised in France – a striking contrast with the poll taken in March 1986.

In the spring of 1988 François Mitterrand was re-elected to a second term as President, and subsequent legislative elections returned a socialist majority to the National Assembly. The Pasqua Law was immediately replaced by the *loi Joxe* which made it more difficult to expel immigrants by taking the expulsion process out of the hands of the Ministry of Interior and placing it in the hands of the courts. Family immigration, '*le regroupement familial*', was restarted. For the longer term, government policy has two aims. The first is to prevent further immigration except that of family members, a policy which other European leaders see with President Mitterrand as being increasingly a European Community matter. The 1990 Schengen Agreement is a step in this direction. The signatories (France, Germany, Italy, Holland, Belgium and Luxembourg) have agreed to form a single area for the purposes of frontier controls effected on non-EC citizens. People admitted to the area will have the right to move freely from one jurisdiction to another provided that they are not on any member state's list of undesirables. Thus, a non-EC citizen admitted in Naples will have the right to move freely to Berlin or Brussels. The right to work, however, is not included in the Schengen-style visa.

The second major ambition of the second Mitterrand administration is the integration into French society of settled immigrants and their children:

> *Considérant que la très grande majorité des étrangers résidant dans notre pays souhaite y demeurer et aspire à participer à la vie collective française, le Premier ministre a souligné que l'intégration de ces populations devait se faire dans le respect des principes de la République: laïcité, tolérance, solidarité.*

(Cabinet press communiqué, 7 February 1990)

That this approach will succeed remains open to doubt. The socialists entered the last decade of the century with their popularity – including that of M. Mitterrand – at a new low. The replacement of Prime Minister Michel Rocard by Edith Cresson in 1991 failed to reverse the government's fortunes, and Jean-Marie Le Pen's *Front national* continued to attract support. A shift to the right was detected among French opinion, and it became so compelling that the other main conservative parties, which normally kept their distance from the Front began to clamour for a more rigorous approach to the immigrant problem in an effort to capture some of the support that was flowing to the extreme right. If the political pendulum comes to rest on the right, it is probable that repressive legislation will be introduced by a conservative successor to the socialists.

Immigrants in French society – from isolation to integration?

Immigrants have come to the forefront of the political debate in France in a negative manner. While there was sustained economic growth and a labour shortage, they were largely ignored and left to their own devices. Few politicians or citizens paid any attention to what was in effect an underclass living in shanty towns (*bidonvilles*) on the fringes of industrial centres, cramped eight or ten to a dilapidated room in run-down boarding houses, drawing the minimum wage and frequently cut off from contact with normal French life by a language barrier.

When, in the 1970s, the size of the immigrant population became a political issue because of rising unemployment, the cultural gap which divided French and immigrants was as great as it ever had been, and relations were guided by mutual incomprehension and suspicion. Immigrants were a 'soft target' for those who saw security and prosperity evaporating after a generation of growth. Insecurity and a feeling of impotence in the face of adverse conditions have played a considerable role in the resurgence of xenophobia in France.

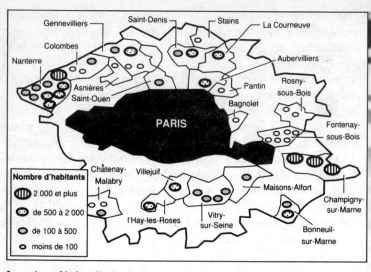

Location of *bidonvilles* in the Paris region, at 1 January 1970. From a map in *Dossier Immigration* (Les cahiers de *L'Express*), 1990.

Omnipresent, though marginalized by neglect and cultural barriers, immigrants, particularly blacks and north Africans, quickly and easily became the scapegoat. And there were politicians who were ready to articulate and capitalize on the fears and anxieties which had affected parts of French society, particularly since the late 1960s. They offered simple answers and simple solutions: '*deux millions de chômeurs, c'est deux millions d'immigrés de trop*', was one such solution offered in the 1970s, while rioting involving *Beurs* in the Paris suburbs in 1991 elicited the response, '*foutez-les dehors!*' from the editor of the right-wing weekly *Minute*.

The views of the *Front national* are predictable. But are they representative of much public opinion? In November 1989 a SOFRES survey carried out for *Nouvel Observateur* indicated that 51 per cent of the sample questioned believed that immigrants could not be integrated. When asked which political leaders – twelve were proposed – offered the most satisfactory solution to the immigrant question, Jean-Marie Le Pen came top of the poll of those who gave an opinion (28 per cent had no opinion) with 17 per cent, beating François

Mitterrand (14 per cent). A year later, the paper, generally sympathetic to integration, commissioned another poll, but was astute enough not to ask such blunt questions. The results of the second poll demonstrated what many French people resent. Sixty-eight per cent of those questioned thought there were too many immigrants; 49 per cent believed that their way of life (*coutumes*) was the main obstacle to *cohabitation*; while 44 per cent said it was their religion – a clear allusion to Islam. Thirty per cent of those questioned felt insecure because they lived in or near large concentrations of immigrants. To put the matter in a wider context, 41 per cent said that immigration was the country's main political problem against 66 per cent who gave unemployment and 37 per cent who gave the environment as the major problem. (The total of the percentages does not add up to 100 because subjects were allowed to give up to four ranked replies.)

Many non-European immigrants have integrated well, and one can find *Beurs* and *Beurettes* in all the professions, in business and in the arts. Nevertheless, the occupation statistics reproduced in Table 6 on page 106 indicate that these are the exceptions rather than the rule. A poll of immigrants carried out in 1982 on behalf of the liberal weekly *L'Express* (overleaf) provides some idea of how immigrants perceived themselves in relation to France and the French. One feature of the responses to the questions asked was the difference between Europeans' attitudes and those of the north Africans.

Even allowing for the desire to 'please' a French interviewer by saying what the subject thinks he or she wanted to hear, the replies demonstrate that it is still much easier for European immigrants to 'fit in'. Indeed, it is clear from news coverage and social studies alike that 'immigrant' usually equals black African or simply north African in everyday parlance.

The integration of immigrants was made a priority of the second Mitterrand administration. It is an immense undertaking. Some critics observe that integration is a spontaneous, 'organic' process which cannot be imposed in a Jacobin fashion from Paris. But it is hard to imagine anything other than a concerted, centrally directed effort to overcome the obstacles which have accumulated over the years. It is also an embarrassing political issue which the government would like

Q Avez-vous l'impression qu'à votre égard les Français sont:

	Latins	*Maghrébins*
chaleureux	11%	10%
plutôt agréables	55	39
indifférents	29	35
plutôt hostiles	5	11
agressifs	—	5

Q Dans les différentes occasions suivantes, vous sentez-vous en situation d'égalité avec les Français?

	Latins		*Maghrébins*	
	oui	non	oui	non
Dans les magasins	91%	9%	76%	23%
Dans un bureau de poste	86	13	79	21
A la mairie	84	14	76	20
Dans la rue, avec la police	78	21	65	34
Pour trouver un logement	74	25	39	58
Pour trouver du travail	77	22	49	49
Pour vos enfants, à l'école	85	15	73	26

Q S'il y avait actuellement un travail pour vous dans votre pays et que vous ayez le choix entre rester en France et y retourner, que feriez-vous?

	Latins	*Maghrébins*
Rester en France	48%	36%
Retourner au pays	39	54

Source: © *L'Express*, 28 January 1983

to see laid to rest. An opinion poll carried out to assess François Mitterrand's first decade in office indicated that the immigrant problem ranked only slightly behind unemployment as the President's most glaring failure (*Nouvel Observateur*, no. 1382, 2–8 May 1991).

Integration on the scale proposed requires considerable sums of money and great sensitivity. Immigrant families tend to be housed in modern high-rise ghettos on the outskirts of towns. The concentration of immigrants drives out French people, making the immigrants' isolation worse. In schools, many immigrants' children are handicapped through their parents' illiteracy in French and by the generally deprived conditions in which so many live. The isolation is increased as French parents withdraw their children from schools in which the numbers of immigrant children rise: it is widely held that a large immigrant minority lowers the attainment level of a school. The *Beurs* involved in suburban rioting are largely the 'no hopers', unable to use the education system to gain qualifications, and condemned to chronic unemployment, as are the *Zoulous*, the bands of African youths who congregate around suburban shopping centres and parts of Paris, often armed with baseball bats and prepared for gang warfare. Many have an acute identity problem. Failures in France, and rejected by the French, they have no prospect of integrating into a north or black African setting.

What steps are being taken to promote the integration of immigrants? The *loi Joxe* was intended to create a greater climate of security for those immigrants in France. If they are legal, they can be joined by their immediate family. In 1990, the *loi Gayssot* enlarged the scope of a 1972 law covering incitement to racial hatred and extended the range of penalties which can be incurred for words and deeds deemed offensive in their reference to a person's religious or ethnic identity. This, too, was intended to enhance foreigners' rights. More constructively, at the end of 1989, a *Comité interministériel à l'Intégration*, chaired by the Prime Minister, and a *Haut Conseil à l'Intégration* to advise the Prime Minister were set up. In 1991, Kofi Yamgnane, a native of Togo who became an engineer in France before being elected mayor of Saint-Coulitz in Brittany, was appointed to the new position of Secretary of State for Integration. In the same year a *Ministre à la Ville* was appointed to tackle the problems associated with the sprawling housing developments which have proliferated around most French cities since the 1960s.

Housing and education have been designated priority areas for action. The old *Fonds d'Action sociale* (FAS) was reanimated, its budget somewhat increased (from 1,075,000 francs in 1985 to 1,284,000 francs in 1990), its brief extended to encourage housing, resettlement and education projects. Local authorities (*communes*) are offered financial inducement (*contrats d'agglomération*) to take part in urban development projects which involve housing, youth training and the provision of neighbourhood facilities (*animation des quartiers*). There is no sure formula, of course. Already a wide range of ethnic permutations have been tried with varying degrees of success in apartment complexes (*cités*) with a view to minimizing the ghetto effect. In Paris, fifteen out of the twenty *arrondissements* simply refuse to allow the construction of HLM (*Habitations à loyer modéré*) blocks.

Eight per cent of the pupils in French schools are the children of immigrants. In the secondary streams leading to the *baccalauréat*, however, they are down to 4 per cent; and they are significantly over-represented in the non-academic and special streams where they make up 19 per cent. In an attempt to redress the imbalance, *Zones d'education prioritaire* (ZEPs) are being identified, areas where school performance can be related to social and cultural deprivation, and where the educational level of the pupils needs to be significantly improved in order to give them an acceptable educational base. The teachers in these areas are selected from volunteers and may receive higher salaries than their colleagues in 'normal' schools. Already there are some 800 preparatory classes in which immigrants' children are taught basic French before filtering into normal classes.

Job training schemes have been given a high priority as many immigrants' children leave school with few qualifications, and their parents are frequently unskilled or in need of retraining. Yet again, immigrants are grossly under-represented on training and retraining schemes. Of the 321,442 people who took a course in 1989, only one in ten was a foreigner, while north Africans accounted for only one in twenty, and black Africans less than one in fifty.

The armed forces, too, have been instructed to accommodate *jeunes Français d'origine maghrébine* (JFOM). Many Franco-Algerian youths had been put off the French forces by rumours of racism, and, using their dual nationality, opted to do their military service in Algeria. The forces' new approach involves presentations in schools and colleges, aptitude tests for conscripts in order to match them to duties, a more reasonable distribution of JFOM among the different branches of the forces, including the *Gendarmerie nationale* – most *Beurs* were consigned to the infantry –, the appointment of Moslem chaplains to the forces, and the provision of Halal rations, and the possibility of education as well as training during the period of military service, including encouragement to follow officer-training courses where appropriate.

However well-intentioned and thorough these reforms may be, the success or failure of the integration project depends very largely on the response of the immigrants themselves. The government has a number of immigrant advisory bodies, and no doubt it was correct in its 1990 statement that '*la très grande majorité des étrangers résidant dans notre pays souhaite y demeurer et aspire à participer à la vie collective française*'. But it is not at all clear that they wish to do so '*dans le respect des principes de la République: laïcité, tolérance, solidarité*'. About 3 million immigrants and their children are Moslems, including 800,000 Algerian citizens, 500,000 Franco-Algerian *Beurs*, and 500,000 *Harkis* and their children. Over the years, devout Moslem immigrants have made growing demands for recognition of their customs and religious practices. Against the background of the spread of Islamic fundamentalism, the Moslem phenomenon in France has become cause for concern. The growing number of strict and 'born again' Moslems is becoming a force against integration, particularly integration into a secular state, and Islam could easily become a rallying point in times of crisis.

While most Moslems in France are Sunni rather than the Shia associated with Iranian-style fundamentalism, the early 1990s have witnessed the emergence of a powerful fundamentalist party in Algeria, the *Front islamique du Salut*, a party which seeks openly to subordinate the state to Koranic law. In elections held in Algeria in 1990, the FIS won control of more than half the local councils in the country, including the major cities and, in January 1992, elections were cancelled in a military-backed effort to prevent the party from taking power in national government. There is some evidence that this party is making progress in France among the most marginalized, least educated Moslem groups for whom Islamic fundamentalism offers an uncomplicated certainty, a consolation against the injustices of Western society. As the Paris Mosque is controlled directly from Algiers, there are suspicions that it will become a vehicle of Islamic extremism.

Even though only 5 or 6 per cent of the Moslem population practise their religion regularly and strictly, already there have been clashes between Islamic and Republican principles. In defiance of the laws banning symbols intended to advertise religious beliefs from school rooms, a number of schoolgirls have insisted on wearing scarfs to school to conform to the Koran. They have all come from strict and militant Moslem families who refuse to accept the norms established for state schools. Female teachers frequently find that they are abused by Moslem pupils because their dress does not correspond to Koranic standards, the study of 'secular' subjects is contested, and history lessons are disrupted because of their 'Christian bias' in studying Medieval Europe and the Crusades, for example.

It is this growing intransigence – some call it fanaticism – within the Moslem population, combined with the bitter memories of the Algerian war between 1954 and 1962, which provides the right with themes that appeal to the insecurity felt by many French people. French culture and civilization submerged by a new barbarian invasion; the erosion of national identity. Photographs of entire streets in Marseille brought to a halt when the Moslem faithful are called to prayer by an *imam* using loudspeakers, the appearance of mosques in every large town give the image of a strident, combative challenge to French norms. The missionary, indeed militant rhetoric of the more radical *imams*, does nothing to reassure French opinion: '*Un vrai croyant ne doit jamais consentir. Il doit ordonner et interdire. Mais jamais consentir.*' Their rigid and exclusive social attitudes, particularly with regard to women, are equally rebarbative in a liberal democracy; '*Tu laisses ta fille se promener à moitié nue! et tu t'appelles croyant*', so said a preacher in a mosque in the tenth *arrondissement* of Paris (*L'Express*, 15 December, 1989).

There is concern that this fundamentalism will attract more Moslem immigrants if they cannot be more thoroughly integrated into French society. Certainly the government is seeking to encourage a more liberal Islamic tradition, one which could coexist with contemporary French values. There are proposals to establish an Islamic theological college at Strasbourg, and to examine ways of incorporating certain Islamic precepts into French law.

Conclusion

The 1990s are witnessing the first concerted attempt to bring France's foreign population into the *pays légal*. It has taken almost twenty years of growing tension and violence to produce the will to do so. Even so, integration, indeed the very presence of large numbers of foreigners on French soil drives a deep wedge between left and right, and it might be argued that it was largely the spectre of '*Lepenisme*' that pushed the Mitterrand administration into seeking an urgent and practical solution. If this is the case, the leader of the *Front national* may achieve the very opposite of what he sought: integration instead of expulsion.

A successful integration programme would have consequences for France's institutions and values. It would be unreasonable and impractical to expect total conformism from immigrants. Integration cannot mean assimilation. It must mean equal rights and opportunities, compromise, respect and toleration of diversity. Thus France's legal system is already being scrutinized with an eye towards the integration of certain Islamic principles. There may follow a dilution, if not the abandonment, of the principle of *laïcité* in state-controlled schools, or the establishment of a genuinely pluralist education system *à l'anglaise*.

Such goals would not appear easy to realize in a country which has a history of competing orthodoxies, each as rigid in its own way as the other in its concept of citizenship and the nation. The left's views are informed by a rational philosophical universalism which dates from 1789; those of the right by a sense of France's Christian, national culture, of a *patrie* based on blood, soil and ancient rights and customs which are 'natural' and which cannot successfully be replaced by rational constructs. The two orthodoxies have struggled for supremacy over two centuries, and no 'pluralist' tradition had a chance to develop. Integration of immigrants has proved difficult enough in countries like the United Kingdom whose political debate is far less ideologically informed than that in France.

At the same time, immigration is becoming a European concern. The wealth of the Community is a magnet that attracts considerable numbers of people from the areas on its fringes – eastern Europe, the Balkans and north Africa, notably. The Single Market and the Schengen Agreements, permitting considerable freedom of movement within the Community, have made a Community policy on immigration inevitable. As things stand, it looks as though European policy will have to envisage the very policies that France has adopted in recent years, namely the closure of frontiers to new immigration, and efforts to integrate more satisfactorily those settled within the territory of the Community.

The task will be far from simple. Considerable population movements have been taking place since the beginning of the 1990s. Anti-foreign feeling has increased in the new unified Germany, while the old spectre of anti-semitism has resurfaced in France and in Germany. From the Baltic to the Mediterranean, extremist right-wing groups are taking advantage of the upheavals and uncertainties following the collapse of the Soviet empire and German unification in order to articulate racial and ethnic prejudices which totalitarianism had suppressed but not eradicated.

Bibliography

Immigration is a subject with demographic, economic, social and political dimensions. Consequently it is dealt with in a wide range of publications. The following are merely some of the more accessible ones. Many contain more detailed bibliographies.

Lebon, A., *Regard sur l'immigration et la présence étrangère en France*. Published annually for the Ministère des Affaires sociales et de la Solidarité by La Documentation française, Paris. Bibliography.

Les Cahiers de *L'Express. Dossier immigration.* Hors série no. 3 (1990).

Ogden, P. and White, E., (eds), *Migrants in Modern France: population mobility in the later 19th and 20th centuries.* Unwin Hyman, London, 1989. Extensive bibliography.

Regards sur l'actualité. Monthly review published by La Documentation française, Paris.

Current affairs magazines regularly carry descriptive and analytical articles concerning most aspects of immigration, also specially commissioned opinion polls (particularly the *Nouvel Observateur*). The weekly *Nouvel Observateur* is on the political left; *L'Express* and *Le Point* are liberal 'centrist' weeklies with no specific political attachment; the monthly *Choc du mois* and the bi-monthly *Identité* are on the right and express *Front national* views.

Le Monde continues to provide the most accurate reporting of important issues. It has a valuable tradition of inviting specialists – lawyers, academics, doctors, community leaders – to write occasional articles.

The Economist publishes well-informed analytical articles on the European dimension of immigration.

5

Foreign policy
Alan Clark and Robert Elgie

The Gaullist heritage (1958–1969)

The essential principles of de Gaulle's foreign policy in the 1960s were few and uncomplicated. Their vital initial postulate was the paramount importance of national independence, the re-establishment of which would enable France to regain its traditional position of international eminence. In independence, France would be free to enter into multiform co-operation with other nations and thus to fulfil its historical 'vocation' of promoting peace and certain civilized values. Without independence, valid international co-operation would not be possible, since it would inevitably involve the subordination of one of the co-operating partners. National indignity apart, such co-operation-in-subordination would in practice be bound to fail.

From 1958 French foreign policy quickly became *le domaine réservé* of the President of the Republic who accorded it prime importance, determining its major orientations and deciding particular, often crucial issues. De Gaulle conducted a personal policy in an individual fashion. For some it was a policy characterized more by its diplomatic style – its gesture and its rhetoric – than by the solidity of its achievements. Yet, substantial or stylistic, important changes in French foreign policy did take place under de Gaulle. Following the broadly successful and rapid decolonization of France's African possessions, and the settlement of the Algerian war by 1962, de Gaulle had worked to establish national independence on the only basis that, in his mind, was valid: French control of an effective national security system. This led him in 1966 to withdraw France from the integrated military command of a NATO dominated by the USA, and to develop a French nuclear strategy and strike capacity. As the converse of this disengagement from the American orbit, a policy of co-operation and *détente* with the USSR and the 'satellite' countries of eastern Europe was pursued with enthusiasm.

In European affairs, French intransigence concerning the implementation in the EC of a common agricultural policy (CAP), effective though it proved to be, took second place in de Gaulle's estimation behind his political ambition to establish a confederal association of west European states, a 'Europe of nations' in which France would play a leading political role. Between, and distinct from, the superpowers of East and West, de Gaulle's western Europe was to have become indispensable to world stability. In practice, his political Europeanism was eventually reduced to an unshakeable opposition to any proposals which might lead to the emergence of a supranationalist Europe, more or less aligned with the USA.

The Gaullist gospel of the independence of nation states was appreciatively received in many parts of the Third World. France's international standing was enhanced by the vigorous co-operation and aid policies it pursued, particularly in the newly independent African Francophone states. Nevertheless, the function of arbiter in international conflicts which de Gaulle had on occasion loudly assigned to a 'neutral' France lost credibility at least with Israel as, in the Middle East, French sympathies came increasingly to lie with the Arab oil-supplying states.

For Couve de Murville (Minister of Foreign Affairs, 1958–68) de Gaulle was beyond doubt *'un homme d'une passion intransigeante et sa passion était la France'*; his foreign policy pursued *'l'intérêt national au sens le plus élevé du terme'*. Couve de Murville's assessment should not be accepted uncritically. Critics within and outside France have accused de Gaulle's foreign policy of being anachronistic, unrealistic and therefore dangerous, merely negative, or – most damning – of being the product of an old man's idiosyncrasies. But, in principle, the pursuit of national independence by de Gaulle was never a matter of ignoring harsh world realities; rather, he constantly affirmed the priority of the national reality as the vital precondition of international dealings. His basic position was not inevitably nationalist in the pejorative sense of the word, to the extent that France's 'nationalness' sought peaceful rather than conflicting relations with other nations. Until very recent years, de Gaulle's ideas and priorities have exercized easily the single most powerful influence on the foreign policy of succeeding Presidents of the Republic – *'le dogme le plus envahissant de la Ve République'*, Alain Duhamel recently called them. More than thirty years later, in the hugely changed international context of the 1990s, President Mitterrand's foreign policy is far from having achieved complete emancipation from its Gaullist heritage.

Foreign policy under Pompidou (1969–74)

At de Gaulle's resignation (April 1969) French prestige stood higher than at any time since 1940 and, arguably, since before the First World War. During the 1960s France had exerted a determining influence on the economic and political evolution of Europe and of a large portion of Africa. The voice of France had been heard – if not always listened to – in far wider fields, from Washington to Moscow and in many capitals of the Third World. Foreign reaction to the new French standing in the world was doubtless an unstable amalgam of resentment and respect, envy and affection. Complaints at the cost of Gaullist co-operation and nuclear policies apart, the French at home were on balance appreciative of de Gaulle's endeavours to restore national dignity.

In defence policy, Pompidou was faithful to his predecessor's approach: in contrast to the high rigidity of France's 1966 position, he adopted the more moderate line perceptible since 1968, but without, however, taking any positive initiatives. Criticism of the tiny size and doubtful efficacy of *la force de frappe* grew. The cost of the nuclear effort weighed more heavily both financially and, as the left increased its electoral following, politically.

France had not signed the 1963 and 1968 international treaties on nuclear disarmament and arms control, and the agreement on the prevention of nuclear war signed between the USA and the USSR in June 1973 justified, in Pompidou's eyes, the earlier intransigence of de Gaulle. For France, the June treaty was tantamount to the self-promotion of the two superpowers to the shared office of nuclear policeman for the rest of the world. It was, according to Pompidou's Foreign Minister, Michel Jobert, a condominium which should not be confused with genuine progress towards international *détente*. The final twelve months of Pompidou's presidency amply underlined basic Gaullist principles and attitudes relating to national security. At the Helsinki conference on European security and defence (July 1973), and elsewhere, France emphasized the need for each nation, and for a united Europe, to exercise defensive responsibilities; subjugation to the superpowers of East or West in so vital an area as defence was unacceptable.

Pompidou's relations with the superpowers were not always as difficult as they became in 1973 and were at no stage sharply marked by the temperamental anti-Americanism to which de Gaulle on occasion succumbed. However, relations deteriorated considerably in 1973 when, as well as the USA-USSR treaty on the prevention of nuclear war, further discord emerged. In an effort to ensure agreement with a Europe working more or less slowly towards economic and political union, the USA proposed (June 1973) a 'new Atlantic charter' designed to promote an Atlanticist orientation of Europe. For the USA and for France's European partners the project had its merits: quite apart from its substantial economic interests in western Europe, the USA provided the lion's share of a NATO defensive system which sooner or later would be affected by the decisions of any politically united Europe of the future. For France the move constituted yet another attempt at domination by the Americans; this time not only the sovereignty of France but also the autonomy of a possible union of Europe were threatened. By the end of Pompidou's presidency (he died in office, April 1974) France appeared again in the familiar Gaullist stance of isolated opposition to American intentions in several fields.

Pompidou continued to develop political links with the USSR in the context of Gaullist 'balanced' relations with the superpowers. Until 1973, exchanges remained cordial and limited progress was made in Franco-Soviet commercial and technical exchanges. But the treaty of June 1973 demonstrated that in matters of importance the USSR preferred to leave France out of account and deal directly with its American rival/partner. On his visit to Peking (September 1973), Pompidou found himself talking the same diplomatic language as the Chinese leaders: both disapproved of the 'collusion' between the USA and the USSR. For Pompidou, their joint 'imperialism' was no less potentially dangerous than had been the conflict between the two blocs in the 1950s and 1960s.

From 1971, the bulk of Pompidou's activity was given to the promotion of greater European union, especially in the monetary and political spheres. Pompidou's desire to set Europe in motion again was evident at the European summit at The Hague (December 1969) which agreed to open negotiations with candidate countries, notably Britain. Following a meeting in Paris between Pompidou and the British Prime Minister, Heath (May 1971), it was decided in Luxembourg that Britain (and Ireland and Denmark) should enter the EC on 1 January 1973. Called at the French President's suggestion, the Paris meeting of the Nine (October 1972) went further and drew up a calendar for a political union that was to be achieved by 1980. Pompidou did not depart from de Gaulle's insistence on a confederal union of states, although he was more sensitive to the isolation of France that was liable to result if that policy was promoted in too absolute a fashion. His temperamental preference was for progressive, concrete realizations. Only ineffectual goodwill was plentiful however, and 1973 ended with Europe struggling in the aftermath of a global oil crisis, still unable to agree on common monetary, energy and raw materials policies.

Pompidou remained firm in the pro-Arab stance adopted by de Gaulle in 1967, conducting his Middle East policy with a sure sense of national economic interests. The diplomatic position remained much as before (namely, guarantees for both Israel and the Palestinian people, and a negotiated settlement based on mutual concessions), but French energy supplies were also involved and had to be protected. Pompidou's pragmatism became apparent when, while maintaining the embargo on arms to Israel, he agreed that France should supply Libya with 100 Mirages (January 1970). Gaullist claims to impartiality fell to pieces: Pompidou's France was no longer a peacemaker but was concerned rather to exert influence and cultivate interests. French diplomats covered the Middle Eastern states thoroughly in the context of a long-term policy intended to develop French industrial, commercial and cultural interests in the region.

Pompidou's action in the Middle East should be seen within his wider policy context of expanding France's role in the Mediterranean region. By emphasising southern interests, Pompidou thought France could re-balance the northern predominance that would result from the Europe of Nine, and regain some of its lost importance by occupying a prominent position in the 'new' Mediterranean that might emerge. Efforts made from 1969 met with moderate success. Contacts with Morocco, Spain and Portugal improved. Relations with Algeria were often difficult: the loss of French oil concessions in the Algerian nationalisations of 1971 was a heavy blow, the proportion of French aid going to Algeria declined steadily and, following racial tension in Marseille in 1973, Algeria suspended the heavy emigration of its workers to France. Pompidou nevertheless persisted in his efforts to cultivate good relations, looking to France's longer-term economic and strategic interests. His concept of an Arab-Latin Mediterranean was far-sighted and perhaps feasible, although it was not without its opportunism. It was a policy defensible as prudent manoeuvring, but one which also contained the implicit admission that France's role, after being played on the world stage, might in future be limited effectively to western Europe and the Mediterranean. And to a presence in Africa.

While President, Pompidou visited, at least once, most of the former French territories in black Africa; after 1958 de Gaulle had not ventured further south than the countries of the Maghreb. The contrast illustrates Pompidou's greater concern for a co-operation policy that was less paternalistic, more open to the evolving circumstances of the Third World. Wherever possible the privileged relations between France and its former colonies were maintained. While it increased in volume, the proportion of the French budget given to co-operation declined to 1974; aid from the private sector (banks, industry, and so on) became almost as important as public aid – and less disinterested. Further, the French co-operation programme began to spread its funds and expertise beyond its traditional African spheres of influence: in 1970, 40 per cent of aid from Paris went to developing countries outside the French franc zone.

As the oil crisis deepened, Pompidou saw the problems of the Third World (the stability of prices received for raw materials, trade relations with the developed world) in global, long-term perspectives and, by 1974, the familiar Gaullist thesis of an international mediatory role for France had cropped up again. France's refusal to follow the American 'common front' strategy on oil prices (October 1973), and its stress on the necessity for developing countries to be fully involved in discussions related to international trade, were welcomed by the many countries of the Third World dependent on prices received for their exports to the West.

Foreign policy under Giscard d'Estaing (1974–81)

A number of features of Giscard's reputation in the field of foreign policy were widely acknowledged at the start of his term of office. He was first and foremost a convinced European who looked to a politically united Europe having its own defence, currency and foreign policy. Although he always denied it, critics (many Gaullists, most socialists and all the communists) accused him of Atlanticist leanings, of working for greater French and European association with the USA, particularly with regard to economic and defence structures. By his own admission Giscard was more deliberately internationalist in his approach to foreign policy: problems now posed themselves on a world scale, state-to-state relations '*à la de Gaulle*' were no longer sufficient in many cases and what he termed '*une politique mondiale*' was vital, although national sovereignty was to be firmly preserved. Such a global perspective necessitated what Giscard regularly referred to as a policy of '*concertation*', that is of dialogue and harmonious co-ordination rather than intimidation and conflict ('*la confrontation*'). To what extent an implied criticism of de Gaulle's resolute defence of (his version of) national interests was to be detected in these Giscardian emphases was a matter of political opinion.

Change was undeniable too in Giscard's own political position. As leader of the *Républicains indépendants* (RI), a minority party of the centre-right, he was the first non-Gaullist President of the Fifth Republic. It was clear from the start that the Gaullists in parliament would see that departures, real or imagined, from their founder's principles (in particular with regard to defence and national independence within Europe) did not pass uncriticized. The narrowness of his electoral victory (fewer than 2 per cent more votes than François Mitterrand, the candidate of the combined left in 1974) might have been expected to restrict Giscard's freedom to conduct his own foreign policy. In fact Giscard's political base expanded significantly later in his term: gains were made by the Giscardian UDF both in the 1978 legislative elections and in the European Assembly elections of the following year. Presidential foreign policy in the three years to May 1981 often appeared in consequence innovative and dynamic, particularly concerning disarmament, Africa and Europe.

Giscard came to power at a time of serious and persistent international difficulties. The oil crisis from late 1973 promised to involve other raw materials and threatened shaky international financial systems. Europe was in conflict, stagnant if not actually regressive. The USA was in the final throes of the Watergate scandal. The new French President's wide financial experience (Giscard had been a liberal Finance Minister under de Gaulle, 1962–66, and under Pompidou, 1969–74) was expected to produce in the conduct of foreign policy an intensification of Pompidou-style sensitivity to French economic interests. Complex and rapid change on all sides also encouraged Giscard to develop his predecessor's pragmatism: in a world characterized more by chaos than by order, '*le pilotage à vue*' and '*la gestion de l'imprévisible*' (the phrases are Giscard's) became the only effective attitudes to adopt. Critics nostalgic for de Gaulle's loudly affirmed basic principles and long-term strategies were reluctant to admit Giscard's constant emphasis on change and on what he called '*le grand réaménagement des relations internationales*' in the late 1970s. The same critics could have been more sensitive to the sombre conflict that underlay Giscardian foreign policy: on the one hand, the advocacy of a humanitarian *mondialisme*, biased towards the indispensable implementation of greater international economic justice and the needs of the developing world; on the other, the no less necessary defence of national strategic and economic interests.

Even had he wanted to do otherwise, Giscard would have been under pressure, for reasons at once political and technological, to adopt a defence policy acceptable to the Gaullists. Before election he promised to maintain and develop French nuclear weapons and guaranteed the absence of France from disarmament and non-proliferation talks which sought only to maintain the blocs of the superpowers. Between 1974 and 1977, however, perceived deviations from established defence policy occurred with disconcerting frequency. Nuclear tests at Mururoa were confined underground and their frequency reduced. Presidential declarations in 1976 implied a geographical extension of the hitherto strictly national dissuasion policy and an increased degree of French involvement in NATO's military structures. Giscard's insistence on the need to modernize France's conventional forces and in particular to develop mobile, multi-purpose interventionist units was also seen to be symptomatic of a relative departure from de Gaulle's priorities.

Deviation in defence policy was in fact more apparent than real. Following the relative pause of 1976–8, nuclear dissuasion policy was substantially redefined along Gaullist lines. Commissioned in 1979, France's sixth strategic nuclear submarine, *Inflexible*, was programmed to enter service in 1985 armed with the M4, a new generation of longer-range, multi-headed missiles. Existing FOST (*Force océanique stratégique*) submarines were to be renovated and similarly equipped from the later 1980s. As a result the megaton capacity of France's strategic forces was projected to quadruple in the seven years to 1985. More specifically, Giscardian emphases on flexibility and innovation were discernible in longer-term projects announced in mid-1980: mobile, land-based strategic missiles for the 1990s, the technological development of enhanced radiation weapons (the so-called 'neutron bomb'). Consequences of Giscard's energetic reaffirmation of defence policy were soon evident. Underground nuclear testing in the Pacific expanded again. French defence costs rose significantly: by 30 per cent in real terms between 1977 and 1981, a rate of expenditure not achieved by most European NATO countries.

International interest was stimulated by Giscard's presentation to the UN (May 1978) of a number of disarmament proposals. His address, which marked France's return to the world disarmament scene after some twenty years' absence, was characterized by a typically subtle combination of Gaullist orthodoxy and Eurocentric innovation. His efforts to regionalize, and in particular to Europeanize progress in international disarmament (Giscard proposed to the UN a pan-European conference on conventional disarmament) were as idealistic as they were necessary. Not only French but west European disquiet intensified as, in a context marked by increased Soviet military power in eastern Europe, the signing of SALT 2 (June 1979) brought into question the long-term reliability of American nuclear commitment to European security. Subsequent deterioration of strategic tensions in Europe served to intensify fears in French political circles, from the Gaullist RPR to the PCF, that the superpowers of East and West were effectively disposing between themselves of European security. It did not diminish the potential value of Giscard's Europeanist approach to security problems which in fact, in 1981, continued to underlie much of the work of the Madrid conference on disarmament in Europe.

Giscard's predicted determination to effect a *rapprochement* with the USA became evident during the months following his election. Even before the considerable public success of the presidential visit to Washington in celebration of the

American bicentenary (May 1976), a more positive tone in bilateral relations had been established. In the aftermath of Carter's visit to France (January 1978) relations between the two nations were, Giscard claimed, '*cordiaux, ouverts et respectueux des droits de l'autre*' – that is, to a degree never previously equalled, the USA recognized France's right to pursue autonomous national policies. However, such formal assertions of the excellence of Franco-American relations became increasingly difficult to reconcile with multiplying points of conflict of a commercial or industrial nature; differences of position over energy and security matters also emerged. By 1979 France had become prominent (for example, at the Tokyo summit of industrialized nations, June 1979) in voicing EC resentment at the absence of a concerted American policy on oil imports.

As with the USA, France's relations with the USSR from 1974 were characterized by an evolution towards uncertainty and, especially after 1977, prolonged ambivalence. At first, France stressed its determination to develop further the policy of *détente* and co-operation which, initiated by de Gaulle, had become established by the mid-1970s as a central figure of its foreign policy. Indeed the triple formula of *détente, entente et coopération* was still employed by France, at the end of the decade, to convey the essence of its formal relations with the USSR. Nor was this a mere diplomatic nicety, for Franco-Soviet co-operation had, by the later 1970s, become varied, substantial and, ultimately, expanding. In late 1974, extensive energy and industrial agreements were concluded, together with a general accord on economic co-operation intended to triple bilateral trade to 1980. In 1976 the value of industrial contracts between the two countries was the highest ever. By mid-1979, wide-ranging co-operation agreements to 1990 were in place; all seemed set fair for the next decade.

Subsequent diplomatic relations proved to be decidedly less smooth. Following almost three years of Soviet disquiet at both the confused evolution of French defence policy and Giscard's more conciliatory attitude towards the USA, 1977–8 was marked by a deterioration in relations so serious as to temporarily hamper commercial exchanges. Secondary areas of dispute were not lacking: Soviet rejection of the French disarmament proposals of May 1978, the Middle East, human rights, China. However, central to Franco-Soviet dissension were Moscow's virulent attacks on Giscard's African policy, and in particular its criticism of French 'imperialist' intervention against 'progressivist' forces in Zaire and Chad (see p. 140–1). Then of some fourteen years' standing, the Franco-Soviet *détente* may, as Giscard claimed, have made a significant contribution to peace and stability in Europe: but just as clearly, no French impingement on the USSR's African strategies would be tolerated. So vulnerable a dichotomy between *entente* and *coopération*, diplomacy and trade, constituted at best an unpredictable basis on which to build Franco-Soviet relations in the future.

The numerous uncertainties of relations with both the USA and the USSR reflected the recent shift in France's foreign policy perspectives away from the bipolar world of the superpowers towards an international scene conceived, where possible, in multipolar, regionalist terms. Complex and subject to constant redefinition, it was a movement compatible both with de Gaulle's criticism in the 1960s of the superpowers' hegemony and with his largely symbolic recognition of the importance of Third World nations. Pompidou's initiatives in Africa, the Mediterranean and the Arab world had maintained the movement. In his turn Giscard attempted to co-ordinate French foreign policy more tightly than ever around the triple regional 'poles' of Europe, the Arab states and the Third World, especially Africa.

As Pompidou had done in 1969, Giscard set out with an ambition to relaunch Europe. Even more than his predecessor, Giscard was obliged from the mid-1970s to pit his ideals against a Europe that was retrogressive and disunited. In particular, common monetary and energy policies were still lacking at a time when member countries were experiencing more or less acute economic difficulties. Pessimistic analyses of the impotent condition of the Nine flourished, and late in 1976 French observers even speculated sceptically on the survival of the EC's fundamental customs union.

Particularly from 1977, however, Franco-German relations materially underpinned European development, providing much needed stability and stimulus. It was, for example, a text jointly presented by Giscard and West German Chancellor Schmidt to the European Council (July 1978) that supplied the basis for the European Monetary System (EMS) which came into operation in March 1979. After a difficult birth, the EMS's early functioning was sound. A substantial advance in monetary co-operation had been achieved.

Persistent French efforts were made from 1974 to promote a politically more united Europe. Giscard's early tactics in this field owed much to de Gaulle's European 'union of states': the new President suggested that the nine heads of government should meet regularly and informally in order to discuss current or longer-term matters of European concern. Prominent among Giscard's intentions in initiating this European Council was the idea of progressively accustoming the Nine to top-level political discussion from which co-ordination and perhaps, by accretion as it were, greater unity might emerge. At the same time such a process was to be supplemented by institutional change, in particular by a European Assembly elected by universal suffrage. After initial moves in 1975–76, smooth formal progress towards the realization of this major Giscardian ambition was made, culminating in the inauguration, in mid-1979, of the first democratically based European Parliament.

In the 1979 Euro-elections almost 40 per cent of the French electorate abstained from voting. With economic interests more pressingly at stake, the next stage in the construction of Europe – the expansion of the EC to twelve members by the inclusion of Greece (from January 1981), Spain and Portugal – did not benefit from such broadly sympathetic public disinterest. Giscard's unequivocal, if not unconditional, support for the Europe of Twelve was exceptional in the France of 1978–9; to the PCF, parts of the PS, the RPR, to farmers' groups and some industrialists in the Midi, the entry of Spain in particular threatened French social and economic interests. If to such hostility were added both left-wing and Gaullist charges that Giscard intended to establish an 'Atlanticized', supranationalist Europe, and the necessity for sweeping institutional reform of an enlarged EC, it seemed probable that the qualified success achieved by Giscardian European policy to 1981 would be difficult to equal, or even to maintain.

For both economic and strategic reasons, Giscard developed relations with the Arab world to a point far beyond that reached by Pompidou. The French diplomatic position with regard to Israel shifted in emphasis if not in fundamentals when, by late 1974, Giscard had already stressed the vital importance of arriving at a durable settlement of the Palestinian problem; a settlement which had to include the establishment of sure and recognized frontiers for all concerned, and in particular for Israel and the Palestinian people. By 1977, France maintained that Israel should withdraw to its territorial limits of 1967, while the Palestinians should have access to a homeland (*une patrie*). The need for a global settlement in the Middle East caused France to share the majority of the Arab world's anxiety and reserve about the Camp David agreements (between Israel and Egypt, March 1979), seeing in them – a further point of Franco-American dissension – a fragmentary and potentially divisive response to what in reality was a much wider issue.

If relations with Israel were eventually normalized (in 1977) after France's effective recognition of the Palestine Liberation Organization (UN debate, October 1974), French identification and involvement with the Arab world expanded enormously throughout the 1970s. Such association ranged in later years from mercenary pro-Arab reactions (the Abou Daoud affair, January 1977) to the promotion of dialogue between the EC and the OPEC states. Above all, however, Franco-Arab relations were governed by economic constraint. Obliged since 1973 to pay escalating prices for its oil imports, France, as other industrialized countries, strove as never before to increase its industrial and technological sales to the Arab states. The inevitable identification of French policy towards the Arab world with the promotion of commercial and strategic interests was firmly underscored by Prime Minister Raymond Barre's productive visit to Iraq (July 1979). Iraq undertook to guarantee up to one-third of France's annual oil imports, thereby more than doubling its rate of supply. In return France was to sell to Iraq a range of arms and military equipment, and a civil nuclear research centre. If in the wake of the Iranian revolution and the Gulf war between Iran and Iraq France redefined some of its strategic relations in the Arab region, the perilous and fragile formula of 'oil for arms' had not outlived its usefulness, or its necessity.

France's relations with the Third World in the 1970s were characterized by an unstable combination, not unknown in de Gaulle's day, of generous intentions and imperfect realizations of those intentions. Giscard consistently presented himself as a renovator of French co-operation policy. Long-established links with North and black African countries were to be retained, but also revised. More importantly, the taint of imperialism was to be removed from co-operation in all its forms, technical, cultural or merely linguistic: *l'Afrique aux Africains*' was the slogan Giscard brandished in talks with African leaders from 1975. In consequence, the numbers of French medical, teaching and administrative personnel based in Africa diminished gradually as greater emphasis was placed on co-operation through investment and the establishment of self-sufficient structures within the developing countries: formation rather than assistance.

This revamped policy did not hinder the expansion and revival of French bilateral relations in Africa and elsewhere. Complementing significant *rapprochement* with previously critical 'progressivist' states such as Angola, Ethiopia and Madagascar, Giscard's historic visit to Guinea (December 1978) restored relations between Paris and Conakry (which had been ruptured in 1958 at the start of de Gaulle's presidency), symbolized the more dynamic, outgoing character of Giscardian co-operation – and promised to be profitable. Unprecedented French initiatives were subsequently undertaken in former British and Portuguese territories with a view to expanding and co-ordinating French co-operation on a broader regionalist basis throughout West Africa. Of potentially equal importance was the long overdue revival of French diplomatic, industrial and economic interest in South and Central America, as evidenced by presidential visits to Brazil and Mexico, and by various ministerial tours of Argentina, Colombia and Panama.

More controversial was Giscard's policy of military intervention in Africa. In western Sahara, Chad, and the Shaba province of Zaire in particular, French military personnel and equipment were repeatedly engaged in stabilizing chaotic internal situations. But at what point did stabilizing assistance end and 'neo-colonialist' interference begin? Reactions were divided and often extremist. The USSR and 'progressivist' African states (for example Tanzania and Madagascar) were unreservedly hostile. Among Arab nations, Libya denounced French policy in Chad as archaic colonialism, while Franco-Algerian diplomatic and economic relations went into serious decline from mid-1977 in the face of French assistance to Morocco and Mauritania, and after the Algeria-backed Polisario Front held several French civilians hostage. On the other hand, numerous black African states, not invariably Francophone, expressed varying degrees of relieved approval of the French supportive actions. More discreetly, the EC, the USA and even sections of the OAU associated themselves sympathetically with Giscard's initiatives.

By 1978 the risks inherent in such interventionism were felt, not least by the ascendant French left led by Mitterrand, to be acute: the prolongation and escalation of military involvement (in response to the civil war there, French troops in Chad were doubled to 2,500 in March 1979), the detrimental identification of France with repressive regimes (Mobutu's Zaire, Bokassa's Central African Empire) and unenlightened policies (continued French intervention in the Comores and presence in Réunion, and ambiguous commercial relations with South Africa). If by 1979–81 French interventionism in Africa appeared less militarily activist, diplomatically more balanced and reserved, the longer-term coherence of what Giscard termed 'la fidélité africaine de la France' was still not evident. Many in France feared that the need to protect French economic and Western strategic interests, as well as African security, could give rise to further piecemeal responses.

More durably innovatory was the importance Giscard repeatedly attached to the need to adopt international regionalist perspectives when responding to the Third World. While France still had a useful role to play in Africa and elsewhere, often limitedly national, bilateral action was now insufficient: economic, political and strategic problems posed themselves on so complex and extensive a scale that only multilateral approaches, involving effective negotiations between industrialized and developing nations, were appropriate. Unfortunately, Giscard's various proposals in this vein too often remained at the level of prestigious diplomatic initiatives, with little or no practical application. The North-South conference on international economic co-operation was launched in 1974 at the joint suggestion of France and Saudi Arabia. It ended (in June 1977) with the participating Third World countries disillusioned by the industrialized world's reluctance to agree to extensive structural reform of international financial and trade systems. Fundamental problems – energy supplies, prices for raw materials, Third World indebtedness – remained virtually unchanged. Two years later, Giscardian assertions of *'concertation'* and *'interdépendance'* as the keys to a more just and workable international economic order were still more numerous than effective. The Lomé Convention (between the EC and African, Caribbean and Pacific countries) was renewed only with difficulty and in confusion (June 1979).

Giscard's major address to the sixth Franco-African Conference (Kigali, Rwanda, May 1979) underlined the three principal interest areas of contemporary French policy, and encapsulated the undoubted farsightedness, the idealist ambition but also the disconcerting ambiguity of that policy. Fusing ideas of Euro-Arab and Euro-African association regularly mooted since 1974, Giscard proposed a Euro-African-Arab 'trilogue' (the elaboration by carefully prepared stages of a triangular charter of solidarity). Potentially no fewer than seventy-eight states were to be involved. Such a vast project in multilateral political and economic co-operation (technology / raw materials / oil) would not, however, supplant Franco-African bilateral relations, nor reduce French commitment to African security. Having recently cancelled the debts of eight African states, France announced at Kigali an increase of almost 50 per cent in its co-operation budget from 1980, as well as substantial additional contributions to African development bodies. Yet, a few months later, the decisive role played by the French Army in the overthrow of Bokassa's tyrannical Central African Empire

(September 1979), while it stabilized a deteriorating situation, exposed Giscard to charges of old-fashioned manipulation of the internal affairs of former colonial territories.

Foreign policy under Mitterrand (1981–   )

The May 1981 presidential election seemed to provide the opportunity for major changes in the course of French foreign policy. The election of François Mitterrand, the first socialist President in the (short) history of the Fifth Republic, was met with jubilation on the left and trepidation on the right. For Mitterrand's supporters there was the hope that the wrongs of the Gaullist and Giscardian past might be righted. For Mitterrand's opponents there was the fear that socialist mismanagement would further weaken France's already precarious position of influence in the world. More than that, there was the fear that Mitterrand's socialist idealism and the presence of four communist ministers in the new cabinet would mean that France might draw closer to the Soviet Union, so upsetting the fragile balance of power in the world. In fact, neither the hopes nor the fears of either side were realized. The direction of foreign policy under Mitterrand bears both *la marque et la trace* of his three presidential predecessors.

The first two years of the Mitterrand presidency were peppered with foreign policy initiatives, many of which were deliberately designed to differentiate the new socialist regime from its Giscardian forebear. Mitterrand wanted to prove that it was possible to pursue a foreign policy which was morally right, rather than one which was based upon what he saw as being greed and self-interest. The most eloquent expression of Mitterrand's foreign policy idealism came at the North-South summit of world leaders at Cancun in Mexico in October 1981. To all the oppressed peoples of the world he sent the message, '*Courage! la liberté vaincra*'. Much to the annoyance of the US however, Mitterrand welcomed the prospect of many of these people being liberated from regimes which were heavily backed by Washington. For example, in August 1981, a joint Franco-Mexican declaration recognized the rebel anti-governmental and, hence, anti-American opposition in El Salvador as a legitimate force. In 1982, France agreed to sell arms to the left-wing Sandinista regime in Nicaragua in the knowledge that these arms would be used to fight the US-backed *contra* rebels. However, Mitterrand's foreign policy was not simply knee-jerk anti-Americanism. For example, on his first visit to Moscow in 1984, the President also severely criticized the Soviet regime for its record of human rights' abuses, calling, in particular, for the release of the prominent Soviet dissident, Andrei Sakharov.

These foreign policy initiatives certainly bore Mitterrand's personal imprint, but they were also partly inspired by the new Minister for External Relations, Claude Cheysson, and the new Minister for Co-operation and Development, Jean-Pierre Cot. In their different ways both Ministers were political mavericks. As a former French Commissioner to the European Community, Cheysson had been in charge of the EC's dealings with poor African, Caribbean and Pacific countries. This background made him particularly instrumental, for example, in helping to draw up a contract with Algeria, whereby France agreed to buy Algerian natural gas at a rate which was substantially above the market price. Nevertheless, Cheysson was also adept at making diplomatic *gaffes*, notably after the assassination of the Egyptian President, Anwar Sadat. Jean-Pierre Cot had been the Socialist Party's spokesperson on foreign affairs before the 1981 election and had the reputation of being a champion of the Third World. He saw the Ministry of Co-operation as having a moral mission. He claimed that he never went to a Third World country without having read its entry in the Amnesty International yearbook. He ensured that overseas aid was extended beyond France's former colonies. However, just to show that Mitterrand was the real master of foreign policy, Cot resigned in 1982 when the President refused to endorse his bid to reorganize his department in a way which would have given it greater powers.

Cot's resignation was one of a series of incidents which soon

The Europeanist aspirations of Mitterrand's defence policy cause anxiety in his presidential predecessors, de Gaulle (left) and Pompidou. (From *Le Monde*, 12–13 January 1992.)

demonstrated the limits to Mitterrand's exercise of foreign policy. For example, the attempt to develop closer relations with Israel was shattered by the Israeli invasion of Lebanon in 1982. In Chad, French forces intervened to prevent Colonel Gaddafi's Libyan troops from taking over the country. An agreement was subsequently reached between Mitterrand and Gaddafi for a mutual withdrawal of forces. However, the French troops left only for Gaddafi to renege on the deal and for Libyan troops to remain in Chad. Not surprisingly, Mitterrand was criticized for having met Gaddafi in the first place (Crete 1984) and then for having naively trusted him to withdraw his forces. France suffered a further humiliation in July 1985 when it was discovered that the sinking of the Greenpeace ship, *Rainbow Warrior*, whilst it was docked in Auckland harbour had been carried out by agents of the French secret service. Although there was insufficient evidence to prove that Mitterrand had personally ordered the sinking, the Defence Minister, Charles Hernu, was clearly implicated and had to resign.

Partly because of the poor results of some of Mitterrand's early foreign policy initiatives, the President soon began to concentrate his efforts upon Europe. In 1981, there were fears that the new government would destabilize the good relations that Giscard had forged with France's EC partners. Prior to 1981, the socialists had been critical of Giscard's policies and particularly of the emphasis that he placed on the Paris-Bonn axis as the motor of European development (see page 137–8). It was also the case that the reflationary economic policy, which the socialists pursued in 1981, ran contrary to the economic orthodoxy which was in vogue in all other EC countries at that time. At first, therefore, it seemed as if good relations with France's EC partners came low down upon Mitterrand's list of priorities. However, by 1983, Europe had been placed at the top of the foreign policy agenda. The turning point was the decision in March 1983 to keep the franc in the EMS. Several of Mitterrand's closest advisers wanted the President to withdraw the franc from the EMS, so as to allow the currency to depreciate and protectionist tariff barriers to be erected, thus helping French exports and discouraging imports. After much hesitation, Mitterrand finally decided against this course of action believing that France's economic and diplomatic interests were best served within the EMS as a full partner in Europe.

This new-found Euro-enthusiasm was particularly in evidence from January to June 1984 during France's presidency of the EC's Council of Ministers. Mitterrand and his newly appointed Minister for European Affairs, Roland Dumas, spent much of their time during this period trying to resolve the long-standing problem of Britain's contributions to the EC's budget. An agreement on this issue was finally reached in time for the Fontainebleau summit in June 1984 and much of the credit for this agreement went to Mitterrand. The French presidency of the Council also paved the way for the entry of Spain and Portugal into the Community in January 1986. In addition, from 1983 to 1986, France was at the centre of some, if not all, of the EC's most important initiatives. Mitterrand personally championed projects such as ESPRIT (information technology), RACE (telecommunications) and Eureka (a joint EC-EFTA scheme for high technology collaboration). Mitterrand proposed that majority voting should replace unanimous decision-making for certain areas of EC policy-making. He also played a major part in the negotiations which surrounded the formulation of the Single European Act (SEA) in December 1985. The SEA was designed to remove all internal barriers between EC partners so as to create a genuine common market by January 1993. At the same time, Mitterrand balanced the economic development of the EC by calls for greater co-operation on social and environmental policy. More symbolically, in his television interviews, Mitterrand started to be flanked by both the French tricolour and the EC flag.

Contrary to some initial fears, Franco-German relations also thrived after 1981. This was due in the main to the coincidence of interests and, in particular, the common defence interests between the two countries that transcended the ideologies of individual presidents. However, it was also due in part to the particularly good personal relationship that Mitterrand enjoyed with Schmidt's successor as German Chancellor from 1982, the Christian Democrat, Helmut Kohl. Undoubtedly, the relationship between the two was helped by Mitterrand's speech to mark the twentieth anniversary of the Franco-German Treaty of Co-operation, which he delivered to the German parliament, the Bundestag, in January 1983. In his speech, Mitterrand supported the deployment of US Cruise and Pershing missiles on German soil as the most effective counter to the presence of Soviet SS-20 missiles in the East. Mitterrand's famous dictum, *'les missiles sont à l'Est, les pacifistes à l'Ouest'*, served to bolster Kohl's election campaign and the German Chancellor was duly grateful.

Such statements, however, were also music to the ears of the Americans. Initially, the newly elected Reagan administration was suspicious of the intentions of Mitterrand's government. Indeed, pressure was (unsuccessfully) placed on the President by the Americans to try and stop the appointment of communist ministers to the government in 1981. Similar pressure was also placed on the French not to sign a deal with

USSR for the supply of cheap Soviet gas. Once again, this pressure was unsuccessful and an agreement was reached in January 1982, just a month after the imposition of martial law in Poland. Despite these and other points of conflict, Franco-American relations under the Mitterrand presidency closely resembled those under the de Gaulle, Pompidou and Giscard presidencies previously. That is to say, there was neither overt Atlanticism, nor rampant anti-Americanism. France was half-in, half-out of the US camp. For example, Mitterrand supported NATO's deployment of US missiles in Europe, but was critical of American research on the Strategic Defence Initiative, the 'Star Wars' project.

There was a similarly ambivalent relationship towards the Soviet Union. Mitterrand's longstanding anti-communism meant that there was never any doubt after 1981 that France was anything other than allied with the West. For example, forty-seven Soviet agents were expelled from France in 1983. However, in a similar fashion to de Gaulle and Giscard, Mitterrand was willing at least to talk to the Soviets. Indeed, arguably, Mitterrand was one of the first Western leaders to recognize the reforming potential of Mikhail Gorbachev after his appointment as leader of the Soviet Communist Party in March 1985. Indeed, Gorbachev's first visit to Western Europe after his appointment was to Paris, in October 1985.

Although French foreign policy in the early 1980s bore a striking resemblance to that of the 1960s and 1970s, the potential for disruption increased after the 1986 legislative elections. The victory of the right at these elections and the appointment of the neo-Gaullist Jacques Chirac as Prime Minister meant that, for the first time in the Fifth Republic, there was a socialist President 'cohabiting' with a right-wing Prime Minister. In domestic affairs Chirac took charge of decision-making and Mitterrand was only a spectator. In foreign affairs, matters were slightly different. Partly because of the President's constitutional powers, Mitterrand was still able to preserve a certain amount of influence over foreign and defence policy. For example, it was the President who decided in November 1986 that submarines with a nuclear capacity should continue to be the mainstay of the French independent deterrent. However, Chirac certainly influenced the course of foreign policy-making to a greater extent than any of his prime-ministerial predecessors. For example, it was his decision to send back the French ambassador to South Africa after he had been recalled the previous year. Chirac worked more closely with the Spanish government, so as to extradite from France Basque gunmen wanted by the Spanish police. He also restored diplomatic links with Iran. In the main, however, these were changes at the margins. There was insufficient disagreement over foreign policy between Mitterrand and Chirac for the two to clash in this area (the same was not true for domestic policy). Indeed, the agreement between them was such that when, for example, France refused to allow American bombers to cross French air space on their way to bomb Colonel Ghadaffi in Tripoli in 1986, both Mitterrand and Chirac claimed the responsibility for having taken the decision.

The main disagreements between the two protagonists came in April and May 1988 in the two weeks before the second round of the presidential election. The election pitted Mitterrand against Chirac and, with his popularity ratings lagging behind those of his rival, Chirac embarked upon several diplomatic stunts in an attempt to reverse the decline in his electoral fortunes. He negotiated with the hostage takers in the Lebanon and secured (that is to say, bought) the release of the remaining French hostages there. He also released from exile, well before the prescribed date, Dominique Prieur, one of the secret service agents incarcerated after the sinking of the *Rainbow Warrior*. In addition, he ordered the storming of the hideout where a group of *indépendantistes canaques*, fighting for the independence of the French overseas territory of New Caledonia, had killed four *gendarmes*, and were holding twenty-six more hostage. Overall, two soldiers and nineteen *canaques* were killed in the operation and the relations between the indigenous population, the French settlers and representatives of the French state remained tense.

These spectacular decisions had little impact on the result of the presidential election. They put off as many people from voting for Chirac as they attracted to him. In the end, Mitterrand was comfortably re-elected. Following his re-election, he appointed Michel Rocard as Prime Minister and re-appointed Roland Dumas as Minister for Foreign Affairs (he had replaced Cheysson in December 1984). One of Rocard's first tasks was to try to end the bloodshed in New Caledonia and, in an historic meeting in June 1988, the *Accords de Matignon* were signed, whereby all sides agreed to end what amounted to a civil war. The President might have been excused for thinking, after the New Caledonian settlement, that his second term would pass off peacefully and relatively uneventfully. However, three things were to prevent any such complacency from setting in: the collapse of the communist regimes of eastern Europe; the acceleration of European integration; and the Gulf war.

Undoubtedly, the French government was as surprised as anyone else at the speed at which the communist governments in the former Iron Curtain countries collapsed. In fact, it might be said that the French government was more surprised than most as, on occasions, it appeared to have been left behind by the course of events in these countries. On 15 November 1989, six days after the fall of the Berlin Wall, Dumas stated to the *Assemblée nationale*, '*la réunification [de l'Allemagne] ne peut être un problème d'actualité*'. On 6 December, Mitterrand met Gorbachev in Kiev and both leaders agreed to warn Chancellor Kohl against any hasty moves towards the reunification of East and West Germany. Mitterrand seemed to confirm this attitude a few days later by going to East Berlin himself and meeting Hans Modrow, the new and short-lived East German communist leader. As subsequent events showed, however, Mitterrand's concern at the speed of re-unification was at odds with the policy of the West German government and with the wishes of the East German people. Mitterrand was forced to accept Kohl's timetable for re-unification and the relationship between the two leaders was temporarily soured.

In his reactions to the fall of the Berlin Wall and to the communist regimes in eastern Europe in general, Mitterrand showed his fear that the breakdown of the post-war division of the world into two opposed blocks would lead to the rise of national and ethnic conflicts. Even though Mitterrand had no nostalgia for the communist system, he felt it was better, as he said, to '*laisser le temps au temps*', than to precipitate a headlong rush to democracy without knowing what the consequences of such a policy might be. For example, in the Yugoslav crisis from mid-1991, Mitterrand at first held out for a continuation of the Yugoslav Federation, even though Slovenia and Croatia had already declared their independence. Similarly, Mitterrand's caution was seen again in August 1991 on the day after the coup in the USSR which ousted Gorbachev from power. On television, he called the generals involved 'the new leaders' of the Soviet Union, which seemed to legitimize their actions. Only a few days later, the coup collapsed and Boris Yeltsin was the hero of the hour. It was noticeable that, unlike Gorbachev, Yeltsin on his first trip to the West after the coup did not make Paris his first stop. However, in February 1992 a Franco-Russian Treaty was signed by Mitterrand and Yeltsin, marking an upturn in relations between the two leaders. No doubt this upturn was at least partly due to the fact that Yeltsin returned to Moscow having secured a 3.5 billion francs aid package from the French government.

In his 1988 election manifesto, *Lettre à tous les Français*, Mitterrand clearly signalled his commitment to European integration saying, '*La France est notre patrie, l'Europe est notre avenir*'. In his first post-election press conference on 18 May 1989, Mitterrand laid down five priorities for the EC: economic and monetary union, the social charter, cultural and broadcasting policy, the environment and '*l'Europe des citoyens*'. The period of French presidency of the European Council of Ministers, from July to December 1989, was largely spent dealing with these issues. However, it was the fall of the Berlin Wall which made the question of European integration an increasingly important issue. The worry expressed by both the French and others was that, with the East-West division no longer operative, Germany would look to Central Europe for both its markets and its allies. As such, it risked being detached from the EC and NATO. In order to counter this threat, it was felt to be imperative that EC integration be extended beyond just the removal of internal barriers to trade so as to include full monetary and political union. This deepening of the EC would have the consequence of stopping Germany's drift towards central Europe. In fact, once the timetable for German reunification was assured,

Mitterrand and German Chancellor Helmut Kohl jointly steamroller their way towards European monetary union. (From *Le Monde*, 30 April 1992.)

Chancellor Kohl was happy to calm the fears of his EC partners. On 19 April 1990, France and Germany issued a joint statement on political union in Europe. The relationship between Mitterrand and Kohl was back on track. On 14 October 1991, the two leaders wrote a joint letter to the acting President of the EC Council of Ministers in which they outlined their proposals for an integrated European defence force. At Maastricht in December 1991, a timetable was fixed for monetary union and the first steps towards political union were taken.

It would be wrong, however, to paint the French government and the French as being idealists dreaming of a federal Europe. Mitterrand has held up the process of European integration when he has considered it to be in France's interests to do so; for example, over the issue of reform of the CAP. In addition, he has been reluctant to give further law-making powers to the European parliament, as France's interests are best expressed through the present structure of the Council of Ministers. It is also the case that, while Mitterrand championed a deepening of the EC, he has been reluctant to accept a widening of it. Much to the annoyance of, amongst others, the Czech president, Vaclav Havel, Mitterrand has said that it would take '*des dizaines et des dizaines d'années*' for the former communist countries to be in a position to join the EC. Instead, on 31 December 1989, Mitterrand launched the vague and grand idea of a European Confederation, rather similar to de Gaulle's idea of a 'Europe of the nations.' To date, both initiatives remain unrealized. Nevertheless, Mitterrand has tried to accelerate the pace of European integration, notably forcing through an agreement on social policy at Maastricht, even though this meant isolating the British government. Mitterrand has undoubtedly been a good European, even if his actions have often been motivated by what he has seen as being in the interests of France, rather than by pure Euro-idealism.

The other great test of Mitterrand's statecraft was the Gulf war. In the eyes of most observers, Mitterrand came through this period with flying colours. His personal popularity remained high throughout the crisis. He gave eight televized press conferences from August 1990 until the end of the hostilities in February 1991 in which he carefully presented the government's arguments to the public. He also kept leading opposition personalities informed of the state of events. Partly as a result, and with the exception of the communists, the leader of the *Front national* and the socialist Defence Minister, Jean-Pierre Chevènement, there was all-party support for the decision to join the allied coalition against Iraq and for French forces to be used as part of the offensive to recapture Kuwait.

The decision for French forces to co-operate in an international military operation clearly marks out Mitterrand from his Gaullist, if not his Giscardian, presidential predecessors. Where would French independence be in an operation dominated by the US? In fact, a distinctive French voice was to be heard in the diplomatic initiatives which preceded the outbreak of hostilities in January 1991. Mitterrand's willingness to accept that there was a link between the Iraqi presence in Kuwait and the Israeli presence in the Palestinian Occupied Territories was anathema to the US. The presidential envoys which Mitterrand sent to Iraq and other Arab countries before the allied offensive in January 1991 were seen by the US as another example of France's 'freelance diplomacy'. Similarly, in a last minute attempt to avoid the outbreak of war, the French delegation to the United Nations wanted the Iraqis merely to signal their intention of withdrawing from Kuwait. Once again, this initiative did not endear the French to either the British or the Americans. In this sense, Mitterrand's exercise of foreign policy during the Gulf war is reminiscent of the general conduct of French foreign policy since 1958. As a medium-sized world power, France has the opportunity to make its voice heard in the defence of its interests. At the same time, however, it is not powerful enough to be able to dictate the course of events. It has to forge alliances and comply with policies which it sometimes finds unappealing. The principled pragmatism of the Gaullist past is echoed in the Mitterrand present.

Bibliography

Aldrich, R. and Connell, J., *France in World Politics*. London, Routledge, 1989. Nine chapters on various aspects of France's international relations – defence issues, European unity, Africa and the Third World, the DOM-TOM, *francophonie*, among others. An invaluable introduction.

Clark, A., 'François Mitterrand and the idea of Europe', in Nelson, B. (ed.), *The Idea of Europe: problems of national and transnational identity*, New York, Berg, 1992.

Duhamel, A., *De Gaulle-Mitterrand: la marque et la trace*. Paris, Flammarion, 1991. See Chapters 3 and 4 for a recent comparison between the foreign policies of De Gaulle and Mitterrand.

Favier, P. and Martin-Roland, M., *La Décennie Mitterrand*, vol. 1: 'Les ruptures'. Paris, Seuil 1990. Part 3 gives a highly readable overview of Mitterrand's foreign policy to 1986.

Frears, J. R., *France in the Giscard Presidency*. London, George

Allen & Unwin, 1981. Chapters 5 and 6 on foreign policy and defence under Giscard.

Giscard d'Estaing, V., *Démocratie française. Préface inédite*. London, Methuen, 1983. Chapter 12 reviews the principal areas of Giscard's foreign policy.

Godt, P. (ed.), *Policy-Making in France – from de Gaulle to Mitterrand*. London, Pinter, 1989. Section V contains chapters on France's relations (1958–1988) with the USSR, Europe, and the Third World.

Hollifield, J. and Ross, G., *Searching for the New France*. London, Routledge, 1991. Chapter 10 provides a good summary of foreign policy since 1958.

Mitterrand, F., *Ici et maintenant*. Paris, Livre de Poche, 1981. Chapters 6 and 7: a lively *tour d'horizon* of major international questions, conducted a few months before Mitterrand was first elected President.

—*Réflexions sur la politique extérieure de la France*. Paris, Fayard, 1986. The Introduction pp. 7–135 contains an extended account of French defence, European and Third World policies.

—'The Future of Europe', in *The World Today*, vol. 43, no. 3 (March 1987) pp. 40–2. A speech made in London in January 1987 which contains much of Mitterrand's policy views and vision of Europe.

Pickles, D., *The Government and Politics of France*, vol. 2 'Politics'. London, Methuen, 1973. Part 2 offers a full and stimulating account of foreign policy under de Gaulle and Pompidou. A list of related French and English titles is included, pp. 481–3.

—*Problems of Contemporary French Politics*. London, Methuen, 1982. Chapter 5: 'The decline of Gaullist foreign policy'; Chapters 6 and 7 discuss Giscardian European and defence problems.

Ross, G., Hoffmann, S. and Malzacher, S., *The Mitterrand Experiment: continuity and change in modern France*. Cambridge, Polity Press, 1987. Section V, 'France and the world under Mitterrand', contains essays on Mitterrand's foreign and defence policies, and on France's relations with the Third World.

6

Education
Roger Duclaud-Williams

Introduction

There is no one best way in which to organize a discussion of
the French education system; each approach to this subject
has its strengths and weaknesses.

This chapter adopts an approach which concentrates on
five problems which the education system must confront. We
might call this a problem-centred approach. The first advantage of such an approach is that it recognizes that policy-
makers behave as problem-solvers. The identification of
problems helps us to understand the reasoning processes and
solutions adopted by those who control education.

The second advantage is that it facilitates comparison.
Many of the problems which French education confronts are
also present elsewhere, and an emphasis on such problems
helps us to avoid the common misconception that everything
which occurs in France is peculiarly French.

Education and the economy

All education systems accept some responsibility for preparing young people for the world of work. If this world changes,
then so too must education if it is to continue to be effective.

The most dramatic of the relevant changes has certainly

been the emergence since the mid-1970s of a persistent problem of youth unemployment in France. Tables 9a and 9b illustrate the rise of youth unemployment and also clearly demonstrate how those who are not so well-qualified have suffered most. Unemployment of any kind was relatively unusual and often of short duration in the period between 1945 and 1973. The government response to this problem does not necessarily take an educational form. Employers may be provided with a financial incentive to take on young people and economic policies may be adopted whose object is to reduce unemployment, but there are also important educational repercussions of youth unemployment. The existence of this problem has certainly encouraged the governments in France to make increased efforts to encourage more young people to stay on at school, thereby reducing the unemployment figures and enhancing their own future prospects. French governments have also responded by creating, with the help of employers and trade unions, new forms of training and apprenticeship for young people who have left school but whose education ought to be continued.

A second major change concerns the international division of labour. A number of countries which were once predominantly agricultural have become important industrial producers and exporters in the last twenty or thirty years. This means that the older industrial economies of Europe must face up to new competition to which they were not previously exposed. The most successful European economies have met this challenge by moving away from the production of simple goods towards the production of goods and services which involve the use of more sophisticated technologies. Because these goods are more difficult and more costly to produce they can often be sold with greater profit. This in turn requires the creation of a more skilled labour force and this is where the education system may have to adapt in training young people in new skills and in raising the level of many traditional skills.

A third economic change which has important educational implications concerns the organization of work within the firm. The typical manufacturing company of the first half of the twentieth century had a small number of qualified and

Tables 9a and b
Chômage des jeunes

a Taux de chômage des jeunes débutants
par grands niveaux de diplômes (1973–83)

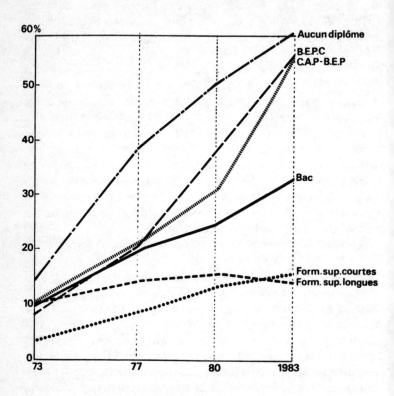

Source: Bilans Formation-Emploi INSEE, CEREQ, SIGES (SPRESE)

b Taux de chômage, en pourcentage des jeunes débutants*
en 1973, 1977, 1980, 1983
selon le niveau scolaire et le sexe (Apprentissages exclus)

	Hommes				Femmes				Ensemble			
	1973	1977	1980	1983	1973	1977	1980	1983	1973	1977	1980	1983
Sans diplômes	12	31	42	59	18	46	63	63	15	38	52	61
B.E.P.C.	5	22	29		16	20	43		11	21	37	56
C.A.P.-B.E.P.	6	17	21	49	10	26	42	62	8	21	32	55
Baccalauréat	9	15	19	32	10	22	28	35	10	20	25	33
Etudes supérieures courtes	3	7	12	17	4	9	13	11	4	8	13	16
Etudes supérieures longues	10	14	11		12	14	21		11	14	16	14
Ensemble	9	20	26	44	13	26	39	44	11	23	36	44

*Jeunes débutants: élèves ou étudiants sortant lors de l'année N qui se déclarent actifs occupés ou à la recherche d'un emploi en mars de l'année N + 1.

Source: Bilans Formation-Emploi INSEE, CEREQ, SIGES (devenu SPRESE) Données sociales édition 1984 (INSEE) p. 74

Both tables taken from: C. Dubar et al., *L'Autre Jeunesse: des jeunes sans diplômes dans un dispositif de socialisation*, Presses universitaires de Lille, 1987.

responsible individuals at its head and a very much larger number of less skilled and responsible operatives performing unskilled work at its base. Many industries and companies are still organized very much in this way but there is a growing sector of companies whose products and philosophy are moving in a quite new direction. These companies have found it useful to extend the responsibilities and skills of many employees who were previously confined to narrowly defined and relatively unskilled tasks. As this trend develops, the general level of education and skill within the workforce must be increased.

Finally, modern education systems must prepare young

people for a labour market in which they will change jobs a number of times during their career. Products become outdated, industries decline and new forms of employment replace older forms. In these circumstances they must be able to learn new skills in adult life and this is only possible when earlier education has been carried forward to a sufficiently high level. These are some of the economic factors which are particularly important for education and training.

The most important recent initiative in the area of training is contained in the law of 24 February 1984. This law was based on an agreement negotiated the previous year between employer organizations and the trade unions. The law provides for three levels of traineeship. The young people concerned spend some time working on the employers' premises and some time in a local school or training centre. The law and the agreement specify the number of hours of training which must be provided and the pay which young people will receive. The higher levels of traineeship lead on to recognized qualifications. It is also possible to progress from the shorter, less demanding traineeships to the longer and more difficult training courses.

The details of these arrangements are constantly changing. The 1983 agreement and the 1984 law accord official recognition to the role of the firm as an agent of education. The education system, as officially defined, is no longer therefore confined to schools and universities, but extends into the economy in a quite new way. One of the consequences of this extension is that organizations which previously were not very involved in providing education, are now becoming more so. Trade unions and employers' organizations are often critical of the over-theoretical and over-academic education which is provided in schools, and they are therefore keen to protect and expand this new area. One of the strongest arguments which they can use in this connection is that many of the young people who are taken on to the new traineeships (*stages*) have left school with either no or very few qualifications. Many of these young people left because they felt school had nothing more to offer, and yet they are willing to work and study in a new setting in which training and future employment are closely linked. Any consideration of the relationship between education and the economy in France must carefully assess technical education at secondary level and the way in which this education is developing.

The secondary technical schools, now called *lycées profession-nels*, have not been created recently in order to deal with new economic challenges. They have their origins in the inter-war period but have expanded rapidly since the Liberation. Most young people go to a *lycée professionnel* having completed four years of secondary education in a *collège*. Aged fifteen or sixteen, they spend usually two or possibly three years in secondary technical education. They work towards qualifica-tions of two kinds: the more specialized and less academic qualification is the *certificat d'aptitude professionnelle*; the slightly less specialized, and more theoretical, qualification is called the *brevet d'études professionnelles* (BEP).

Although great efforts have been made to improve the atmos-phere and working conditions in these schools in recent years, they nevertheless continue to suffer from a great number of handicaps. A large number of the pupils in the *lycées professionnels* have joined because they were unable to gain admission to the general *lycées*. This means that pupils and teachers alike are conscious that, for many of them, the *lycée professionnel* is second best. A further difficulty is that many young people cannot get into the type of training in the *lycées professionnels* which they would prefer. Some forms of training are heavily over-subscribed and pupils therefore have to be turned away.

A number of changes are taking place in the *lycées profession-nels* with a view to dealing with some of these problems. Every effort is being made to inform new arrivals as fully as possible about employment prospects, so that as many young people as possible will prepare for qualifications which give them the maximum chance of employment once they leave school. The course content is in a constant process of revision and here the aim has been to reduce the number of CAPs, which are thought to be rather too narrow, and to increase the number and attractiveness of the BEPs which prepare pupils better for the more fluid labour market referred to above. Periods of work experience related to the kind of courses that young people are studying have also been organized for almost all pupils in the *lycées professionnels* since 1979. But the most important recent reform which, it is hoped, will make these schools more attractive, has been the creation of a new type of *baccalauréat* (*baccalauréat professionnel*) which will offer those leaving the *lycées professionnels* the possibility of continuing their studies at a higher technical school or a university. Although all of these reforms are necessary and useful, a note of caution may be sounded. There is no reason why standards and achievements in the *lycées professionnels* should not be raised considerably, and more and more young people may well be encouraged to stay on the extra year required to obtain the *baccalauréat professionnel*. But most of these pupils are conscious of the fact that they have already been eliminated from the mainstream of the education system. Their performance has been judged not promising enough to allow them to go on to the general *lycées* to prepare one of the more familiar and longer established general *baccalauréats*. In these conditions it is difficult to create the kind of enthusiasm and commitment necessary for success.

In the 1950s the study of classical languages was, as it had been for more than a century, the subject which enjoyed the highest regard and prestige. Since the 1960s this has no longer been the case. What now attracts the most able pupils and enjoys the highest prestige is undoubtedly mathematics. Every pupil who has the necessary mathematical ability enters the 'C' stream in his or her penultimate year. One of the principal reasons for this is that success in the competitive examinations for entry into the higher business and engineering schools (*grandes écoles*) depends to a very great degree on mathematical ability. Pupils who have not followed the 'C' stream, and have therefore studied much less mathematics, are at a substantial disadvantage. Of course, anyone successfully passing the *baccalauréat* is entitled to a university place in France, but the schools of engineering and business studies offer their graduates career possibilities which are considerably more attractive than those which university graduates are likely to obtain. Hence the attraction of mathematics and the 'C' stream.

We have seen that higher education in France is of two quite different varieties: firstly there are vocationally oriented engineering and business schools which offer their graduates attractive career prospects and, secondly, the universities with many more students, and much less attractive conditions for study. They also experience high drop-out and failure rates, and produce graduates whose career opportunities do not compare with those from the *grandes écoles*. This two-tier system of higher education provides a very strong incentive for secondary school pupils to study those subjects which are economically most useful. At this level then, there seems no need for governments to intervene in order to encourage the study of those subjects which they regard as most important for the expansion of the national economy. What recent governments have succeeded in doing, and will continue to do for the forseeable future, is to increase the number of places available to these *grandes écoles* so as to provide the country with a much increased supply of administrators and engineers.

Some critics of recent government policy on the left and the right disapprove of attempts to link education more closely to the economy. Left-wing critics argue that there is little point in improving technical education if many of those who leave school have no jobs to go to. They feel that many of the young people taken on as apprentices or trainees are poorly paid, exploited and often provided with inferior training facilities. They argue also that much that is not economically useful in education is nevertheless extremely valuable, and that education and educational institutions ought to enjoy some real independence so that they may resist the demands of employers and governments who are too narrowly interested in economic success. In other words, these critics argue that there is more to life than high pay and promotion, and that it is the business of the school especially to make young people aware of these other values. Of course, it is conceded, schools should prepare young people for the world of work, but they should also prepare them for their role as citizens in a democracy, for leisure and for their role as family members.

Some of this stress on human values is also present in right-wing criticisms. Some on the traditional right are particularly scandalized by the neglect of subjects like philosophy, ancient languages and history, which have no obvious or immediate

Confrontation between students and police, Paris, May 1968.

economic utility. They also criticize what they see as a lowering of standards and the undesirable practice of resorting to continuous assessment. It is important to be aware of these dissenting voices but we should remember that, for the time being at least, there is very widespread agreement in support of those educational reforms which aim to produce a closer relationship between the worlds of education and work. Young people are anxious to avoid unemployment and so are their parents. Employers are keen to recruit well-educated and highly motivated young people. Opposition from teachers to more career-oriented schooling was strongly and repeatedly voiced in the 1960s and 1970s but are seldom heard today. It seems probable that the trends towards a closer relationship between education and work will continue for the foreseeable future.

Overcentralization and decentralization

The rulers of France in the nineteenth and the first half of the twentieth century maintained strict central control over most aspects of education. This was largely because they wished to impose and encourage a sense of belonging to one nation, and because the education system was an effective tool with which to discourage the use of regional languages and create the greatest possible degree of linguistic unity. The sense of national unity is now strongly developed in all French regions, with the exception of Corsica, and a once crucial foundation of centralized administration has therefore been removed. The problem of linguistic diversity has also disappeared.

But there are also positive arguments in favour of greater decentralization for which there is strong support in France. Many French observers of foreign education systems, especially those familiar with English and American schools, have been struck by the contrast. They have criticized French schools for concentrating too narrowly on the academic function and undervaluing extra-curricular activities and the pastoral role of the school. Those who argue in this way would like to turn French schools from academic institutions into self-governing communities. As matters stand, however, one cannot expect teachers who have been posted to schools which are not of their own choosing to show any great loyalty or attachment to them. If, for example, schools could play some part in the appointment of their own teachers, then a team spirit of co-operation might be more easily developed.

This emphasis on schools as self-governing communities, rather than impersonal institutions controlled from afar, is strongly supported by many on the left and in the centre of political life. A rather different perspective, but one which is equally supportive of decentralization, appeals more to those on the right. In this line of argument the analogy between the school as a provider of education and the firm as a provider of goods and services plays an important part. The argument is that greater efficiency and responsiveness to local demand would be encouraged if head teachers and their staff enjoyed more independence in the management of their schools. The same kind of free market logic underlies the argument that, if parents had more choice as to the schools attended by their children, schools might be encouraged to compete with one another and in the process pay more attention to parents' and even perhaps pupils' demands.

A final element in the case for decentralization relates to the role of local authorities. Between 1981 and 1986 an attempt was made to extend the responsibilities and independence of local authorities by transferring to them functions previously exercised by government departments in Paris. Many local politicians would like to see this process applied in education just as it has been already in areas such as town planning and the social services.

When we compare universities with schools we are immediately struck by the greater scale and complexity of the former. Both of these characteristics can be cited as strong arguments for greater decentralization and university autonomy. Students have also often demanded greater self-government and autonomy for universities. However, student opinion and student organizations are not really the strong supporters of university autonomy that they appear to be.

Since 1986, local authorities have become responsible for

the building of new schools and the maintenance and repair of existing ones. The *lycées* are the responsibility of regional authorities; *collèges* are the responsibility of the departments and primary schools are left to the communes. Recent legislation has also provided for local authority representation on the governing bodies (*conseils d'administration*) of schools, and authorities are permitted and encouraged to organize after-school and out-of-school activities of an educational character. Finally, in the outline law (*loi d'orientation*) enacted in July of 1989, provision is made for secondary schools of all types to prepare what is described as a *projet d'établissement*, or school plan. Each school must prepare its own and it is intended that parents, pupils and local politicians should play some part in this process alongside teachers and headteachers. The same law provides for the creation in all *lycées* of a pupil council which will be elected by the pupils, will meet three times a year and will be consulted on school rules and regulations.

Many commentators on these developments have come to the conclusion that they do not yet amount to very much. Teachers are still posted to schools rather than recruited by them. The content of the national curriculum and the internal organization of schools are still centrally determined. Only a cautious move has been made towards allowing parents more choice of schools for their children. There is a widespread feeling that the school plans which have been prepared are theoretical documents which are unlikely to have much impact on practice because of the inability of schools to take control of their own future. How can the widespread commitment to decentralization, but the failure to do very much in this direction, be explained?

Part of the explanation is that it is easy to praise decentralization in general terms, but more difficult to accept that schools and universities should be allowed to do things which are controversial and to which powerful groups and interests may object. But there are more specific obstacles to the progress of decentralization. Teacher organizations, either based on particular subjects, or in the form of unions, are generally either lukewarm supporters of decentralization or outright opponents. It is not too difficult to see why this is so, trade unions are concerned to protect their members from the exercise of arbitrary power by superiors. Under present arrangements, teachers' appointments and promotions are governed by rules which protect teachers' rights. If decentralization were to become a reality it would almost certainly mean that headteachers, or perhaps even local politicians, would come to possess new powers which they might exercise in unpredictable ways to the detriment of teachers' interests.

A further cause for doubt about decentralization is the fear that it might lead to greater inequalities between institutions and regions. Those who fear this see existing arrangements as providing an effective guarantee that the same quality of education is available to all pupils wherever they live and regardless of the school they attend. This may be an illusion but there is still a widespread sentiment that whatever unintended inequalities exist within the present school system, these might become more acute if schools were made more self-governing.

Through much of the debate about decentralization in education runs a set of mixed and contradictory feelings about the role of the state. Some see the state as the heavy hand of distant bureaucracy stifling local initiative and presenting obstacles to genuine pupil and parent involvement. This view is hostile to the state and seeks to promote decentralization. A second group sees the state as the impartial external arbiter whose power prevents the outbreak of local conflicts and ensures fair play and respect for the rules. This position is much more sympathetic to existing arrangements and sees more danger than advantage in the promotion of decentralization. Finally, a particularly influential group cannot quite decide whether to sympathize with the anti-state or the pro-state faction. Many who find themselves in this camp have confused and contradictory ideas about decentralization, often demonstrating support in principle but opposition in practice. With public and expert opinion divided in this way it is not surprising that reform in this area has so far proceeded with much caution and hesitation.

The equality debate

This debate focuses on the early years of secondary school. In France this means the *collège* which is attended by most children between the ages of eleven and fifteen. Since the 1950s, the belief has been that there is no justification or need for different kinds of school for children of primary school age. At the other end of the scale, arrangements for the teaching of the over-fifteens are highly differentiated, and this differentiation between general, technical and vocational education, is broadly supported. The difficulty and the controversy arise over exactly at what point and in what form differentiated education ought to begin.

In the early 1960s French children between the ages of eleven and fifteen attended one of three kinds of school. The most academically able children were admitted to the *lycée*. These children were expected to stay in the *lycée* until the age of eighteen when they would take the *baccalauréat* and continue their studies at the university. The least academically able children remained in special classes provided for the older children in primary schools. They were expected to leave without qualifications at the earliest possible date. Between these two groups of pupils existed a third group who were received by the newly created *collège d'enseignement général*, or CEG. The CEGs had been created in order to offer a form of secondary education to those families who were not content for their children to simply stay on at primary school after eleven.

French governments in the 1960s agreed with many of the criticisms which were made of these arrangements. They felt that much talent was going to waste in the extension classes of the primary schools and in the CEGs. There was considerable political pressure for the expansion of secondary education and the prosperity of the 1950s and 1960s made it possible to satisfy this demand. Associated with the expansion of secondary provision was the reform of its structure. In 1963 the Minister of Education, Christian Fouchet, established the *collège d'enseignement secondaire* or CES. The CES was what used to be described in England as a 'multi-lateral school', catering for all abilities within a single institution but in a differentiated manner. In fact, Fouchet decided that he would recreate within the CES the three-fold division of staff, curriculum and ability level which had previously existed within separate institutions.

Between 1963 and 1977 this system was gradually established, thereby providing within a single institution what had previously been provided in three. Critics of the CES continued to argue during this period that it was not enough to bring all pupils together under one roof, and that a single curriculum for all could be taught without disadvantage to the more able pupils. From the beginning of the school year in 1977 and starting with the first year of secondary education, the jump was made from segregated provision to a common syllabus and mixed ability teaching in all the CESs now relabelled *collèges*.

In English terminology, 1977 marked the triumph of the comprehensive school. It is true that some pupils continued to leave the *collège* for technical education at thirteen and that there was limited separate provision in some *collèges* for the least able pupils, but by and large the comprehensive ideal was adopted. For most pupils selection would now occur only at fifteen at which point some would go on to the *lycée* to prepare for the *baccalauréat* and others would go into technical education.

Since 1977 there has been no major reorganization of the structure of French secondary education but there has been some more piecemeal evolution. Many teachers complained of the difficulties which they encountered in teaching the new mixed ability classes. The number of secondary pupils who were required to repeat a year because of unsatisfactory academic performance increased. There were also complaints that some parents and schools connived at the creation of selective streams which were contrary to the spirit of the 1977 reform. These complaints produced a state of affairs in which most people were convinced that it was impossible and undesirable to return to the segregated arrangements which had existed before 1977 but that, on the other hand, existing mixed ability arrangements needed modifying in some way.

When a socialist President and government were elected in 1981 they were faced with this difficult problem. The approach they adopted is spelt out in the Legrande report. The Legrande report and the socialist government were very sympathetic to the comprehensive principle but the report argued that mixed ability teaching was not working for certain fundamental subjects. Legrande therefore recommended that separate ability groups could be constituted, if schools so desired, for mathematics, science and French but reunited for the rest of the timetable. Legrande was also successful in persuading the Minister, Alain Savary, that there should be some shift of emphasis in the *collège* away from traditional academic subjects so as to allow more time and attention for the moral, aesthetic and sporting sides of the curriculum. One of the justifications for this shift was that it might provide more encouragement for less academic pupils and in this way provide them with an incentive to work harder. Legrande also hoped that each *collège* would be allowed some flexibility as to the precise form of the compromise it adopted as between mixed ability and differentiated forms of education. In practice, this autonomy has not always been realized but there is at least now some variation in organization and teaching style between French *collèges*.

A pessimistic view of such developments as these is possible. The work of statisticians and sociologists of education makes it quite clear that there is still a close correlation between social origins and academic success. Table 10 gives some indication of the scale of these inequalities as they affect pupils in the first year of primary schooling. The sons and daughters of workers are still heavily under-represented in the *lycées* and universities. More seriously, the academically able child who comes from a working-class family is less likely to fulfil his or her full potential than a child of similar ability from a professional or business background. Governments have found it easier to equalize opportunities for entry into education and to standardize the education system than to secure equality of results.

But a more optimistic interpretation of these events is also possible. Achievements might be assessed not so much in terms of equality and inequality as in terms of the numbers of pupils who achieve a particular level of qualification. Those with this point of view feel that genuine progress has been

Table 10
Taux de redoublement du cours préparatoire en 1979–1980 des enfants entrés à six ans, selon l'origine socio-professionnelle (enseignement public)

Salariés agricole	29.9
Ouvriers sans qualification	23.9
Non actifs, non déclarés	22.9
Ouvriers spécialisés	22.5
Personnels de service	21.4
Ouvriers qualifiés	14.9
Agriculteurs, exploitants	11.1
Employés	10.7
Artisans, petits commerçants	9.8
Autres catégories	5.7
Cadres moyens	4.4
Industriels, gros commerçants	3.7
Cadres supérieurs, professions libérales	2.4
Ensemble	13.8

Source: J.-M. Favret, *Consultation-réflexion sur l'école,* ministère de l'Education nationale, avril 1984, p. 144.

Taken from: J. Lesourne, *Education et Société. Les Défis de l'An 2000*, 1988 (Editions La Découverte et Journal), p. 211.

made because, whereas in 1960 10 per cent of each age group obtained the *baccalauréat,* today the figure has reached 40 per cent. This is a benefit which has been enjoyed by young people from all social classes even if some groups have been able to exploit the new opportunities more successfully than others. From this more optimistic perspective one may take satisfaction in the rise in the general level of education, and worry less about inequalities in academic achievement between social classes. It is difficult to imagine a society in which family advantages or disadvantages do not have some impact on the educational and career prospects of young people. As long as family characteristics (whether biological or cultural or influenced by wealth) continue to have such an impact on children, it cannot be expected that equal opportunities in schooling will produce equal results. One may also argue, in defence of existing French arrangements, that it is more important to do all that is practicable to eliminate inequalities entirely: that is, it may be politically more important to make every effort to eliminate inequalities than to ensure success in all areas. Any French observer of English education would also remark that the most prestigious French *lycées* are state schools, not fee-paying, and that at secondary level there is no French parallel to the English public school phenomenon with its associated social and educational inequalities.

The state and private sectors

An examination of this subject is important because it helps us to understand to what extent a genuine partnership between state and private interests has been created in the provision of education. In other words, it helps us to determine whether power is concentrated within the state or dispersed. The greater the role of the private sector, the more likely it is that some variety, experiment, or even choice may be introduced into the education system. This is particularly the case in France because of the uniformity of the state sector.

Throughout the nineteenth and early twentieth centuries the most important challenge to the state's dominant position in education came from the Catholic Church, and conflict and rivalry were often acute and sometimes violent. We must remember that throughout the nineteenth century, and during the early years of the twentieth century, the Catholic Church in France was a declared enemy of parliamentary democracy. Those anti-clericals who attacked the educational role of the Catholic Church did so in the name of democracy and republicanism, making the conflict more political than educational.

In the 1980s and 1990s these great questions of political principle no longer divide French Catholics from non-Catholics, but this does not mean that Church and state have been able to establish an easy relationship in the sphere of education. During his election campaign in 1981, François Mitterrand promised to create a single education system, which would include state and Catholic schools but which would be created by negotiation with the representatives of the Catholic Church. Since the Church no longer represented a threat to the democratic constitutional order, we may well ask why the new President and his allies in the socialist, communist and radical parties, were intent on tightening the links between the state non-denominational and the private religious parts of the education system.

Those who worked within and sympathized with the state education system harboured a number of grievances against their competitors in the Catholic sector. They felt that the latter occupied a privileged financial position because they could freely attract new pupils, and then effectively oblige the state to finance expansion from public funds. Schools in the state sector could not do this. They had to obtain permission for any expansion in advance. There were also complaints because whereas parents could choose freely between the state and religious schools, they were not able to choose between different state schools. There were also objections, particularly from the teachers' trade unions. Teachers employed in the Catholic sector, for example, did not in practice enjoy the same freedom and the same degree of professional recognition as those within the state sector. Headteachers in Catholic schools were occasionally open to criticism for interfering in the private lives of those whom they employed as teachers. We must remember that these establishments were not self-supporting but received state support approximately proportional to the numbers of pupils for whom they were responsible. Many on the left felt that it was only right and proper that in return for this substantial public financial support, the Catholic schools should be bound by the same rules as the schools in the state sector.

These grievances may not seem of overwhelming importance, especially when one remembers that negotiations and legislation on a question of this kind were very likely to prove politically controversial and possibly damaging to a left-wing government. An explanation of the risks which a left-wing government was willing to incur in this area must take account of some less tangible considerations. Although the great issues of freedom of conscience and the legitimacy of parliamentary institutions were no longer at stake, many on the left were still emotionally affected by the memory of these conflicting principles. Tradition had outlived the reality to which it related, but was still an important influence on the behaviour of those involved. A less emotional and more honourable argument in favour of legislation to create a single system by agreement with the Catholic Church, which appealed to some on the left and on the right, was that France had long been divided by the secular/Church question and, if this difficulty could be settled amicably, it could have advantages for the nation in terms of co-operation between state and private sectors. This, it would seem, was the argument which principally appealed to Alain Savary, François Mitterrand's first Minister of Education and the man entrusted with implementing the President's electoral undertaking.

The one question which was never answered in the 1981 election campaign was, what would happen if it proved impossible to reach an agreement with the Church about the closer relationship desired between the two sectors. Would the government press on regardless and use its majority to impose legislation in the name of the majority, or would it give way to Catholic objections, thereby effectively conceding that a minority was entitled to exercise a veto over government policy of which it strongly disapproved? The events of 1984 demonstrated that it was the second option which Mitterrand preferred. When legislation to which the Church took strong exception was in the process of being discussed in parliament, there were demonstrations in Paris culminating in late June with more than a million demonstrators present, and so the President concluded that it was too electorally risky to continue.

Although this was a major political set-back for the socialist government we should not be too quick to conclude that it was quite such a major triumph for the Catholic Church. Polls designed to test the attitudes of parents who sent their children to Catholic schools make it quite clear that their choice is not made for purely religious reasons. They more often take the view that the Catholic school is simply a better school: it is the educational qualities of the school rather than its religious character which attract them.

In interpreting the events of 1984 and the government's decision not to proceed with legislation, we must also ask ourselves exactly how Catholic were the Catholic schools whose character the Church had fought to protect. The major difficulty which the Church faces in this area is one of recruitment. Before 1945, Catholic schools generally had no difficulty in finding the teachers they required. It was assumed that everyone who taught in a Catholic school was a practising Catholic and that the school would therefore have a markedly Catholic character. Since the War it has become more and more difficult to find appropriately qualified Catholic teachers, and as a result many of those who teach in the French Catholic schools of the 1990s are indistinguishable in terms of attitude and belief from those teaching in the state sector. The progressive de-Christianization of post-war France has made it impossible to fully maintain the Catholic character of nominally Catholic institutions. In interpreting the Catholic 'victory' of 1984 we should not forget the very limited degree of educational independence which these schools enjoy. They must apply the national curriculum in exactly the same way as schools within the state sector. We might well ask ourselves how far there was any genuine independence to defend. In fact, under the terms of the Debray law of 1959, in order to obtain the public financial support which was necessary for survival, the Catholic Church had already given up most of the real independence it had once enjoyed – and to a right-wing government not a left-wing one. There was a large measure of hypocrisy in the left's case against the Catholic schools just as there was a similar degree of empty rhetoric in the Catholic defence.

One of the most important areas of recent expansion in private education concerns adults as well as young people. Under the law of 16 July 1971, all companies in France employing more than ten people must devote 1.1 per cent of their wage budget to education and training. Many of the smaller employers, rather than attempt to provide training themselves, pay this levy to private organizations of various sorts who then offer courses to the private sector on a profit-making or cost-covering basis. As mentioned above, new forms of traineeship are being provided by the larger companies under the law of 24 February 1984. Nor should we forget that many smaller businesses, especially retailers, offer apprenticeship to young people and are required to allow apprentices time off for study at college. Finally, although the most prestigious *grandes écoles* are state establishments, there is an increasing number of private institutions often administered and partially financed by the Chambers of Commerce, who provide higher education for which parents are willing to pay substantially. These private institutions of higher education often enjoy a much more genuine independence than the more notorious and politically controversial primary and secondary schools within the Catholic sector.

The question of how state education ought to respond to forms of religious practice which are relatively new in France was raised in the autumn of 1989 when three young Moslem girls were turned away from their *collège* in Creil because they wished to wear the veil in class. The controversial and heated debates to which this incident gave rise can best be understood by contrasting the views of two opposed camps. We shall describe these as integrationist and pluralist. The solution that was finally adopted was a compromise between the two extremes.

The integrationist position is most strongly defended by the teachers' unions, the right-wing opposition to the present socialist government, and a large number of members of left-wing parties. The integrationist position is more popular in France than the pluralist. The integrationists supported the exclusion of the Tunisian and Morroccan girls. They felt that a strict defence of the non-denominational principle was necessary in state schools. They argued that education would be obstructed if religious controversy, associated with the wearing of particular forms of dress, was allowed to enter the school. They also insisted that Moslems had no right to request exemption from aspects of the curriculum to which they took objection. Among the integrationists many on the left adopted the feminist position that the girls in question were almost certainly being compelled to wear a veil and that therefore their exclusion from class could be justified as assisting their emancipation from improper parental influence.

The weaker, pluralist camp was represented by the Minister of Education at the time, Lionel Jospin, some of the organizations representing the French Moslem population (although Moslems were sharply divided over this question), and representatives of other religious minorities in France, in particular Jews and Protestants. The strongest pluralist argument, and an argument often repeated by the Minister, was that exclusion would probably deprive these young women of the education which was necessary to their future. The pluralists felt that the dangers of religious division, if particular forms of dress were accepted, were greatly exaggerated by the intregationists. They felt that French society was sufficiently mature to recognize '*le droit à la différence*'.

In practical terms the integrationists had their way because the young women in question were eventually persuaded to discard their veils and were subsequently re-admitted to school. However, with respect to the new rules for dealing with similar situations in future, something closer to a compromise has been reached. The *Conseil d'état*, the supreme French administrative tribunal, has ruled that the law does not permit pupils to wear ostentatious signs of political or religious belief; but the court declined to specify what 'ostentatious' means. It is clear, for example, that some distinctive forms of dress are not necessarily objectionable under this ruling. A discreet badge or other minor indication of political or religious preference might not be a proper basis for excluding a pupil from school. The question then arises of how to distinguish between 'ostentatious' and 'discreet' dress or decoration. Here the court said that it was the responsibility of the governing body of each school to lay down general rules and make particular decisions. This seems to leave the field wide open for a variety of interpretations. In practice this is probably a solution which leans more towards the integrationist than the pluralist position because experience suggests that, largely as a result of teachers' influence on school governing bodies, almost any sign of religious or political belief will be locally designated 'ostentatious' and can therefore serve as a proper basis for exclusion. Nevertheless, if opinion should evolve in a more tolerant and pluralistic direction, it is possible to imagine that local decisions at the school level will relax the application of the court's ruling so as to allow the display of religious and political beliefs in school.

Neither side can claim an outright victory in this conflict although, on balance, those who feel that the obligation rests on religious minorities to accept a degree of conformity in the interests of social and national unity certainly seem to have gained the upper hand. Commentators on the position of minorities in French society often observed in the 1970s and 1980s a trend to what they regarded as a more pluralistic and tolerant approach. They argued that, whereas pre-war and nineteenth-century French society had insisted on a high degree of linguistic and religious conformity, this was proving less and less necessary. The controversy of 1989 over the wearing of the veil seems at least to have set back this trend. Many politicians are sensitive to the hostility which a vociferous minority of French voters exhibits towards Moslems, Arabs and foreigners in general. The steady support by 10 per cent of the electorate for the extreme right-wing and anti-immigrant National Front is a constant reminder to politicians of the dangers they might run with the electorate if they are perceived to be too sympathetic to immigrants and their children.

Protest in schools and universities

Student and pupil protest has been a recurrent feature of the educational scene in France since at least 1968. The student protests of 1968, with widespread support from the trade union movement, came near to overthrowing the government and even perhaps the whole regime. The student unrest of November and December 1986 damaged the prestige and credibility of the newly elected right-wing government led by Jacques Chirac and caused reform legislation relating to the universities to be abandoned. Most recently we have seen a movement of protest led by younger pupils in the *lycées* in the autumn of 1990 which led to a commitment by the Education

The *lycéens* protest, 1990.

Minister and government to spend the equivalent of £400 million on improving the facilities in *lycées*.

In attempting to understand why protest occurs in French schools and universities it is important to take account of two rather different contributory traditions. The first is a tradition of political protest on questions of principle. The second is a tradition of protest designed to press claims (often of a material kind) on behalf of particular groups. The first type of protest tends to be associated with radical critiques of contemporary society coming either from the left or the right, whilst the second is simply an instrument used in the defence of particular interests. Frequently these two traditional forms of protest combine in complicated ways. In 1968 both forms of protest were present, but the political and revolutionary demands were very much to the fore. In 1986, on the other hand, radical critiques of contemporary society were almost entirely absent and the student protest movement concentrated very narrowly on opposing prospective legislation which was thought likely to be inimical to student interests.

The 1990 pupil protests were more difficult to classify. On the one hand these pupils were clearly not interested in revolutionary objectives, but on the other they did not seem to have any specific demands which they wished to press.

In trying to understand the protest phenomenon, we should also take account of the important social changes of attitude and behaviour which are evident in the post-war history of the French family. Parental control is clearly now exercised with much greater restraint. Young people enjoy a degree of independence to which they did not feel entitled forty or fifty years ago. The tendency of young people to stay on much longer at school, and in higher education, also means that many young people who in the past would have been at work, and therefore subject to employer and market disciplines, now enjoy the free atmosphere of secondary or higher education.

Overcrowding and consequent deteriorating conditions for study have also contributed to arousing protest. In the five years from 1983 to 1988 the number of *lycée* classes with more than thirty-five pupils rose from 15.3 per cent to 38.8 per cent in the public sector and from 5.6 per cent to 14.4 per cent in the non-secular sector. Institutions at the secondary and higher level are often rather impersonal, if only because the pressure of numbers requires teachers to define their responsibilities rather narrowly.

Yet student protest is not a uniquely French phenomenon. Student protest (less often pupil protest), is a quite common feature of educational life in many advanced industrial countries, and we should therefore not expend too much effort in trying to explain why this phenomenon is present in France. What we need to ask ourselves additionally is why it is absent in come countries such as the United Kingdom.

In examining the official response to protest we need to distinguish between the short term and the long term. The official short-term response has usually been to attempt to negotiate with student leaders. Meetings and negotiations certainly occurred in 1986 and 1990 which led to legislative and financial concessions by the government. In the longer term, the government is promoting a number of measures to make student life, and life in the *lycées*, more attractive, comfortable and purposeful. We have already mentioned the new advisory councils which are to be established in each *lycée*. Students already elect their representative to university governing councils. Money has also recently been made available to pay teachers on an hourly basis, for out-of-school activities. It is also hoped that the anxiety and uncertainty of student life can be reduced in a number of ways. If the quality of advice and information which students receive, especially when first arriving in the university, can be improved, then perhaps students will be able to make wiser choices and avoid preparing for examinations which they have little chance of passing. It may also be possible to persuade more students to follow vocational courses which offer more secure employment prospects. The morale of students on courses of this type is usually higher than that of young people pursuing studies of a purely academic character. There are few who believe that these measures, though undoubtedly desirable, can ever turn volatile students into compliant and obedient young people. There seems every possibility that, from time to time, protest movements will re-emerge, especially where large numbers of students are crowded together and obliged to work under difficult conditions.

Conclusion

There is a great deal which cannot be discussed in a chapter of this length. We have said nothing about the moves to create a more united teaching profession by doing away with the existing distinction between *instituteurs* and *professeurs* through a common training programme. Nor have we referred to the attempts to reduce working hours in the *lycées* by removing irrelevant material from syllabuses. Radical suggestions are also under consideration for reorganizing the school year and the school week, involving perhaps the abolition of Saturday school which is at present normal in both the primary and secondary sectors. Nor have we said anything about the controversies which have affected the teaching of particular subjects: spelling and grammar with respect to the teaching of French, chronological versus thematic approaches to the teaching of history, traditional versus modern mathematics, and many others.

But one theme does emerge from the above discussion, namely the shift away from a remote and rather authoritarian state towards a more extensive but more responsive one. We can find evidence for this trend in the development of the new forms of privately provided education and training. The same is true of the so far rather tentative moves towards greater decentralization. The willingness of the administration to permit parental choice in a rather larger number of localities also implies a move in the direction of greater responsiveness. Only with regard to the acceptance of cultural and religious diversity does this movement seem to be making limited progress or none at all.

But although there is undeniably a trend of development in this direction it does not go uncontested. There is still a strong temptation for politicians and religious leaders to use schools as instruments of control rather than organizations designed to serve. Teaches are often sceptical about the value of innovation in education and doubtful about the new forms of decentralization and privatization. It is natural that this should be so. Those in positions of authority make decisions but the cost of implementing them and adjusting to new arrangements often falls principally on those who work at the chalkface. Educational policy is made and change occurs through a constant dialogue and compromise between those at the summit of the pyramid, who wish to impress and who are never short of new ideas, and those at the base, who are asked to implement these ideas and accept, without compensation, many of the costs which change imposes. It is not surprising then that there is much resistance to change. We should not be too ready to condemn the caution or obstruction of teachers and school administrators. It is their role to try to explain to those on high the complicated realities with which they are confronted day by day, just as it is the role of those in positions of responsibility to convince the teachers and administrators at the base that some changes are necessary in order to adapt to a changing world.

This chapter has concentrated on trying to understand and explain. Little attempt has been made to evaluate the performance of the system. The information which would be necessary for such an evaluation is almost entirely lacking. We may nevertheless conclude by tentatively suggesting that the strength of the French education system lies in the very real demands which it places on young people. Much is expected, especially from the more able pupils, and certainly much is obtained. The system is severely competitive at almost all levels. This is very praiseworthy if one adopts a narrowly academic or economic view of the education system. However, if one takes a broader perspective which pays more attention to the human costs of existing arrangements, one is inclined to be more critical. The personal, the human, and the pastoral are too often neglected. Bureaucratization and centralization too often mean that teachers and administrators refuse to accept responsibility, blaming the government or the ministry for any difficulties that arise. This stiffness and formality of approach probably imposes the greatest costs at primary level where it frequently means that young children of only seven or eight are required to repeat a year because they have not learned to read as rapidly as their classmates. Perhaps we should conclude: '*pourrait mieux faire*'.

Bibliography

The best historical introduction to the French education system is certainly A. Prost, *Histoire générale de l'enseignement et de l'éducation en France*, vol. 4: 'L'école et la famille dans une société en mutation'. Nouvelle Librairie de France, Paris, 1981.

For discussions of the relationship between education and economic performance, see particularly:

OECD, *Youth Unemployment in France*, OECD Paris, 1984.

OECD, *Education and the Economy in a Changing Society*, OECD Paris 1989.

Commissariat général du plan, *Ecole de la 2ᵉ chance de l'école*, vols 1 and 2. Commissariat général du plan, Paris, 1988.

More general and recent studies include:

Devaquet, A., *L'Amibe et l'étudiant*. Éditions Odile Jacob,

Paris, 1988. The first-hand account of the Minister responsible for the unsuccessful attempt to reform French universities in 1986.

Haby, R., *Combat pour les jeunes Français.* Julliard, Paris, 1981. The first-hand account by the Minister of Education from 1974–8.

Prost, A., *Les Lycées et leurs études au seuil du 21ᵉ siècle.* La Documentation française, Paris, 1983. Accessible, moderate and full of common sense.

Raynaud, P. and Thiebaud, P., *La Fin de l'école républicaine.* Calman-Levy, Paris, 1990. A good example of recent conservative attitudes.

Toulemonde, B., *Petite histoire d'un grand ministère.* Albin Michel, Paris, 1988. A revealing first-hand account by a senior civil servant in the Ministry of Education.

7

Religion
John Flower

Introduction

As France advances through the last decade of the twentieth century, there can be little doubt that religious practice itself and the relationship between it and social and political events are going to change. This has already been anticipated by the debate over the *école libre* in 1984 and by the *affaire du foulard* in 1989. While the first of these went beyond the immediate issue and was a reminder of the rich vein of conservatism in much of French society, the second was rather more significantly a pointer to its increasingly multi-national character and to the potential problems to which that could give rise.

Catholics

The Catholic Church of course retains its pre-eminence in a country where over 40 per cent of the population acknowledges a feeling of affinity with a religious faith *of some kind*, but where only 13 per cent claim to practise their religion regularly. According to various polls which have been conducted, about 80 per cent of the population remains baptized into the Catholic Church, and there is evidence that the number of adults seeking to enter or re-enter the Church is increasing very slightly. In general, however, the kind of erosion witnessed over the last twenty years continues. Fewer than 10 per cent of Catholics regularly attend mass, more than a third of newly married couples consider the religious part of the ceremony to be unnecessary (though there is an increasing number of mixed marriages taking place), the divorce rate has grown, and the number of children receiving instruction in the catechism in preparation for confirmation continues to drop steadily. When the Pope visited France in 1983 the estimated number of people who gathered at Lourdes was lower (150,000 per day) than anticipated. Ten years on, even that figure might not be reached.

Within the organization and structure of the Catholic Church the diminution of previous years also continues. For every seven priests who die or retire, only one is ordained, a situation which will lead to a crisis by the end of the century by which time demographic predictions suggest that around 16,000 priests will represent barely more than half those presently in office. The numbers of secular priests are diminishing at an even faster rate and more and more responsibility is being assumed by deacons (*diacres*) of whom there are over 300 and who have the authority to celebrate marriages and baptism, but not mass; and as the total number of priests shrinks so the responsibilities and difficulties for those left increase. There are 38,000 parishes in France of which 22,000 are without their own priest. A single priest usually, and almost always in rural areas, has responsibility for several parishes and on average for 2,000 people, an increase over the last twenty years of 100 per cent. Many churches are in a poor state of repair and are threatened with demolition (though the government is investing considerable sums for the restoration of churches which have significant historic interest) or are being closed. With an official salary of about 4,000 francs per month the priest remains poorly paid, though this income is supplemented by the *denier du culte*, contributions by members of his congregation representing (it is recommended) 1 per cent of their annual salaries. He is faced, as well, with a physically demanding job, especially in rural areas where he may well be obliged to travel as many as 5,000km per month, even though a car is a heavy drain on his slim financial resources. Security of employment, free accommodation and no immediate family expenses do, as some admit, allow them to exist without real hardship, but the growing debate about married priests has only served to underline the expression of misgivings about the difficulty of their tasks and the burden of loneliness. One priest certainly spoke for many when he remarked: '*La boîte de sardines mangée seul, un jour de Noël à midi, a un affreux goût de solitude.*'

Yet whatever the apparent disaffection amongst Catholics, and despite problems of organization and morale, the Church still has a massive presence within French society. Nowhere perhaps is there a better illustration of this today than the decision to build a new cathedral (the first for over a hundred years) at Evry, just over 30km south of Paris. Some government money has been set aside for this but the largest proportion is being raised by private subscription and contribution.

The model for the new cathedral at Evry. It has been scornfully dismissed by the traditionalists as '*à mi-chemin entre la salle des fêtes et le stade coupe du monde . . . tout est symbolique maçonnique.*'

Such a project with that kind of support suggests not only that the position of the Catholic Church remains pre-eminent, but also that its role within French society is growing in importance. Statistically this is so, but in a society whose composition and values are changing, other religions are every day becoming more vital and more influential.

Protestants

There is some evidence to suggest that the number of Protestants in France is growing, with a high percentage in their traditional areas – Alsace, the Cévennes and the southern Rhône valley. There are certainly over 2 million, of whom perhaps 1.3 million are practising, though many do so only irregularly, and large numbers have admitted that they have never even listened to the radio broadcast of a service. Most belong, however informally, to the Reform Church, but the non-conformists and the Lutherans, who adopt a much more fundamentalist interpretation of their faith, constitute important groups. Whatever their doctrinal inclinations, Protestants seem to be bound together by a sense that their religion is more direct and personal than Catholicism. For some the absence of the kind of hierarchy to be found in the Catholic Church is also attractive, and they claim that the Reform Church has none of the ambiguity of Catholicism in its attitude towards certain political issues, and, in recent years, towards education. On occasions relations are strained, but in general most active Protestants seek to engage in a better dialogue with the Catholic Church, all the while remaining constructively critical of it. At the national synod in May 1990 the predominant tone of modern French Protestantism was set by one pastor, Monique Veille: '*Il est souhaitable qu'un vaste public sache que l'on peut être chrétien de plusieurs manières. Il ne s'agit pas de faire du prosélytisme, mais de montrer qu'il y a une alternative possible.*' And yet more recently, in October 1992, at a conference of all French bishops, the President of the *Fédération protestante de France*, Jacques Stewart, criticized the Roman Church for not being more encouraging and for its over-insistence on the '*doctrine catholique très centralisatrice de l'ecclésiologie de communion.*'

Jews and Moslems

The three other major religious communities in France are those of the Orthodox Church (about 250,000), Jews (nearly 750,000) and Moslems. Three quarters of the Jewish community is to be found in the Paris area, with large settlements also in Lyon, Marseille and Provence. Numbers swelled, especially in the mid-1960s with the arrival of many from northern Africa during and after the Algerian war. This increase can be simply illustrated by the fact that in 1962 there were only three kosher butcher's shops in Paris; in 1991 there were over sixty. Jewish schools too have developed apace. Unfortunately with the rise in France in recent years of the extreme political right wing, anti-Semitic activities have increased. Jews have been the target of bomb attacks in Paris and have had their cemeteries desecrated, notably in May 1991 in the Provençal town of Carpentras where graves were opened and tomb stones daubed with Nazi slogans. The Chief Rabbi, Joseph Sitruk, is firm in his orthodoxy (he is opposed to '*la dilution des valeurs juives*') and the tone of a meeting at Le Bourget in November 1989, which attracted 30,000, suggested that there is a growing fundamentalist movement amongst Jews and, perhaps more alarmingly, considerable support for Israel.

This particular development is more pronounced in the Moslem community. More numerous than the Protestants, active and well-organized, Moslems have a right to be considered the second most significant religious group in France. It has been claimed that there are probably nearly 4 million of them, meeting in as many as 1,500 different places of worship, ranging from the splendour of the *Grande mosquée* in Paris to the squalor of a disused garage in the back streets of Marseille. About half of this number are practising, about three quarters of a million are of French nationality and over 30,000 are converts, principally from Catholicism. The renovation and extension of the mosque in Paris so that it will be able to accommodate up to 8,000 has been promised support by Jacques Chirac in his capacity as mayor and a second has been built just outside Paris, at Evry. Michel Noir, Mayor of Lyon, where there are over 5,000 Moslems, gave his permission in 1989, against very considerable local opposition, for a mosque to be built in a residential area not far from the centre of the city. Such moves suggest a climate of tolerance, but this is not always and everywhere the case. In Mulhouse in January 1993 over fifty graves of Moslem soldiers were vandalized by adolescent schoolchildren and in Marseille, where Moslems represent 10 per cent of the city's population, they themselves have considered it unwise (not to say unpractical) to build a second mosque since it will inevitably be blown up! Consultation is still taking place and a final decision is yet to be reached, but there is no doubt that the appearance of a second mosque in a city where extreme right-wing sentiment runs high is likely to be seen as provocation.

In March 1990, Pierre Joxe set up a *Conseil de réflexion sur l'Islam en France* (CORIF), which, while it has no legal status, is an attempt to establish some kind of national overview and, above all, to encourage the emergence of a 'French Islam'. Certainly, as within the Catholic and Protestant Churches, there are different factions within Islam. In 1987 the *Fédération nationale des musulmans de France* (FNMF) led by a French convert to Islam, Daniel Youssof Leclercq, accused the then leader of the Moslem community, Sheik Abbas, not only of favouring Moslems from his own country, Algeria, but of being in the hands of the Algerian government. While Algerian Moslems are certainly the largest group, there are others from all over the Arab world of which the Milli Gorus, a Turkish group in the region around Strasbourg, is probably the most extreme. And it is of this kind of fundamentalism that so many French people are wary. In 1989, Raymonde Girod, herself a *pied-noir*, and president of the residents' association in the eighth *arrondissement* of Lyon where the mosque is to be built, voiced the concern of the opposition to the project when she said: '*Je ne règle pas de comptes avec l'Algérie . . . Dès que j'entends parler arabe, je suis folle de joie. Mais l'Islam a changé. Il n'a plus rien à voir avec celui que j'ai connu là-bas.*'

But it is not only the extremist wing which worries some moderate French people. Islam is more than a religion, it is a way of life. The *imans* (of whom there are about one thousand in France) are not so much priests as guides whose wisdom and authority extend beyond matters of faith. Already as in

Great Britain, the debate over Salman Rushdie's *Satanic Verses* has produced factions and pressure groups which in general have lowered the standing of Islam in the eyes of many. But it was the *affaire du foulard*, between September 1989 and January 1990, which, if only for those few months, went to the heart of the religious issue.

The *foulard* was the name popularly given to the *tchador* or *hidjeb*, the veil worn by Moslem women. In October 1989, at the *Collège Gabriel-Havez* in Creil, a school with nearly 1,000 pupils drawn from twenty-five different nationalities, three girls returned after the summer holidays wearing the veil, having for the previous three years been bareheaded. As this was clearly against the law governing the national *école laïque* they were banned. Over the weeks, interventions by the Prime Minister, Michel Rocard, his Minister for Education, Lionel Jospin, and eventually even by the Moroccan government, produced a series of compromises ending in the girls' acceptance of French law, but not before the matter had caused widespread and often heated debate. Some accused the headmaster of racism; some saw the girls as the pawns of local Moslems who wished to make a political gesture; some extended the issue to women in society generally; some pointed out that since the wearing of a cross or the Jewish cap is tolerated, why should the veil not be. Spokesmen for the religious communities were inevitably drawn in. Lustiger, Archbishop of Paris, warned against discrimination but in general was cautious, interpreting the girls' gesture as teenage rebellion rather than a political statement. He did, however, say that it would take at least thirty years for Moslems to accept the idea of *laïcité* as it existed in France. Sheik Tedjini Haddam, Abbas' successor, also declared himself to be 'indigné par l'attitude discriminatoire', a view shared by Alain Goldmann: '*Aujourd'hui ce ne sont plus les religieux qui font preuve d'intolérance, comme on le leur reproche si souvent, mais les laïques. L'école laïque doit donner l'exemple de la tolérance.*' He was also reported as saying that the wearing of the veil or the *kipa* could be educationally useful: '*La confrontation des petits Français avec la "différence" [leur] apprennent à connaître et à respecter l'autre.*' Such statements as these were perhaps predictable, but behind the events, albeit magnified by the media, the concerns they prompted were very real and it is arguable that the case for integration and tolerance (religious and cultural) was weakened.

Another cause for concern among some French citizens has been the opening of a European Moslem centre in the château of St Leger de Fougeret in the Morvan in Burgundy. This admits about fifty students each year, claims to teach a broad-based liberal Islam and to be intolerant of fundamentalism. As such, this may seem innocent enough but many French Catholics are concerned about the gradual infiltration of more extreme elements and are not reassured by events in Algeria during 1992 and the rise of the FIS.

The Catholic Church: tradition and progression

The rise of traditionalism

While over the last two decades in particular the claims and opinions of progressive Catholics have made themselves heard, traditionalist groups of various kinds have increasingly expressed their concern at what they see as a serious erosion of the Church's authority. Of these, none have been more influential than the supporters of Marcel Lefebvre who, until his death in March 1991, had emerged as the staunchest defender of traditional Roman Catholicism and an outspoken opponent of all liberal and ecumenical tendencies. His traditionalism – *le lefebvrisme* as it has become known – has a number of fundamental tenets: the retention of the Tridentine Mass; opposition to modernization of the liturgy and the catechism, to religious freedom, to links with non-Catholics and to the dismantling of the Church's hierarchy.

Ordained in 1929, Lefebvre rose rapidly through the ranks of the Church hierarchy. At the age of forty-two he was ordained bishop in Senegal in 1947, became Archbishop of Dakar a year later and delegate for the African Churches at the Vatican. In 1962, he returned to France as Archbishop of Tulle. His arrival coincided with the opening of the Second

Vatican Council. At once Lefebvre made his mark as the principal spokesman for minority oppositional groups, declaring in his final intervention in the debates: '*Ce n'est pas le Saint-Esprit qui inspire le concile, mais le diable.*' In 1969, Lefebvre moved to Ecône in Switzerland where he established the *Fraternité sacerdotale de Saint-Pie-X*, a seminary for the training of priests along traditionalist lines. In 1974, his book *Un évêque parle* expressed his position unequivocally: '*nous refusons de suivre Rome dans la tendance néo-moderniste et néo-protestante clairement manifestée au cours du Vatican II et des réformes qui en sont issues.*' Two years later he had his first serious direct conflict with the Vatican by ordaining priests. This led to his being suspended in July 1976 *a divinis*, which in principle barred him from celebrating mass, dispensing the sacrements and preaching. Lefebvre chose to ignore the Pope's ruling and subsequently claimed as well that Paul VI was both misguided and wrongly inspired. Thus in New York in November 1977, for example, he remarked: '*Nous sommes prêts à suivre les instructions du pape. Mais lorsqu'il ne suit pas les instructions des deux cents soixante-deux papes qui l'ont précédé, nous ne pouvons pas suivre les siennes.*'

It was also in 1977 that his first real clash with the established Catholic Church occurred. Late in February, Paul VI announced he would not grant Lefebvre an audience until he had satisfactorily responded to earlier requests to modify his position. On 27 February, as an instant response, traditionalist Catholics, organized by one of Lefebvre's principal supporters, the abbé Ducaud-Bourget, occupied the church of Saint-Nicolas du Chardonnet in the fifth *arrondissement* in Paris. In spite of various 'threats' (notably, of recourse to the civil authorities) by the then Archbishop of Paris, Marty, the occupation continued. In May 1979 the parishioners of Saint-Nicolas wrote to Giscard d'Estaing as President of the Republic demanding action: not only was it a matter of civil liberty, they argued, but also of religious tolerance and political activity. Certainly this last point has been increasingly noticeable. The church of Saint-Nicolas is in the heart of conservative Chirac country and in addition to a large proportion of elderly people, Mass there attracts younger members of extreme right-wing groups, often anti-Semitic and racist in attitude, and others who look somewhat nostalgically back to the period of collaboration during the Occupation and to the values of the OAS during the Algerian crisis.

Faced with these kinds of developments, Marty and later Lustiger found themselves in an impossible position despite their authority as archbishops. Marty tried to distinguish between '*tradition*' and '*fixisme*' and '*passéisme*' but to no avail. He allowed the parish to call in the civil authorities and offered the traditionalists another church – the rather aptly named Marie-Méditrice near the Porte des Lilas – but the problem refused to disappear. Lefebvre's representative, Ducaud-Bourget, proved to be a formidable opponent, an intransigent interpreter of the traditionalists' policies who gathered around him a rapidly growing and admiring congregation. Before ill-health forced him to retire in September 1983, one of his last statements neatly and unambiguously summarized his position. His task – and that of his successors – was to maintain the struggle against '*la dérive protestante de l'Eglise, le devoiement de la religion, les messes sans prêtre où l'on bat des mains comme les nègres*'. And almost as if to ensure that his spirit should live on, his last sermon and his funeral service (he died in May 1985) were recorded. Available on cassette for 50 francs the recording continues to sell well.

Despite impressions given by the media, the positions apparently adopted by Lefebvre and by Rome were not totally immovable. Negotiations for a compromise continued and it seemed likely that one would be reached in the spring of 1988, at a time when Lefebvre announced his intention of ordaining four bishops – an action which would automatically invoke his excommunication. Lefebvre would be allowed to celebrate Mass in Latin and the Pope would ordain one of his nominees as bishop; in turn Lefebvre would have to acknowledge the changes against which he had so firmly set himself in matters of religious freedom, liturgy, hierarchy and ecumenicalism. Despite formal ratification of the general principles in a '*protocole de paix*', Lefebvre appears not to have been satisfied and on 30 June the ordinations took place with much ceremony on a hillside overlooking Ecône.

Excommunication followed and hence a schism within the Catholic Church. From then until his death, Lefebvre, however, continued at least in public to justify his position

1789 - 1989
Va-t-on vraiment fêter cela ?

Soutenez
l'ASSOCIATION 15 AOÛT 1989

Abonnez-vous à **L'ANTI-89**

40 F par an (12 numéros)
B.P. 125 - 92150 Suresnes cedex

and attack Rome: '*On nous a dit excommunication, mais excommunication par qui? Par une Rome moderniste, par une Rome qui n'a plus de foi catholique [. . .] Nous sommes condamnés, par des gens qui devraient être excommuniés publiquement.*'

The national celebrations in France the following year gave Lefebvre and his followers further reason to state their position. The *Association 15 août 1989* organized a mass in Paris attended by several thousands – estimates vary between

10,000 and 40,000. Posters and leaflets recalling '*cette page douloureuse et sanglante dans notre histoire*' were widely distributed. There was perhaps nothing surprising in this. Many opposed to the principles of the Revolution do not share Lefebvre's traditionalist stance, but the expression of latent sympathy indicates an audience to be targeted. In the autumn of the same year the *affaire du foulard* provided an opportunity. Already in July Lefebvre had been fined 5,000 francs for 'religious defamation' towards the Moslem communities in France. His remarks at a press conference on 14 November, while ostensibly focused on the religious dimension of the problem, had a much wider target:

'*Les musulmans vont petit à petit imposer leurs lois. Le droit chrétien ne peut s'accorder avec le droit islamique. Les musulmans ne peuvent vraiment être catholiques. Ils ne peuvent vraiment être français. Il ne faut pas leur permettre de s'organiser, ni sur le plan politique, ni sur le plan religieux.*'

Arguably, during the last years of his life Lefebvre had been driven on, as one British commentator observed, by pride and fear, trapped within his own vision of the Catholic Church as it succumbed, as he said in October 1990, to '*l'anarchie totale*' and was swamped by the tide of ecumenicalism '*contraire à la foi de l'Eglise*' – but neither his movement nor his beliefs died with him. When Ducaud-Bourget retired in 1983 he was replaced at St Nicolas by Philippe Laguérie, described in one survey of the traditionalist Catholic influence as embodying a mixture of faith and fanaticism. Certainly, as is to be expected, there has been no tempering of Lefebvre's message. In *Le Chardonnet*, the Church's newsletter in April 1986, Laguérie dismissed the ecumenical movement as '*cette dissolution de Jésus-Christ, qui est le propre de l'antichrist*'. In the summer of 1989 after Lefebvre's excommunication he wrote:

'*Aujourd'hui le sens de la foi est le seul secours des fidèles devant l'imbroglio inimaginable d'une hiérarchie qui prêche droits de l'homme, œcuménisme, liberté religieuse, Révolution [. . .] et qui trouve le moyen d'excommunier ceux qui ont encore l'audace de croire que Jésus-Christ est Dieu*'.

Six months later he referred to the French episcopacy as '*une bande d'assassins de la Foi*'. Franz Schmidberger, to whom responsibility for the seminary at Ecône was given in September 1982, has followed suit: '*l'esprit de Satan pénètre la société et la détruit*', he wrote in his regular *Lettre aux amis et bienfaiteurs* in October 1990. In the same communication he voiced an impassioned outburst against contemporary society in which '*les médias répandent partout le flux immonde du blasphème et de la pornographie: excès impensable hier, devenu aujourd'hui banalité quotidienne, avec l'approbation des hommes publics*'. Schmidberger has expressed the view that by the end of the century the Church will have ceased to have any significance for most people, a situation that is directly the consequence of the 'errors' of the Second Vatican Council. He sees a rearguard action, a kind of resistance, as necessary and claims (perhaps optimistically) that well over a million people would like to see Lefebvre's excommunication posthumously revoked.

The full extent of sympathy for the movement is impossible to measure with any degree of accuracy, but there is no doubt about its presence. Since the occupation of St Nicolas, other churches and buildings have been appropriated – St Louis at Marly in November 1986 or another by the same name in Boulogne-sur-mer, a disaffected church which until the spring of 1990 had been used as a garage. The *Institut universitaire Saint-Pie-X* in the sixth *arrondissement* in Paris holds regular lecture series, and privately founded schools are being established. The movement has its own radio station and claims a subscription list of around 40,000 for its magazines *Fideliter* and *Anti-89*. Nearly 300 priests are being trained each year at Ecône even though their mission will take them throughout the world. Centres like the one in Flavigny in northern Burgundy continue to expand and virtually every department in France has a '*lieu de culte*' where the traditional Latin mass is celebrated.

Yet not all now are *lefebvriste* in inspiration. After the schism a number of priests refused to follow him and the Vatican has not been slow in trying to encourage them to re-accept the central authority of the Catholic Church. At the same time, some have become even more entrenched in their integrism, such as, for example, the *Comité chrétienté-solidarité* led by

Bernard Antony – or as he is better known Romain Marie – which seeks to establish both a national Catholicism along strict traditionalist lines and links across Europe. Another extension of Lefebvre's movement, *Présent*, in 1990 opposed a move, which had been supported by the government, to create an international medieval centre at Chartres, arguing that it would amount to *'une désacralisation'*. But more significantly, and more worrying than internal discussion over issues based essentially in the expression of faith are the political allegiances and tenets of some of these Catholics.

St Nicolas in Paris is, as we have noted, in the heart of an area predominantly supportive of Jacques Chirac. Many of the regular attenders at mass, and indeed throughout France, have found in the words of both Lefebvre and Laguérie a statement of privately held convictions. One reported remark from a supporter of the former is nicely illustrative:

> *'Pétain, de Gaulle et Monseigneur Lefebvre sont curieusement tous les trois originaires du nord de la France. Je les crois tous les trois également utiles. Ce sont souvent les minoritaires qui ont raison et font avancer les choses.'*

Lefebvre never hid his admiration for either; he also expressed approval for the monarchist movement, the *Action française*, at Lille in 1976 and, in 1987, admired Pinochet's regime in Chile: *'Il n'y a pas un pays où l'on puisse circuler aussi librement.'* Over the last decade too, links with the *Front national* have developed and Jean-Marie Le Pen (also from the north of France) has not been slow in perceiving the advantages. On Lefebvre's death his party's tribute was telling: *'pour avoir su sauvegarder, contre le communisme athée et le matérialisme décadent, l'héritage de nos valeurs occidentales les plus sacrées'.* The traditionalist mass is regularly celebrated at major *Front national* rallies and Bernard Antony is a party member in the European parliament. Any developments considered to be progressive or democratic within the Church are instantly and stridently opposed. In 1988 one extremist (and monarchist) was reported as saying:

> *'Regardez l'Assemblée nationale. Enlevez les protestants et les franc-maçons, qu'est-ce qui reste? Et pourtant ces gens sont terriblement minoritaires dans le pays. C'est le résultat de la démocratie.'*

Another acknowledged that while Jews and Moslems could be converted to Catholicism, without that, '*Ils devront vivre dans des sortes de ghettos. De toute façon il n'est pas question qu'ils puissent librement et publiquement célébrer leur culte.*'

However strong and indeed genuine their sense of mission within the Catholic Church may be, integrists of whatever hue throughout France are in a minority and must surely remain so. At the same time it does seem unlikely, without a substantial shift either in their position or in that of the Vatican, that the rift with Rome will be healed. Yet their form of fundamentalism will not have the wide-ranging impact of the kind exerted by certain Moslem groups, if for no other reason but that Catholicism does not dictate a way of living to quite the same degree as Islam. What is interesting is, that while only a few years ago it was progressive Catholics whose involvement with politics invoked cautionary statements and displeasure from the Church authorities, more recently it is the traditionalists. And it is precisely this, together with their exploitation by extreme right-wing groups, which presents such a threatening prospect.

The progressive legacy

Even though the traditionalist movement within the Catholic Church has been prominent during the last few years, it would be wrong to ignore or diminish the legacy of the activities of progressive Catholicism as it developed during the 1970s.

The *Mission de France* continues its work in industrial areas and despite its relatively small size (278 priests in 1990) is in a healthy condition. The *Action catholique ouvrière* (ACO) retains 17,000 members while the rally of the *Jeunesse catholique ouvrière* (JCO) at La Courneuve in the north of Paris in May 1990 attracted about 40,000 young people in what one journalist described as the atmosphere of '*une vaste kermesse*'. Both movements, as their traditions dictate, are in favour of an increased dialogue between the Church establishment and the underprivileged and working-class areas of French society. The need still remains, the former have argued, for the latter to enjoy '*la possibilité d'exprimer sa foi dans son langage et ses rites*'.

Bishop André Lacrampe, head of the *Mission de France*, went even further:

> '*L'Eglise n'est l'Eglise que dans l'ouverture et le dialogue que si elle aide les chrétiens et les non-chrétiens à vivre au cœur des défis quotidiens: l'éthique, la santé, les droits de l'homme, les choix économiques.*'

The French episcopacy has continued to respond to observations of this nature. Since the annual conference of archbishops and bishops in 1989, increasing attention has been given to the social and educative roles to be played by religion, especially in a world in which '*l'usage de la drogue et la multiplication des suicides sont les symptômes les plus inquiétants*'. In November 1990 concern was expressed once again at the lowering of the Church's general visibility and over the need to revitalize religious life within parishes. Already attempts to meet this need have been put into practice. Training centres like the *Centre d'intelligence de la Foi* (CIF) have been established and it is now possible for people to study part-time for a degree in theology at the *Ecole cathédrale (Notre Dame) institut catholique*. Rather more immediate and practical has been the creation of elected diocesan synods (twenty-eight by the summer of 1990) composed of clerics and lay members of the Church, and normally of three years' duration. Their task is to examine local issues in a spirit of '*coresponsabilité*' and to make recommendations to the national episcopal assembly. Another major step has been the rewriting (since 1985) of the catechism, to produce an '*exposé complet et organique de la foi chrétienne*', dealing not only with matters of faith and exegesis of the Bible, but with moral and social issues such as contraception, for example, as well. The success of this particular venture has been considerable. When it was published in November 1992 it sold over 100,000 copies in that month alone and topped the best-sellers list for several weeks! Along with the revised catechism the question of religious instruction in schools has also been raised. The right to such instruction is guaranteed by French law, but increasingly schools (about 25 per cent so far) have been moving the classes to Saturday morning. The result has been a drop in about 25 per cent attendance, a further proof of what Joseph Duval, archbishop of Rouen and new head of the episcopal assembly, referred to in November 1990 as '*la conception matérialiste du week-end*'. His predecessor, Decourtray, and Lustiger are both opposed to this change, seeing in it the beginning of an erosion of religious education altogether. '*L'enjeu est capital*', said Lustiger. '*Avec une affaire apparemment technique, on touche à un point important de l'équilibre culturel et spirituel du pays.*'

While, over this and other issues, the central authority of the Church has expressed reservation, elsewhere sharper criticism has come from individuals and organizations that not enough has been done. One particular voice, ready to express uncomfortable views, is that of Jacques Gaillot, Bishop of Evreux. Gaillot is openly in favour of contraception, of married priests and of tolerance of homosexuality. In an interview published in *Lui* in January 1989 he remarked in a typically forthright manner: '*Si le préservatif peut sauver des vies, alors utilisons-le.*' Rather more fundamentally disturbing for his colleagues on the episcopal council was a comment made in November 1988: '*L'Evangile est une parole parmi d'autres, une parole contestable, et nous ne devons pas chercher à l'imposer.*' When, in December 1989, the ashes of the abbé Grégoire were moved to the Panthéon, Gaillot was the only senior member of the episcopacy present. Not surprisingly, he has been given the nickname by traditionalist Catholics of '*Camarade Gaillot*'.

Ever ready to use the media to circulate his opinions, Gaillot is not without an audience especially amongst the young. One representative movement is that of the *Jeunes Chrétiens Service* whose rally at the *Parc des Expositions*, north of Paris, in March 1991 drew 10,000 participants. It is ecumenical in outlook and strongly critical of the Church hierarchy for failing still to be properly representative of lay Catholic opinion. As the movement's president, Philippe de Saint-Germain observed: '*Notre expression de laïcs est suspecte dans l'appareil institutionnel de l'Eglise de France*'. Even more outspoken is a group of progressive Catholics from Belgium and Lyon who, through their periodical *Golias*, have maintained a steady flow of criticism. Lustiger in particular has been a target, and in the spring of 1991 an issue entitled '*Les Dix Ans du Cardinal Lustiger à Paris*' accused him of authoritarian behaviour, conservatism and patronage.

The problem, as always, for the national episcopal assembly, as the supreme body of the French Catholic Church, and for Lustiger, as its most significant individual, is balance. Before he retired from the presidency, Decourtray reflected growing support amongst many of his colleagues for the involvement of women in the Church, at the General Synod in Rome in October 1990, only to be met with the Pope's firm reiteration of his preference of '*la discipline du célibat*'. Over AIDS the Supreme Body of the Church has been concerned to dissociate itself from the medieval view expressed in the late 1980s by Cardinal Siri, Archbishop of Genoa, that the illness was a divine punishment. At the same time it has refused to modify its position on the use of contraceptives.

Pivotal in all this activity is Cardinal Jean-Marie Lustiger, Archbishop of Paris. Of Jewish origins (he was baptized in 1940) Lustiger as a child experienced hatred and persecution. His mother was sent to Auschwitz and he had to go into hiding. His decision to enter the priesthood was accepted by his family with reluctance and there can be no doubt that this kind of background had an immensely formative impact on his intellectual and spiritual development. He is not without his opponents. Amongst them, the most outspoken are the traditionalists and, when he was appointed to Notre Dame in June 1981, Lefebvre's reaction was to the point: '*On peut être surpris de penser que se trouve à la tête du plus grand diocèse de France quelqu'un qui n'est pas d'origine vraiment française.*'

Lustiger's presence is characterized by a kind of combative dignity. Ideologically, he is close to John-Paul II with whom he is said to enjoy a warm relationship. He has particular responsibility for the role of the Catholic Church within Europe, has tended to appoint bishops sympathetic to it and has set up a series of committees and organizations to ensure that this work will continue. Lustiger is a man of deep faith. He is generally suspicious of the modern world and of the roles played in it by science and the social sciences. He has spoken out against experimentation with human embryos for example. While he is quick to see the benefit of television he has condemned the manner in which it is responsible (according to him) for encouraging a subculture of anarchy, disrespect and violence. When Scorsese's controversial film *The Last Temptation of Christ* opened in Paris in the autumn of 1988 Lustiger made his opposition clear: '*On n'a pas le droit de choquer les sentiments de millions de gens pour qui Jésus est plus important que leur père et leur mère.*'

Even so, in all probability no Archbishop of Paris during the second half of the twentieth century has enjoyed such a high public profile and had such influence. His opinions, if not always popular, nevertheless command respect and such is his impact that the words *lustigérophile* and *lustigérophobie* have become part of current French.

Conclusion

In October 1989 the French episcopacy invited the European President, Jacques Delors, to attend their assembly. His response was predictable: grateful for being asked and encouraged by the way in which the French Catholic Church could be instrumental in easing European and multi-nation relationships. While there is doubtless some truth in this prospect, it is not without its problems. At present the traditionalist movement around Ecône has a much more prominent European identity than any other element within the French Catholic Church and has become associated with (or is used by) extremist political groups. More important for the French Church, certainly in the immediate future, is its relationship with other religions and cultures within France. Here again Lustiger is to the fore, encouraging dialogue with the representatives of Islam in particular. Movements and groups have been formed. In January 1991, *Promouvoir la Fraternité* brought together Christians, Moslems and Jews, Protestants and members of the Orthodox Church in an expression of opposition to the Gulf war and to the proliferation of chemical and bacteriological weapons. But differences remain, and as orthodox and fundamentalist tendencies develop, often fired by social and political issues, the debate becomes ever more difficult. At the same time, there is considerable evidence that the claim, made in 1983 by the review *Prier*, that there were signs of renewal of '*spiritualité populaire*' was correct. The ecumenical community at Taizé near Cluny celebrated its fiftieth anniversary in 1990 and continues to draw young people in ever-increasing numbers. In remote areas of the southern Rhône valley groups of hermits – mostly Catholic women – have formed. The first Masonic temple in France opened in Toulon in May 1990. Buddhist centres in the south-west, in Joinville in the south-east suburbs of Paris, and in Burgundy have become well established and attract many, French and foreigners alike. Arguably, many developments of this kind reflect a desire to turn away from a world which is seen as being predominantly materialistic and uncaring, in an attempt to find new, stable values. And the trend may continue. As France approaches the end of the century and is host to an increasingly racially mixed and complex society this religious feeling, however it is expressed, may have a significant role to play. When, as part of his presidential campaign, Mitterrand produced his famous poster depicting a quiet French village and the emotive slogan '*la force tranquille*' he was essentially appealing to the nation's sense of community and family, underpinned by the traditions of Catholicism. Even in as short a time as a decade the phrase has taken on new meanings.

Bibliography

General background information for the history of the Catholic Church in France during the first two-thirds of the twentieth century will be found in:

Dansette, A., *Destin du catholicisme français*. Paris, Flammarion, 1957.

Latreille, A. and Rémond, R. (eds), *Histoire du catholicisme en France*, vol. 3. Paris, Spes, 1962.

Rémond, R., *L'Anticléricalisme en France de 1815 à nos jours*. Paris, Fayard, 1976. The last of these is especially good on the period from the Second Vatican Council to the early 1970s. Chapters in earlier editions of *France Today* provide information on the period from the early 1950s.

Books dealing with specific issues include:

Gilson, G., *Les Prêtres*. Paris, Desclée de Brouwer, 1990.

Hazard, M. J. (ed), *Printemps d'église: aujourd'hui, les laïcs*. Paris, Desclée de Brouwer, 1987. On the resurgence of lay movements.

Kepel, G., *Les Banlieues de l'Islam: naissance d'une religion en France*. Paris, Seuil, 1987.

Mehl, R., *Le Protestantisme français dans la société actuelle*. Paris, Labor et Fides, 1982. A sympathetic, wide-ranging survey; good on 'internal' disputes within Protestantism.

Although now slightly dated, a thorough summary of information about all religions and sects is 'Religions et société en France', in *Problèmes politiques et sociaux*. Paris, La Documentation française, no. 518:6 (Sept. 1985).

The following reviews also contain important and interesting articles:

L'Actualité religieuse dans le monde, no. 55 (15 Apr. 1988). Contains information on the traditionalist movement.

L'Express (19 May 1989). On the presence of Islam.

L'Evénement du jeudi (19–25 Apr. 1990). On the Jewish community in France. The same magazine (12–18 Jul. 1990) contains a supplement on *laïcité*.

Golias (Jun.–Jul. 1990). 'Trombinoscopes pour épiscopes'. A series of pen portraits of all French bishops, not all of them flattering and some amusing.

Histoire (Jul.–Aug. 1990). A special issue, 'Chrétiens, juifs et musulmans en France'.

Le Nouvel Observateur (29 Jul.–4 Aug. 1988). On Lefebvre and the traditionalist movement.

The official 'handbook' of the Catholic Church is *L'Eglise catholique en France*. Information-Communication, 106 rue du Bac, 75341 Paris Cedex 07.

8

The press
Ray Davison

Introduction

The French press faces the challenges of the 1990s in a beleaguered state. In the course of a symposium, held in Paris in October 1988, Pierre Albert, one of France's leading anatomists of the world's press, hesitated between the choice of *'une crise'* or *'une maladie de langueur'* as the more appropriate description of the present state of his country's press. Despite the odd counter-expression of optimism, captured notably in a widely discussed article in *Le Monde* (28 April 1989) by Jean Marie Dupont entitled *'La Revanche de Gutenberg'*, the general consensus among media specialists is one of decline and even of entropy. France is now placed thirtieth in the world tables of newspapers consumed per one thousand inhabitants, with a figure of 178 (Japan leads with 562, more than treble the French total, whilst France is also well behind Britain, 398, Germany, 345, and the Netherlands, 314; France does, however, lead over Spain, 78, and Italy, 116).

The scale of this decline in consumption from the turn of the century is dramatic. In 1914, France with America headed the world tables with a rate of 344 papers sold per thousand population. It then possessed eighty Parisian dailies producing 5.5 million copies and 242 provincial dailies with a print run of 4 million. By 1988, there were just eleven Parisian and sixty-five provincial dailies with a combined production of 10 million copies, despite an increased population of 56 million. Because of these figures, the sense that the glorious years are over and that, in the 350-year history of the French press, the golden age has long since vanished, is not the least significant of the problems affecting the industry.

This general pattern of declining titles and circulation since 1914 has, it is true, been interrupted on occasions. The immediate post-Second World War years, 1945–6, which witnessed the vigorous relaunching of the industry, produced a boom in circulation to 15 million and a consumption rate of 370 per thousand for a population of 41 million – there were then twenty-eight Parisian and 175 provincial dailies. However, these figures have not been matched in the years subsequent to 1946 and both titles and circulation have declined annually since that date, although there were inter-mittent booms between 1962 and 1973; the events of May 1968 augmented sales to a record post-Second World War level of 13 million. The latest figures record the seventeenth successive year of declining titles and circulation and further slippage on the world tables (France was twenty-second in 1986 and thirtieth in 1990).

Such statistics tend to mask the even more dramatic decline of the Parisian daily papers. In 1939, the circulation of the provincial dailies equalled that of the Parisian ones for the first time in the history of the French press (6 million each). By 1945 the figure for the Parisian papers was 4.606 million with twenty-six titles and for the regional dailies 7.532 with 153 titles. The 1988 figures record 2.942 million and eleven titles for the Parisian papers with 7.155 and sixty-five titles for the provincial ones. The French provincial press has thus out-stripped in importance the contracting Paris dailies and indeed it now controls some 70 per cent of that market. It is the Rennes-based provincial daily *Ouest-France* which is now France's most popular daily paper.

Furthermore, it should not be forgotten that the percentage share of the press market held by daily papers is also declin-ing: for example, in 1965, daily papers constituted 57.3 per cent of the total press market. By 1988 the figures had reversed to 41.2 per cent. This is not to overlook the relative strength of the periodical press. In 1987, if a French person consumed 2.2

fewer daily papers than a British person and two less than a German, magazine sales were much more encouraging: 1,022 copies were sold per thousand inhabitants compared to 1,517 in Germany and 996 in Great Britain. The prosperity and dynamism of this section of the French press will be examined later.

This history of decline threatens pluralism and diversity in a country which has been anxious, particularly since 1945, to restrict both press monopoly and over-concentration of press ownership, especially in the area of the dailies. *Francoscopie* now estimates that within the last ten years, the number of readers of a daily newspaper in France has declined by a massive 25 per cent. In 1989, 47 per cent of French people read at least one daily newspaper, although variations in readership by age group should not be forgotten, (17 per cent of fifteen to twenty-four year olds, 19 per cent of twenty-five to thirty-four year olds, 28 per cent of thirty-five to forty-nine year olds, 19 per cent of fifty to sixty-four year olds, 17 per cent of over-sixty-fives).

Explanations for these falling circulation figures and the declining range of titles, especially in the vital area of the national dailies, are plentiful among media specialists but not always convergent. They range from the rudimentary to the sophisticated. For example, some commentators point to the high cost of French newspapers in the post-war period and regret the absence in France of the cheaper tabloids available in Britain (they do not appear to regret the absence of the particular modes of journalism practised by such tabloids). Admittedly, since 1975, the price of French daily papers, which until 1982 was fixed by the government, has increased at twice the rate of the general cost of living, whilst the percentage of the French family budget allocated to newspapers has remained static. In 1991 a Paris daily costs between five and six francs, although the regional dailies are cheaper and their circulation has not declined so much. However, it is interesting to note that, despite price deregulation in 1982, there has been no attempt at a price war, nor has the much talked-about emergence of a cheap tabloid come to anything.

More sophisticated explanations tend to concentrate on the

history of the French press and its complacent relationship with French political life in the inter-war years and especially during the period of the Vichy regime and collaboration. According to this thesis, daily papers and notably the Parisian dailies, became publicly discredited through collusion with the bankrupt politics of the Third Republic and the Nazi propaganda machine. Cut off from Paris, the regional dailies were spared some of this opprobrium and have not declined to the same extent. Such an explanation may have some cogency for it is certainly true that the French do not appear to like or to trust their journalists very much at all; surveys frequently point out that the French distrust what they read in the papers and that they treat the whole press medium with touching suspicion. Yet it is also true that the French distrust the written word much less than the language of radio or television journalists who are nevertheless absorbing a growing proportion of the leisure time activities of the French, compared to the journalists on the daily papers.

While no clear or single explanation exists, it may be possible to define further both the features of this undoubted decline and to comment more precisely upon its possible causes. For this purpose an overall analysis of the main characteristics of the press as an industry in France today, together with a profile of its general daily and periodical production, is necessary.

Cartoon by Barbe from an article entitled 'La révolution des médias', *Le Monde*, 1984.

The French press as an industry

The economic and industrial situation of the French press embodies areas of weakness which may offer some parallel explanation of the decline of circulation and titles. The press had a turnover in France of 48,200 million francs in 1988, well behind England (60,000 million) and Germany (70,000 million). This figure represents about 1 per cent of PIB (GDP) and makes the press industry between the twelfth and seventeenth largest sector of the French economy.

It has been argued, perhaps paradoxically, that the relative weakness of the French press industry's financial base compared to, say, Britain and Germany is linked to the many direct and indirect state subventions to the industry. France protects its newspaper industry more generously than any other European country apart from Italy. State subventions, amounting to some 12 per cent of the industry's turnover, were designed along with a whole series of judicial regulations in 1945 to resist the tendency to economic concentration and monopoly and thus to protect pluralism and diversity of informational viewpoints. With the general movement of capital concentration in Europe in the post-war period and especially over the last fifteen years, the industrial and financial base of the French press has perhaps found itself weakened by such protectionist policies, and thus outstripped on the capital front by more powerful European conglomerates. For example, the turnover of the German Bertelsmann group was itself equal to the total turnover of the whole French press in 1988. Such an argument is often linked to another factor tending to check development of concentration: the relative strength of France's regional newspapers. Paris simply does not dominate France in terms of papers in the same way that London dominates England and the emergence of large powerful grouping may well have been further checked by this fact. With European and global competition for markets intensifying all the time, the diminutive stature in relative terms of the top French press financial groupings will certainly put the industry's growth at a disadvantage.

Slowness in both modernization and diversification is also

adding to the industry's problems as is the historical separation of the various components of the media industry, preventing the rapid rise of multi-media conglomerates.

Be that as it may, the French press currently employs more than 150,000 people, almost half of them journalists. The numerical strength of the journalistic staff has actually increased by 50 per cent over every decade of the post-war period and the largest growth area has been the increasing number of female journalists in the profession. The development of television and radio has also provided the industry with a rising number of cross-media journalists. The industry now generates some 3,000 publications, providing 7.9 million copies, of which some 6.7 million are sold. The rather large margin of unsold copies in France is linked to distribution problems, for household deliveries and subscriptions are relatively undeveloped compared to sales at kiosks.

A further important dimension of the industry is its paper consumption. It uses 1.3 million tons of paper annually, France being twelfth in the world tables of paper consumed per inhabitant for press purposes. Sixty-four per cent of the paper for newspapers is imported and 45 per cent is magazine quality paper.

The profit margins of the French press generally are also depressed relative to the larger European groups. Worker–management relations, the already cited slowness in adapting to technical advances, rigidity of practice in production leading to increased costs are among the reasons most often given to explain this low level of profitability. Such phenomena render the French industry increasingly vulnerable to competitive advances from Britain and Germany after the events of 1992 and the implementation of the Single European Act.

If under-capitalization and depressed profit margins have obstructed the growth of the French press industry, developments in the advertising world have also contributed to its enfeebled state. Although the advertising market in France, as in many places in the world, is expanding – indeed its rate of expansion is faster than in other countries – this is because the present size of the industry itself is quite small. France, in 1986, devoted only 1.2 per cent of GDP to the advertising

industry compared, for example, with the USA's 2.4 per cent and Finland's 1.7 per cent. Advertising expenditure per head of population was $81, placing France fourteenth in the world (America is naturally in first place with $424 per head and Britain ninth with $145 per head). In terms of the world market in advertising, France has a 4 per cent share (the USA has over 50 per cent, Europe generally 25 per cent). Competition for advertising revenue in France tends to be extremely fierce because of this restricted scale of the market in general. At the same time, however, the French press is becoming increasingly reliant on advertising revenue, as opposed to sales, for its viability. In 1975, for example, 36.8 per cent of its revenue came from advertising; by 1988 this had risen to 43.2 per cent (this should be compared to the figures of 70 per cent in the USA and 65 per cent in Britain). Simultaneously, however, the market share of advertising revenue held by the press has been falling, partly because of declining sales, partly because of the growing stake of television in the advertising world since deregulation in 1981. In 1967, 78.8 per cent of advertising expenditure in France was directed at the written press with 15 per cent going to radio and 3.5 per cent to television. By 1987, the television share had risen to 22 per cent whilst the press received 57 per cent and radio 7.5 per cent. Of course, everywhere in Europe television is making inroads into the advertising revenue market, although the rate of progress is by no means as swift as many anticipated. Nevertheless, in the last twenty-five years the press has lost some 20 per cent of its advertising market whilst in Britain and Germany the press maintains much higher shares of the market.

This decline in advertising revenue is particularly marked in respect of the daily press which has seen its share of advertising dwindle from 30.5 per cent in 1975 to 24 per cent in 1983, whilst in the same period the periodical press share has remained stable. The growth of *la presse gratuite* since 1960 and the erosion of the small ads market by the ever-expanding number of *Minitel* terminals have also added to the financial difficulties of the big dailies in terms of advertising revenue.

The press industry today is largely composed of fourteen groups whose annual turnover exceeds a thousand million francs. The main group is Hachette-Presse, founded in 1829 as a publishing business. Its annual turnover has augmented from 7.8 thousand million francs in 1981 to 24.4 thousand million francs in 1988, some two-fifths of this increase coming from expansion abroad. This is a multimedia consortium which in 1986 made an unsuccessful bid for TF1. About a third of its activities relate to the press proper. It has a one-third stake in the Parisian daily, *Le Parisien*, and controls the provincial dailies, *Dernières Nouvelles d'Alsace*, *Le Provençal* and *L'Echo républicain*. It also owns nine weeklies including the Sunday papers *France-Dimanche* and *Le Journal du Dimanche* as well as the very popular *Télé 7 Jours*, *TV Hebdo*, *TV Couleur*, *Elle*, *Ici Paris* and *Le Journal de Mickey*. Sixteen monthly magazines are also under the group's control including *Max*, *Onze*, *Parents*, *Vitae*, *Fortune* and *Première*. It was this group which envisaged launching a new national daily in the 1980s but it abandoned the project in 1987.

The second largest group is the Groupe Hersant, controlling some 22 per cent of the regional and 33 per cent of the Parisian dailies and with an estimated turnover in 1987 of over 7,000 million francs. The group was established in 1950 with *L'Auto journal*. From this small beginning the group has grown spectacularly by taking stakes first in the regional press (*Le Havre libre*, *La Liberté du Morbihan*, *L'Eclair* and finally in 1972 *Paris Normandie*). Then in the 1970s, the group took control of *Le Figaro* (1975), *France-Soir* (from Hachette in 1976) and *L'Aurore* (1978, and absorbed by *Le Figaro* in 1979). This sudden expansion of the group in the 1970s led to the accusation in 1978 that it had breached the Liberation monopoly laws but nothing came of the case against it. In 1983, the group expanded again taking control of *Le Dauphiné libéré*, *Le Progrès de Lyon* in 1985 and *L'Union de Reims* in 1986. The laws of 15 August and 27 November prohibited a single press grouping from controlling more than 30 per cent of total circulation, so the group's further expansion cannot be so spectacular. Hersant controls some twelve magazines including *Le Figaro magazine* and the French racing weekly *Paris-Turf*. Hersant too, like Hachette, has talked of launching a new daily, *Paris-Star*, but it has not yet twinkled.

Other large groupings with some of their better known titles include:

– Editions Mondiales (turnover 2,100 million francs). *Télépoche, Intimité, Nous deux, Bonnes soirées, Caméra vidéo, Auto-Plus*.

– Ouest-France (turnover 1,700 million francs) controls the regional daily *Ouest-France*, France's best-selling paper, *La Presse de la Manche* and the large group of free papers called '*le Carillon*'.

– CEP Communication (turnover 1,760 million francs). Created in 1988 this group controls some seventy specialist publications but it also owns *L'Express, Lire* and *Biba*.

– Prisma Presse (turnover 1,680 million francs) is the French arm of the German group, Grüner und Jahr, and its titles include some of the most popular magazines such as *Géo, Télé loisir, Femme actuelle* and *Cuisine nouvelles*.

– Editions Amaury (turnover 1,642 million francs) controls *Le Parisien libéré*.

– Groupe Filipacchi (turnover 1,619 million francs) owns *Paris-Match*.

– Bayard-Presse (turnover 1,336 million francs) owns the

Catholic papers *La Croix, Le Pèlerin magazine* and a whole range of periodical titles.

Two smaller but self-evidently important groupings should also be mentioned: the Groupes de presse communistes. This is directly controlled by the French Communist Party and is responsible for the four communist dailies *L'Humanité, Liberté* (Lille), *L'Echo du centre* (Limoges) and *La Marseillaise*; it also owns the weeklies *L'Humanité-Dimanche, Révolution* and *La Terre*; the monthly *Heures claires* (for women) and numerous other locally based militant papers. Finally, there is the Groupe Le Monde which has a turnover of 1.239 thousand million francs and produces *Le Monde, Le Monde de l'éducation, Le Monde diplomatique* and *Le Monde des philatélistes*.

Such groupings, as already indicated, are not on the scale of their German and British counterparts but that does not reduce the ferocity of the competition for market share in all domains. New titles, especially in the magazine press, come and quite often go (the *De Profundis* pages list the major deaths annually in the *Guide de la presse*) and shifting arrangements and alliances between groups make their precise description uncertain. It should be said that the growth rates of these larger groupings seem sound and healthy, notwithstanding the problems outlined above. However the relationship between capital infrastructure and a varied and reliable news service is never far from the minds of press analysts who fear that further contractions of pluralism will result from inter-group competition.

This press profile would not be complete without mentioning that the development of large capital groupings has also created the conditions for the growth of a multitude of press agencies in France. Despite the increasing numbers of journalists, the actual gathering and supplying of news is more and more channelled through agency services, again leading to fears of excessive uniformity and repetition in the selection and presentation of news items. The use of specialist foreign correspondence in international news reporting is declining (*Le Monde* is a notable exception to this and the benefits are all too evident in the brilliance of detail and penetration of its foreign coverage). The international agencies, Associated Press, Reuters, Tass and the French-based *Agence France Presse* (created in 1945 as a successor to *Agence Havas*, the first international news agency established in France in 1832) are increasingly strengthening their grip on world news information processing. National and local news coverage, however, is also rapidly being sucked into agency systems undermining the role of locally-based individual reporters. At the last count there were some hundred such agencies. News as an industry in the intensely competitive capital markets is running the risk of becoming a processed and packaged commodity. Thus pluralism and diversity are threatened not just in terms of the shrinking number of titles but also in terms of the systems of news dissemination which are growing up as a response to economic developments. This does not augur well for the future of the French press as it confronts the problem of loss of readership.

A survey of the French press

Our survey will concentrate on three key areas: the Parisian and the regional dailies and the periodical press.

The Parisian dailies

There are now just nine general daily newspapers which are Paris based, together with one specialist sporting daily, *L'Equipe*, one racing daily, *Paris-Turf* and three specialist financial dailies *Les Echos*, *La Tribune de l'expansion*, *Le Temps de la finance* (*La Cote Desfossés* with a circulation of just 25,000, is also published on a daily basis; founded in 1825, it is the specialist stock exchange paper). The combined circulation of the Paris dailies is now just under 3 million and it has declined yearly since the peak post-war figure in 1968 of just over 5 million. A substantial proportion of all sales is in the Paris region which curiously has the least active readership levels of all the regions of France. Many titles have disappeared: *Le Quotidien du peuple*, launched in 1975, ceased publication in 1980. *Rouge* lasted only three years and was withdrawn in 1979. *J'informe*, a centre-right daily appeared for just a few months in 1977. A similar fate was reserved for *Combat socialiste*, 1981, *Paris ce soir*, 1984, *Forum international*, 1980 (a financial daily) and *Le Sport*, 1988. Three of the most important casualties were the popular *Paris-Presse* in 1970, *Paris-Jour* in 1972 and, of course, *L'Aurore* in 1980.

With the falling sales of *France-Soir* since 1967 and of the *Parisien libéré* subsequent to its modernization troubles in 1977 and 1978, it is no longer really possible to claim that France has a *popular* national daily newspaper.

Le Figaro

This is France's oldest daily newspaper. It was founded in 1826, became a daily in 1866 and calls itself *'le premier quotidien national français'*, although over 50 per cent of its sales are in the Paris area. It has a circulation of over 400,000 and, since 1975, has been part of the Hersant group. Its finances are relatively healthy – its economic strength partly derives from its successful weekend supplements *Le Figaro magazine*, *Madame Figaro* and *TV magazine*, totalling some five hundred pages and sold as a package for 20 francs on a Saturday. *Le Figaro* is printed in the larger format and includes three other supplements: *Le Figaro économie* (daily), *Figaroscope* (Wednesday) and *Le Figaro littéraire* (Monday). It is basically a conservative paper, which savaged the French socialist President over the *Rainbow Warrior*, immigration policy and law and order issues. After Mitterrand's re-election in 1988, it somewhat softened its opposition to the socialists and to government policy. Under its new editor, Olivier Giesbert, the paper increasingly resembles the British *Daily Telegraph* or the American publication the *Herald Tribune*. Its economic pages are readable and informative, as is its literary supplement and the paper certainly appeals to the French people's sense of their own pragmatism. *Le Figaro* is probably not quite as good as it was under its post-war editor, Pierre Brisson, who died in 1964. Nevertheless, it is a quality paper with a touch of cultural distinction which speaks for the right-wing intelligentsia of France. *Le Figaro* also strives to be useful by providing sources of practical information in its well-documented *'pages pratiques'* and its jobs and property advertisements. As it confronts the 1990s, *Le Figaro* aims to be the voice of the modern, pragmatic France.

Le Parisien (libéré)

This is the only French newspaper which remotely resembles a popular national daily. It was founded in 1945 and by 1975 its circulation of 785,000 made it France's leading daily. Its long-time owner, Emilien Amaury, killed in a riding accident in 1977, had built up the paper on strong anti-communist lines and engaged it in continuous populist and sensationalist polemics against immigrants, delinquents and left-wing activists. It repeatedly called for the reintroduction of the death sentence. It never wished, however, to sink to the level of the *Sun*, nor did it adopt the tabloid format. A long industrial dispute, including an all-out strike between 1975 and 1977 over Amaury's decision to modernize the paper's production methods, led to a boycott by distributors and this halved its circulation. Neither were the paper's finances helped by family squabbles about political direction after Amaury's death. Finally, Hachette took a 50 per cent stake in the paper in 1983 and helped resolve the difficulties. Since then, sales have increased to 405,000 in 1989 and it has a target figure of half a million in 1991. The paper introduced colour in 1985 and dropped '*libéré*' from its title in 1986. Paradoxically, *Le Parisien* has become increasingly liberal since that date and tries now to be informative and balanced, although it is still a right-wing paper. It does not offer in-depth analysis but specializes in short, punchy reporting aimed at swift readability. It is abundantly illustrated, uses quite a lot of cartoons and graphics and has the sort of sporting, games and advice pages associated with the popular press. Over 75 per cent of its sales are in Paris, making it more like the regional daily paper of the area than the national daily it aspires to be. It is reasonably priced at 4.50 francs.

Le Monde

Arguably the best newspaper in the world, *Le Monde* impresses by the range and depth of its news coverage, by the brilliance of its foreign affairs columns and the intelligence of its approach to reliable and informed journalism. It achieved a circulation figure of 381,558 in 1988 from 110,000 in 1946 and 200,000 in 1957. It manages a high level of sales abroad (17.09 per cent compared with 3.68 per cent for *Le Figaro*). Its coverage of developments in the Soviet Union has been in a class of its own and the paper generally lives up to its name by providing insights into political realities which sometimes challenge the reader's grasp of geography. Regular exposure to the paper's concentrated text, until recently unadorned by any diverting photographs or graphics, would ensure a well-informed and comprehensive grasp of world political events. However, *Le Monde* with its '*belle écriture*' is an austere paper, not meant for the faint-hearted and swift readability is not one of its attributes.

Le Monde appears in the evening with the following day's date on it. It first appeared on 18 December 1944 and saw itself as the successor to the pre-war daily, *Le Temps* (1861–1942). Its founder and editor until 1969 was Hubert Beuve Méry who worked for *Le Temps* and had a distinguished record in the Resistance movement. Politically the paper is centre-left: in the 1950s it supported Mendès-France, questioned the return to power of de Gaulle and condemned torture in Algeria. In 1974 and 1981, the paper backed the Mitterrand presidential campaigns and it also celebrated the liberation of South Vietnam. The paper was widely read by young students during May 1968 and it maintains an enlightened and progressive line on matters relating to world famine, debt and conservation, thus guaranteeing it a continuing audience among educated youth. Its independence of judgement and depth of analysis often give its journalists considerable influence over economic and political affairs, causing displeasure to professional politicians on all sides. André Fontaine and Robert Guillain are very respected voices in the world of foreign affairs, whilst the likes of Pierre Drouin and Gilbert Mathieu have built up considerable reputations on the economic front.

Over the last ten years *Le Monde* has had to face the challenges of modernization, European-scale competition and of finding a replacement for Beuve Méry – editors are elected by the journalists themselves at *Le Monde*. The retirement of Jacques Fauvet in 1982 (Méry's successor) brought financial difficulties which the new editor, André Fontaine, had to address with his famous rescue package in 1985. This involved selling the paper's premises in the Rue des Italiens and a restructuring of its capital base with a novel organizational format and increased outside shareholdings. Its total market value is divided into 1,240 share parts distributed among the founders' group, the journalists' trust, a new readers' trust, a management trust and a white and blue collar workers' trust. *Le Monde entreprise*, set up in 1985 to promote the paper, is also a shareholder.

The paper has now put most of its difficulties behind it. It has a new headquarters in the Rue Falguière, a new modern printworks at Ivry and is fully equipped with new technology. It faces the future with considerable confidence, aiming to be the third strongest French daily after *Ouest-France* and *Le Figaro*. *Le Monde*, like *Le Figaro*, produces supplements: arts and entertainment (Thursday), books and ideas (Friday), radio and TV (Saturday). It also publishes a number of successful magazines entitled *Dossiers et documents*, and the monthlies, *Le Monde diplomatique*, *Le Monde de l'éducation*, *Le Monde des philatélistes*. There is also *Le Monde hebdomadaire*, a selection of articles designed for the overseas market, published in French and English.

France-Soir

Under the editorship of Pierre Lazareff, this was once France's strongest daily paper, achieving high circulation levels in the 1950s and 1960s. Its slogan, '*Faites comme tout le monde, lisez France-Soir*', underlined its aspiration to be a readable, somewhat dramatic popular daily. It is now part of the Hersant group but faces an uncertain future. Although one of Paris' big four dailies in terms of circulation (301,000 plus in 1988) its readership is declining and is currently below 3 million. The paper is also in deficit. Its political affiliations are still insistently conservative, although its political coverage has generally been reduced. It delights in eye-catching scoop headlines involving scandals, frauds or national disasters and, since 1988, it has appeared with front-page colour. It is now really a morning newspaper (there is some talk of changing its title to *France-Matin*). *France-Soir* appears to be losing a circulation battle with *Le Parisien* and *Libération* which are eclipsing it in the use of *faits divers*. It does have the advantage of swift readability and the latest estimate of average reading time is three minutes. *France-Soir* was founded after the Liberation in 1944 and was successor to the Resistance journal, *Défense de la France*.

Libération

Established in 1973 as a political left-wing daily, part successor to the Maoist *La Cause du peuple*, *Libération* was split by internal divisions in 1981 and ceased publication in February that year. It reappeared in May 1981, under the editorship of Serge July, with a much more moderate but basically left political stance. Its circulation then grew from 70,000 to 165,000 in 1986 and 180,000 in 1989. The paper is now a long way from its roots in 1968 student sensibility and from its preoccupation with left-wing intellectual and ideological issues. It has established itself as a quality paper with a serious and professional approach to analysis of political, cultural and international events. It maintains a degree of non-conformism and freshness in its reporting and its leader-writers are always interesting. It would appear to be slowly attracting students to its pages and is now challenging *Le Monde* for that audience. *Libération*, unlike the other left dailies – *Rouge*, *Le Quotidien du peuple* and *L'Humanité rouge* – which have all disappeared, lives to fight another day.

L'Humanité

Established by Jean Jaurès in 1904 as the paper of the SFIO, *L'Humanité* was the first French newspaper of the socialist movement and of the working class. It quickly established itself as a paper of working-class militancy and peace. Since 1920 it has been the organ of the PCF. Between 1939, when it was banned, and 1944, the paper operated clandestinely. It reached a peak circulation in 1946 with a readership of 400,000. Since then its circulation has declined regularly to a level of 109,000 in 1988, with 14 per cent of its sales abroad. Its annual losses are covered by receipts from the world famous *fête annuelle de l'Huma*. It has repeatedly embarked on modernization strategies to check falling sales. It became a tabloid in 1985 and acquired new headquarters in Saint-Denis in 1989. The paper is designed to arm party members all over France with the ideologies and political weapons which they need and to brief them on official party policy lines. Developments in the Soviet Union are putting severe pressure on its ideological perspectives and the future of the party itself is the subject of much recent debate. Always interesting and always doctrinaire, *L'Humanité* has given exceptional coverage to South Africa and to Nelson Mandela. Its cultural pages are among the best available in the daily press.

La Croix

This is the only other Paris daily paper with a circulation of over 100,000. *La Croix* is a Catholic evening paper founded in 1883. Its readers mainly pay by subscription (some 80 per cent) and four-fifths of them live in the provinces. It is the only national Catholic daily and is part of the leading religious press group, Bayard Presse. It enjoys a reputation for serious, reliable and concise journalism and has a discreet mission to promote Christian values. It has a good letters page and often pursues detailed debates on current political issues. It naturally also has a profound interest in matters of personal freedom concerning abortion and contraception, although it is arguably too close to the Vatican for modern French tastes. The paper's sales are declining and it is in deficit, subsidized by Bayard Presse's other more successful publications.

Le Quotidien de Paris

Born in 1974 with two-thirds of its editorial team former journalists on *Combat, Le Quotidien de Paris* is now a struggling anti-socialist paper with a small circulation of some 30,000. It has a lively, acerbic style but seems out of phase with France's political consensus at the moment. It enjoyed the period of *cohabitation* between Mitterrand and Chirac but its political ideology now looks decidedly bankrupt and the future of the paper is uncertain.

Other Parisian newspapers

The remaining Paris dailies are all specialist papers. *Présent* is an ultra right-wing, Catholic daily appearing five times a week. It operated until recently on a subscription-only basis but, under the slogan '*Dieu, famille, patrie*', it is beginning to appear in the newsagents. Its present circulation is about 8,000. *L'Equipe* is the leading sporting paper of France. It has an 87.57 per cent male readership and a circulation of some

230,000, 40 per cent of it in the Paris region. *Paris-Turf*, the racing daily, sells about 126,000 copies. The specialist economic dailies – *Les Echos*, '*le quotidien de l'économie*', founded in 1908, and *Le Temps de la finance*, founded 1981, have circulation figures of 103,000 and 57,000 respectively. No specialist economic paper in France yet matches the British *Financial Times* with its circulation of almost 300,000. The Pearson group, which owns the *Financial Times*, acquired *Les Echos* in 1988 and it will be interesting to chart its progress under new ownership.

The regional dailies

The regional daily papers of France are generally prosperous and much stronger than their Parisian equivalents. Modernization programmes have advanced quite swiftly and the whole regional industry has a certain all-pervasive dynamism. Until 1939 when, with a combined copy total of 6 million, it equalled the production of the Parisian press, the regional press was treated with some contempt and as inferior level journalism by the French intelligentsia. The regional press now accounts for some 70 per cent of the market in dailies, where its supremacy is unchallengeable. Since 1976 it is the regional daily, *Ouest-France*, which is France's best-selling daily paper (it toppled *France-Soir*). Most of the regional dailies have different editions according to their distribution zones, and at present the regional dailies generate some 400 different editions in about 250 different localities. In 1914, there were 242 regional dailies, in 1946, 175 and in 1991 just sixty-five, nineteen with sales averaging over 110,000. Capital concentration is likely to lead to the loss of further titles, whilst competition from the growing numbers of free papers (392 in 1988, with a combined run of 15,000 million annually) in the advertising market is likely to have its financial effect.

The great strength of the regional dailies is, of course, their local news component which takes up some 50 per cent of their space. French people read their local papers seriously and with greater commitment and continuity than the national ones. The regional dailies in general tend to avoid precise political affiliations, even during election periods. They try to balance their coverage of the different political groupings or attempt to avoid politicizing issues altogether. Where a paper has a monopoly or quasi-monopoly, political neutrality is seen as essential to secure the continuing loyalty of all readers.

Space does not allow for detailed examination of all the regional dailies but a synoptic view of the principal ones in each region follows. The geographical areas listed take into account the spheres of influence of the various papers.

Northern region (Pas de Calais, Somme, Aisne, Oise Nord)
With five dailies, *La Voix du nord, Nord-Eclair, Nord matin, Liberté* and *Nord littoral*, the Pas de Calais area can boast a certain pluralism. However, *La Voix du nord* (375,000 copies) is in a crushing position of domination and could eventually achieve monopoly status. It is one of the best-selling French daily papers. Politically of moderate right-wing persuasion, the paper also gives good space to rival parties. Its Saturday editions consist of plentiful advertising and minimum editorial content. It has weak rivals in the Hersant based *Nord matin* (a socialist paper with a declining circulation of 77,000) and *Nord-Eclair* (100,000) a paper selling in both France and Belgium and having the best home-delivery service of any French newspaper. *Liberté* (56,000) is the declining regional daily of the PCF; *Nord littoral* (11,000) sells in the Calais area but was taken over by *La Voix du nord* in 1986.

Normandy (Manche, Calvados, Orne, Eure)
Paris-Normandie (19,000), established in 1944 and now part of the Hersant group, runs twelve different editions from its base in Rouen. Some of its pages are the same as other regional dailies from the Hersant group in the area such as the politically moderate *Le Havre presse* (18,000) and the left-inclined *Le Havre libre* (26,000). *La Presse de la Manche* (28,000), now controlled by *Ouest-France*, operated in Cherbourg and *L'Echo républicain* (34,000), 40 per cent owned by Hachette, in Chartres. The circulation of the regional dailies in this area is depressed by a very strong and flourishing weekly press involving some thirty titles.

Brittany

This is the home of the Rennes based *Ouest-France*, sometimes described as '*le plus impressionnant menhir de la presse quotidienne française*'. It was founded in 1944 and, since 1975, is France's leading daily with a circulation of some 765,000 in 1989. It produces forty local editions. It has quite strong sections on farming and fishing and fairly lengthy sports pages. Political news is concisely and responsibly presented. The paper is the successor to the 1899 Catholic paper, *L'Ouest-Éclair*, launched at the time of the Dreyfus appeal hearing. *Ouest-France* does not have a monopoly. The Morlaix based *Le Télégramme de Brest et de l'Ouest* (181,000) is dominant in le Finistère and is an independent paper, which used to be radical socialist but is now politically anodyne; *Liberté du Morbihan* (91,000, Hersant) operates in Lorient, whilst *Presse océan* (80,000) and *L'Eclair* (17,000), both owned by Hersant, share the market in Nantes.

Eastern region (Alsace-Lorraine)

The regional dailies are all bilingual and benefit from a very well-developed home delivery service, although their circulation is declining. They appear on Sundays but not Mondays and have very extensive coverage of economic matters. *L'Alsace* (124,000) is a bulky forty to forty-eight page paper with a good strong team of journalists. It has operated since 1944 and has a high level of penetration in a restricted area (some 70 per cent of households). *Dernières nouvelles d'Alsace* (237,771) is part of the Hachette group and dominates in the Haut and Bas Rhin with some twenty-eight editions. This is a good quality daily enjoying a peace treaty with *L'Alsace*. The Catholic daily, *Le Nouvel Alsacien*, collapsed in 1988. *L'Est républicain* (280,000) produces a Sunday edition wih a very high level of sales (360,000). Its regional news coverage is excellent but its national reporting is sketchy. It competes in Lorraine with the Metz based *Le Républicain lorrain* (194,000) which partly owns it.

The other dailies in the region are: *La Liberté de l'Est* (35,000) which produces four editions, appears every day of the week and is firmly on the left; *L'Est éclair* (35,000), based in Troyes and increasing its sales; *La Haute-Marne Libéré* (14,000) operates on a subscription basis (72 per cent) and has its own radio station; *Libération Champagne* (15,300) is a socialist paper; *L'Union* (113,000), part of the Hersant group since 1988, is dominant in Champagne; *L'Ardennais* (28,000), originally a socialist paper, now politically neutral if not neutered.

South west

In Aquitaine, the Sud-Ouest group virtually has a monopoly in the five departments. As well as producing the Bordeaux based *Sud-Ouest* (367,000), the third strongest of the regional dailies, the group controls the radical socialist *La Charente libre* (45,000), the Périgueux daily *La Dordogne libre* (4,820), *Sud-Ouest la France* (50,000) and *La République des Pyrénées* (35,000). *Sud-Ouest* itself averages about thirty pages with little or no colour. It is clearly written and very readable. It has twenty local editions and also produces the *Dossiers du quotidien*, special numbers treating in detail regional issues such as the tourist industry of Aquitaine.

Midi, Pyrénées, Languedoc

Two dailies compete for readers – the radical and dominant *La Dépêche du Midi* (277, 955) based in Toulouse and the now free paper, *Le Journal de Toulouse* (36,000). *La Dépêche* specializes in sharply focused interventions into local political debates and has a loyal readership because of this. The paper has a controlling interest in *La Nouvelle République des Pyrénées* (17,000) and a 40 per cent stake in *Le Petit Bleu de l'Agenais* (13,000). The popular *Midi-Libre* (207,508) dominates the five departments of Languedoc-Rousillon, although it faces competition nowadays from *Nîmes-Matin* (110,000), launched in 1989 by Hachette as a centre-right daily. *Midi-Libre* also now owns *L'Indépendant* (84,625), one of the closest French regional papers founded in Perpignan in 1846.

South east

The Marseille-based papers dominate in the Alpes de Haute-Provence, Vaucluse and Var. *Le Provençal* (171,000) is the paper previously owned by the socialist, Gaston Deferre, who died in 1986. It is now part of the Hachette group and is a long way from its political roots. The paper produces an evening edition, *Le Soir* (14,000) and a satellite *Var matin* (85,000) in

Toulon. *La Marseillaise* (45,000), the most important of the three PCF regional dailies, appears to be declining both in circulation and in terms of its share of the advertising market. *Le Méridional-La France* (68,000) is the voice of the right in the region. *Nice-Matin* (265,000) is in the dominant position in the Alpes Maritimes. This is a quality paper with a sound financial base and a staunchly conservative stand. Lack of competition is making the paper slightly colourless in approach. *Vaucluse-Matin* (15,000), part of the Hersant group of *Le Dauphiné libéré*, also now runs three editions in this area.

Rhône-Alpes
This area provided the battleground for a well-documented struggle in 1979 between the Hersant-owned *Le Dauphiné libéré* and *Le Progrès de Lyon*. Both papers are now under the control of Hersant. *Le Dauphiné libéré* (294,000) has a monopoly in Grenoble, *Le Progrès* (304,000) dominates in the Rhône and in the Ain. *Le Progrès* is now really a press group in itself: it controls the daily *L'Espoir* and several weeklies, giving Hersant a powerful position in the Lyon area and reawakening governmental fears of press monopolies. *Lyon libération* (12,000) is the Lyon edition of *Libération*, created in 1986 to rival *Lyon Figaro* (20,000) created a week earlier by Hersant.

Le Massif Central
The Limoges-based *Le Populaire du Centre* (61,514) was launched by the Socialist Party in 1905. It is now part of the Groupe Centre-France, which owns *La Montagne* (285,000), based in Clermont-Ferrand and one of France's oldest regional dailies dating from 1919. *La Montagne* was fiercely anti-Vichy and is proud of its history. The group also produces in Nevers *Le Journal du centre* (37,000) and the Bourges-based *Le Berry républicain* (37,000). Hersant is represented in the region by *Centre presse* (24,000), which has a monopoly in Poitiers. *L'Echo du Centre* (25,000) is the PCF daily for the Limousin. *L'Eveil de la Haute-Loire* (15,000) is the daily of the Puy-de-Dôme.

Val-de-Loire
La République du Centre (60,000), the daily paper of Orléans, remains famous for being the only paper in the world to have

published colour photographs of man's first steps on the moon in June 1989. It has centre-right leanings nowadays, although its founder, Roger Secrétain, was part of the liberal left. *La République* has to compete with the dominant *La Nouvelle République* (296,000). This paper, created in clandestinity in 1944, is dynamic and growing. It has a virtual monopoly in the Touraine. The staff own 35 per cent of the shares of the paper which is very prosperous. *Le Courrier de l'Ouest* (108,423), part of the Amaury group, dominates Maine et Loire from Anger. It publishes seven editions and also controls Radio Anger 101. *La Maine libre* (56,000) is also part of the Amaury group and sells principally in the Sarthe.

Burgundy-Franche Comté

Two daily papers compete for readership in the Côte d'Or: *Bien public* (founded in 1868: 58,797) is 42 per cent owned by the Luxembourg TV company RTL and is very much the mouthpiece of the UDF and the RPR; and *Les Dépêches du Centre-Est* (25,100), a daily of the centre-left. *Le Courrier de Saone-et-Loire* (81,000) is now partly associated with the Hersant group although not owned by it, and operates in that area. *L'Yonne républicaine* (45,228) has a departmental monopoly in Auxerre. It is a left-wing paper with a mainly conservative readership. It contains good coverage of the local political scene, usually giving a lot of space to prominent political activists and notables of all persuasions.

The periodical press

The periodical press in France is much more extensive and important than in other parts of Europe and is the most dynamic and flourishing sector of the press industry, producing a vast and varied range of titles. It is also the sector most open to change and innovation and, as a consequence of this, it is quite impossible to pin down and classify its protean activities. In 1990, weeklies accounted for twelve out of the twenty best-selling press publications in France and also provided the top four best-sellers. Of the remaining twenty, seven were monthly or fortnightly publications. Furthermore the periodical press now accounts for 60 per cent of the industry's turnover and 54.4 per cent of total circulation.

One of the reasons usually given to explain the vigour of the periodical press is the absence in France of anything remotely resembling the English Sunday papers. This would certainly account for the success there of publications with the news magazine format such as *L'Express* and *Le Nouvel Observateur*, modelled on the American publication *Time*. There also seems to be a view in France that a weekly or fortnightly news magazine allows for a more mature and considered assimilation of events than the hustle and bustle of the daily paper. There may thus be a certain intellectual snobbery surrounding the periodical press when it comes to news coverage.

France now possesses over three hundred regional weekly papers and twenty-seven monthlies. Although this figure is a far cry from the several thousand titles recorded in 1914, or even the 900 listed for 1939, it is still a large number. Just twenty-two of these regional weeklies appear on a Sunday but the combined total number of copies printed, even including the Parisian Sunday papers, amounts to only 4 million. Thus, whatever else the French may do on a Sunday, they do not appear to spend much of it reading newspapers.

Weeklies dealing with general news coverage
The Sunday press in France is represented by *Le Journal du Dimanche*: founded in 1944, the paper was originally conceived as the Sunday edition of *France-Soir*. When *France-Soir* was sold to the Hersant group in 1977, the *Journal du Dimanche* remained with Hachette. It has a circulation of over 300,000 and tries to combine a degree of serious reporting with the general characteristics of the popular press – eye-catching headlines, details from the glamorous world of show business, lots of photographs and so forth. In a certain sense it enjoys a virtual monopoly for its only rivals are *L'Humanité-Dimanche* (200,000 copies printed in 1990 but no circulation figures are available) and the sensationalist *France-Dimanche*, a kind of French equivalent to the *Sunday Sport*, but far less offensive. *France-Dimanche* is famous for its bizarre and extravagant headlines about the British Royal Family (among other things), and has a special place in the hearts and minds of the French. It sells about 655,000 copies and is sixteenth in the list of the twenty best-selling press productions in France, outselling all the

dailies apart from *Ouest-France* and all the weekly news magazines apart from *Paris-Match*. It was founded after the Second World War with a mission to cheer up the French after the terrible experience of the Occupation. It has a rival in another sensationalist weekly, *Ici-Paris*, (600,000) which appears on a weekday and specializes in the private lives of film stars.

The main news magazines

Modelled on the American publication, *Time*, France now boasts four weekly news magazines (1984 witnessed the death of both the right-wing *Magazine hebdo* and the left-wing *Nouvelles*). The first weekly to adopt the *Time* format was *L'Express* in 1964. Created in 1953 by Jean Jacques Servan-Schreiber and Françoise Giroud, *L'Express* supported the socialist, Mendès-France, in the early days and took a vigorous anti-colonialist line during the Algerian war. It abandoned its crusading style in 1964 and appeared in its new format, claiming to be a news magazine aiming at an objectivity which quickly revealed itself to be Gaullist (it was then that Jean Daniel left it to establish *Le Nouvel Observateur*). In 1989 it sold 579,858 copies per week making it the leading informational weekly (over 70 per cent of its sales are by subscription). In 1977–8, Servan Schreiber yielded control of the magazine to James Goldsmith who swung the magazine behind Chirac. Goldsmith departed in 1988 and this has not disadvantaged the publication one bit. *Le Point* (319,659) is also on the right and was itself a breakaway formation from *L'Express* in 1972. Originally financed by Hachette, it now belongs to the Société Gaumont. It specializes in easy-to-read, sensible journalism and is attractively laid out. It has actually been a successful publication, although its circulation has been static since 1985. *Le Nouvel Observateur* (403,028) – originally *France Observateur*, founded in 1950 as a voice of the non-communist left, *Le Nouvel Observateur* was launched in 1964 by a breakaway group from *L'Express* as a left news magazine, when the original publication was virtually bankrupt. The renewed strength of the Socialist Party helped the magazine's sales to climb from 340,000 in 1976 to 385,000 in 1981, and after a brief lapse in 1985, its circulation figures are still increasing. This is the news magazine of the intellectual left and was even Jean-Paul Sartre's favourite weekly. It is a substantial magazine and much harder to read than *L'Express* or *Le Point*. It lost its editor, Giesbert, to *Le Figaro* in 1988. The publication is sometimes accused of radical chic and even of left snobbery but, politically, it is tougher and more stimulating than the *New Statesman* to which it is sometimes compared. *L'Evénement du jeudi* (179,762) – since 1991 simply called *l'Evénement* – was founded in 1984 and readership shareholdings constituted a novel part of its launch capital. Its editor, Jean-François Khan, used to write for *Nouvelles littéraires* and wanted to create a high-quality weekly with a progressive approach. It contains excellent sections on literature and culture and its editor writes equally illuminatingly on domestic and international political issues. It is not as infested with advertising as *Le Point* and its sales are increasing, despite its high cost of 20 francs.

Other important weeklies covering current events
Paris-Match, established in 1949 and reaching its zenith in 1960 with a circulation of 1.5 million, is no longer commanding the attention of its readership despite repeated efforts to renew its appeal. It has, however, recovered from the dip to 58,000 in 1975 and sold 875,392 copies in 1989. Recently the magazine has done some excellent photo reportages on events in Iran and Haiti. Its coverage of events, in general, is vivid but a bit sensationalist although invariably claiming to be revelatory. It has the usual panoply of headings of general interest – arts, television, health, diet, problems. Its crosswords have a popular appeal. *Paris-Match*'s readership is slowly being taken over by the growing world of TV magazines. *VSD* (*Vendredi-Samedi-Dimanche*) is also suffering from declining sales: 266,000 in 1989 after a peak in 1986 of 335,000. *VSD* no longer practises the dramatic photojournalism of its earlier years and concentrates now on the lives of the famous, particularly TV personalities and high media profile politicians.

Mention should also be made of the weeklies produced by the political parties, although their circulation rates are generally below 30,000. *National hebdo*, established in 1980, is the organ of the *Front national* and, since 1988, has been available in the kiosks. *La Lettre de la nation* (RPR), *Vendredi* (PS), *Révolution* (PCF) are of interest to the party faithful. *La Vie ouvrière* (1909) is produced by the CGT and provides a weekly insight into the world of trade unionism. Also in this category are a wide range of weeklies from a number of religious groupings, including *Tribune juive, La France catholique* and *Témoignage chrétien*. *Pèlerin-Magazine*, with an estimated readership of 640,000 in 1988 and a lifeline stretching back to 1916, is the dominant Catholic weekly. Seventy-five per cent of its readers are practising Catholics. It is often compared unfavourably to *La Vie*, another Catholic weekly edited by Georges Hourdin. *La Vie* has 280,000 subscriptions and gives a serious account of weekly news items from a Catholic viewpoint.

The satirical press is still championed by the distinguished weekly, *Le Canard enchaîné*. Established in 1916 as *Le Canard déchaîné* by Maurice Maréchal, *Le Canard* was originally intended to be a French news-sheet with a mission to de-mystify, for the common soldier, official government propaganda about the First War. It is now something of a French institution and has never actually been banned by the government for all its satirical verve and impertinence. It is run as a co-operative, refuses advertizing and has as its slogan '*La liberté de la presse ne s'use que si l'on ne s'en sert pas.*' *Le Canard* combines serious investigative polemical journalism with bald and sometimes strained humour about the shortcomings of governments and politicians of all parties. Its language is full of puns and gnomic references which are not that easy to decode for the non-native. It is financially successful and sold 423,100 in 1988. *Le Canard* also produces quarterly *dossiers* which often sell spectacularly well: for example, the one on Giscard and the diamonds sold 337,100 copies.

Minute (established 1962) tries to satirize the French right but from an ultra-right perspective. Ferociously anti-Gaullist in its early days, its closest political ally nowadays is Le Pen. It faces competition from the *Front national*'s own paper, *National hebdo*. Both papers attack what they consider to be the complacency of the parliamentary right on matters of race and immigration. Both favour the restoration of the death sentence. The left counterbalance to these weeklies is *L'Idiot international*. Originally sponsored by Sartre and de Beauvoir in the early 1970s, the paper, named after Dostoevsky's Muichkine, was relaunched in 1988 to be '*informé, indépendant, talentueux, insolent, digne et drôle*'. It often gets taken to court for libel when its outraged innocence gets out of control.

Televison and radio weeklies

This is a readily expanding and flourishing part of the press industry. *Télé 7 jours*, owned by Hachette, is France's best-selling paper, with a circulation of over 3 million. *Télépoche* (Editions Mondiales) takes third place with 1.7 million, *Télé-Star*, fifth place with just under 1.7 million, *Télé-Loisirs*, seventh place with 1,138,520 and *Télé Z*, tenth place with 949,414. In all, there are some nineteen titles in this section with a huge combined circulation of 11.7 million copies per week. This market appears to appeal to everyone.

Women's weeklies

At the last count, some thirteen women's weeklies were in circulation, together with thirty monthly and twelve bimonthly magazines. Their combined annual sales topped 437.4 million. This is another significant area of growth in the periodical press and is naturally the target of much of the advertising market. Second only to *Télé 7 jours* in the national list is *Femme actuelle* with a circulation of 1,915,306. Prisma-owned *Femme actuelle*, like its British and Spanish counterparts *Best* and *Mía*, aims to be both popular and practical. It easily outsells *Madame Figaro* (649,827), *Nous deux* (613,126), *Maxi* (581,416), *Femmes d'aujourd'hui* (417,000), the Hachette-based *Elle* (380,616) and *Intimité* (316,998). Several other women's weeklies sell over 200,000 copies, such as *Voici, Bonne soirée* and *Jours de France*. The dynamism of these weeklies is all the more remarkable given the strength of the women's monthlies, like *Prima* (fifth best-selling press publication throughout the whole of France with a circulation of 1.25 million), *Bonne heure* (1.1 million), *Modes et travaux* (1.07 million), *Marie Claire* (604,000), *Marie France* (316,000) and *Cosmopolitan* (297,000).

The economic and financial press

This sector is less thriving than the British and Italian equivalents. The French, traditionally, have suffered from an underdeveloped financial culture and it is certainly significant that the strongest group in this field, the Groupe des Echos, is owned by the English group, Pearson, whilst the American group, Dow Jones, is responsible for the *Tribune de l'expansion* (see earlier section on the dailies). Now that the dailies are producing their own economic supplements, many analysts are predicting a degree of growth in this market, although it is doubtful that France will ever produce anything like *Business Week*. The most important weeklies are: *La Vie française* (established 1945, circulation 110,000), *Investir* (1974, 106,000), *Le Nouvel Economiste* (1975, 92,000), and *Business bourse* (1987, 40,000). The more notable financial monthlies include: *Le Revenu français* (1968, 171,000); *Science et Vie économie* (1984, 123,000) and *Dynasteurs* (1986, 100,000). The bimonthly *Expansion* was established in 1967 and averages 195,000 copies an issue. Despite predictions that the 1987 '*krach*' would impede the development of the financial press, it is continuing to grow and 1992 could accelerate the process. Europeanization of the press is likely to occur more swiftly in this key sector of the industry, especially if we move to a single currency.

The arts

This is an area where profound changes have occurred over the last twenty-five years. *Arts lettres et spectacles* disappeared as a separate paper in 1967; *Le Figaro littéraire* was withdrawn in 1971, *Les Lettres françaises* in 1972, *Nouvelles littéraires* in 1984. As a consequence of this the dailies have strengthened their arts coverage. The Monday edition of *Le Figaro* now houses a literary supplement; the Wednesday edition of *Le Quotidien de Paris* contains *Le Quotidien des lettres*; the Thursday editions of *Libération* and *Le Monde* include '*Cahiers livres*' and '*Le Monde des idées*' (previously '*Le Monde des livres*') respectively. The best-selling publication in this section is now the monthly magazine *Lire* (part of the *Express* group with a circulation of 150,000). Directed by Bernard Pivot, the magazine publishes, in its '*morceaux choisis*', extracts from recently published literary works and a useful guide to new works, listed under different headings. The '*Carnets de Pivot*' are read with interest, as is the section '*Actualités*', where authors in the news and new books are discussed. *Lire* outstrips in circulation, but not in quality, the thirty-page *La Quinzaine littéraire* (1966, 40,000) which is part of French literary life. The monthly *Magazine littéraire* (80,000) seems to compete with the highly acclaimed television programme *Apostrophes*. The cinema world is covered by: *Cahiers du cinéma* (1951, 34,000), *La Revue du cinéma* (1951, 48,000) and *Positif* (1952, 20,000). More like books than periodicals, France also has its '*grandes revues*'. With a specialist readership and in competition with the wider circulating monthlies, these publications face an uphill struggle. The most important ones are *La Nouvelle Revue des deux mondes*, *La Nouvelle Revue française*, *Esprit*, *Les Temps modernes*, *Etudes* and *Europe*.

To conclude our survey, mention should also be made of some of the other developing sections of this buoyant periodical press market. These include a thriving sports sector, a widely read '*presse du cœur*', the professional and technical press, a varied youth and children's section and the substantial area usually called '*la presse administrative*' (official publications, including the redoubtable *Journal officiel de la république*).

General conclusion

The strengths and weaknesses of the French press revealed by this survey and by the economic and industrial profile, make it difficult to assess with confidence how the fourth estate will respond to the future challenges of the Single European Act and to the advancing pawns of rival European enterprises on a grander scale. It is generally assumed that less state support will probably be made available in the very near future as part of an ideological shift away from interventionist economics in the EC (it is by no means certain that things will continue along non-interventionist lines for a long period). It is doubtful that the phasing out of such subsidies will prohibit the regulation of the whole media industry by a government anxious to protect pluralism within and across each media grouping. Newspapers will have to compete for the loyalty of their readers and their advertizers in an increasingly competitive and diversified media environment which will transcend national boundaries. The dailies, in particular, will have to fight vigorously to check the erosion of their readership and to avoid further casualties. The 1990s will provide a very testing arena for the French press industry.

Bibliography

Albert, P., *La Presse française*. Paris, La Documentation française, 1990.
—*La Presse*. Paris, PUF, 1991.
—*Lexique de la presse écrite*. Paris, Dalloz, 1989.
—*Histoire de la presse*. Paris, PUF, 1970.
Bellanger, C. (ed.), *Histoire générale de la presse française*. 5 vols. Paris, PUF, 1969–76.
Bonvoisin, S. M., and Maignien, M., *La Presse féminine*. Paris, PUF, 1986.
Cayrol, R., *Les Médias – presse écrite, radio, télévision*. Paris, PUF, 1991.
Charon, J. M., *La Presse en France de 1945 à nos jours*. Paris, Seuil, 1991.
—*L'Etat des médias*. Sous la direction de J. M. Charon. Paris, La Découverte (Médiapouvoirs), CFPJ, 1991.
Guéry, L., *Quotidien régional, mon journal*. Paris, CFPJ, 1987.
—*Guide de la presse 1990*. Paris, Office universitaire de presse, 1990.
Guillauma, Y., *La Presse en France*. Paris, La Découverte, 1990.
—*Histoire et médias – journalisme et journalistes français*. Sous la direction de Marc Martin. Paris, Albin Michel, 1991.
—*Média-Sid*. Paris, La Documentation française, 1974–.
Mermet, G., *Francoscopie 1991*. Paris, Larousse, 1990.
Terrou, F., *Annuaire statistique*. Paris, Unesco, 1981–.
Todorov, P., *La Presse française à l'heure de l'Europe*. Paris, La Documentation française, 1990.

Fuller bibliographies are included in Albert, *La Presse française* and Cayrol, *Les Médias*.

9 The Broadcasting media
Geoffrey Hare

Introduction

The recent use of the term *'le PAF'* (*'le paysage audiovisuel français'*) for 'the media' suggests the French situate broadcasting within a broader concept of audiovisual communication than that commonly understood in the UK. The French have indeed sought to combine reform of broadcasting with technological modernization. The 1980s in particular saw wholesale changes in French broadcasting: an enormous increase in the number of radio and television stations and the birth of independent broadcasting, independent both in the sense of relative freedom from government interference and in terms of the creation, for the first time, of a privately owned and financed sector. A combination of ideological and political change inside France, technological developments, and economic pressures (all of these forcing a European dimension onto public and private sector decision-making), have transformed the traditional system of a tightly government-controlled national monopoly into a more open, deregulated, market-oriented system.

Whereas at the beginning of the 1980s there were only three television channels, all in the state sector, and the few pirate radios challenging the state monopoly were being jammed and pursued through the courts, in the early 1990s there exist six national terrestrial or off-air television channels, a handful of French direct broadcast satellite stations (not to mention various European-wide satellite stations), over a hundred city cable networks offering additionally a wide range of European stations, and a small but growing number of local television stations.

As for radio, the cosy competition of a handful of national stations run by Radio-France and the French-language commercial stations broadcasting from across the eastern and southern frontiers, has been rudely disturbed by an explosion of some 1,800 independent local and nationally networked FM stations.

In addition to this multiplication of the supply of media outlets, the other major change has been that the traditional hegemony of the state sector has been shattered during the 1980s, leaving the market open to private enterprise, and France's biggest names in industry and finance have not been slow to invest. The independent television companies, now in the majority, were, in 1991, part owned by, among others, Bouygues (the leading company in the construction industry), the publisher Hachette, the newspaper magnate Robert Hersant, Jérôme Seydoux's *Chargeurs* group (owner of *Pathé Cinéma*), the major food group *Générale occidentale*, the public utilities companies *Compagnie générale des eaux* and *Compagnie Lyonnaise des Eaux-Dumez*, the banking groups Paribas and *Compagnie Indo-Suez*, and the advertising agency Havas, not forgetting foreign media interests such as the companies of Robert Maxwell and Silvio Berlusconi, and the CLT (*Compagnie luxembourgeoise de télédiffusion*). There are, however, limits on monopoly ownership of national stations, making ownership alliances necessary. This explosion of *libéralisme* was, paradoxically, triggered by the socialist governments of 1981–6. The right-wing Chirac government of 1986–8 increased media deregulation, which the post-1988 socialist governments have not gone back on.

State investment in new technologies, whether cable, satellite, high-definition television or videotex (*le Minitel*), has been nonetheless massive. However, changes of political direction, conflicts between economic and cultural objectives, and a reining-in of the over-ambitious plans of the early 1980s have prevented the hoped-for comprehensive integrated planning of national communications. Satellite and cable television, for example, have each been pursued at different times at the expense of the other, and to the detriment of both.

In the early 1990s a political consensus about the new balance between public and private sector broadcasting seemed to have been achieved, as much through exhaustion in the face of such rapid and often unco-ordinated reforms as through real agreement. However, this consensus may prove precarious if, despite the amount of public and private money poured into broadcasting, the quality and range of choice of programmes does not continue the improvement which viewers had perceived during the 1980s. A 1989 *sondage* summed up French views of their television as: '*en progrès, mais peut mieux faire . . .*'.

Regulation and the politics of broadcasting

The frequency of changes to the statutes and regulatory framework of the French broadcasting system (seven major reforms since 1959) shows how much radio and television have been a political football and how the broadcasters have not enjoyed a consensus in public opinion about their position within French society and institutions. Most governments since the War, believing firmly in the power of the media to influence the electorate, have aimed to manipulate the broadcasters, accepting, like President de Gaulle, himself a past master at communicating through television, that the written press was beyond their control. His successor, President Pompidou, even went so far as to say that broadcasters could not be as independent as newspaper journalists, and should never forget they were '*la voix de la France*'. However, after the election of François Mitterrand as President in 1981, the various forms of direct state control of radio and television gave way to a system overseen by a broadcasting regulatory body, *la Haute autorité*. The existence of this buffer organization designed, according to the socialists, to 'cut the umbilical cord' between government and the media, has not prevented

Mitterrand and his ministers from putting heavy political pressure on the regulators at different times.

The state monopoly of broadcasting dated from decrees by the Vichy government in 1941 and 1942. From 1944 to 1949 *Radiodiffusion française* and from 1949 to 1959 *Radiotélévision française* (RTF) were as much an arm of government as was the Department of Posts and Telecommunications. RTF's status as part of the civil service changed in 1959 as it became an autonomous public body with its own budget, but still under the authority of the Minister of Information. The huge sway exercised by government over the broadcasters, with rumours of direct telephone lines between them, is illustrated by the appearance of Minister Alain Peyrefitte one evening in the mid-1960s on the television news to announce how he, the Minister, had decided that the format of the TV news programmes and the approach of the news broadcasters were going to be modified. In the 1960s television was sarcastically referred to as '*le gouvernement dans la salle-à-manger*'. Successive changes of statute, while giving the appearance of distancing broadcasters from government, did not have significant effects on the subservience of hand-picked media managers and presenters, nor did they break the habit of the Directors of News and Current Affairs being changed as governments came and went. In 1964 the RTF became the ORTF, managed by a Director General responsible to a Board of Directors, but still under the 'tutelage' of the Minister.

The *événements* of May 1968 shook the state broadcasting system, with many broadcasters joining the strikes against their masters in the *Maison de l'ORTF* and its stifling bureaucracy, as much as against the Gaullist regime, but their protest ended in dismissal for the ring-leaders. A brief interlude of more liberal treatment by the Chaban-Delmas government (1969–72) was followed by another crackdown, and further changes by President Giscard d'Estaing in 1974–5, involving the splitting up of the constituent parts of the ORTF into three service bodies (SFP for production, TDF for transmission, and INA for conservation) and four programming networks (three television channels and Radio-France). Government retained political control of broadcasting budgets and appointments to key posts, so that a form of self-censorship generally ensured compliant news coverage, even of such potential scandals as President Giscard's evasiveness over a personal gift of diamonds from the African dictator Bokassa in the late 1970s. There were great hopes for a more independent system of broadcasting when Mitterrand and the socialists came to power in 1981. They had consistently criticized their predecessors for the confiscation of freedoms, especially freedom of expression through the broadcasting media. The most important innovations in their 1982 reforms were (a) the creation of a broadcasting regulatory body, independent of government, the *Haute autorité de la Communication audiovisuelle*, and (b) the end of the state monopoly of the air-waves ('*la communication audiovisuelle est libre*'), thus opening up the possibility of commercial broadcasting.

The buffer institution proved less independent than promised: government opted, controversially, for retaining political control of the system of appointment of the nine members of the *Haute autorité*: three being nominated by the President of the Republic (Mitterrand), three by the president of the National Assembly (inevitably a government supporter), and three by the president of the Senate (in the 1980s a right-winger). The length of mandate, nine years and irrevocable, which in principle gave its members great independence, would also conveniently prolong the influence of the initial nominees beyond the five-year term of the National Assembly and the seven-year term of the presidency. Government also retained control of budgets, and made decisions on cable, satellite and new channels. Although the *Haute autorité*'s first president, Michèle Cotta, a former radio and television journalist, worked hard to establish the independence of the body, it was undermined by various events: the government's refusal in 1984 to back its request for judicial sanctions against commercial radio's violation of agreed transmission norms and of the ban on paid advertising; and the appointment of Mitterrand's favoured candidate, Jean-Claude Héberlé, as head of the second channel in 1985, in preference to other well-qualified applicants. A further erosion of its authority was the political decision to set up two new commercial television channels and the award of the franchises simply by presidential diktat in 1986, one to a known supporter of the

Socialist Party, Jérôme Seydoux (in alliance with the Italian, Berlusconi).

The suspicion of lack of independence in the institutions created by the socialists merely served to justify the dismantling of the 1982 reforms by the Chirac government in 1986. Claiming too that the freeing of the air-waves from state regulation had not gone far enough, they privatized television's first channel, TF1. Their reform created a new regulatory body, the CNCL (*Conseil national de la Communication et des libertés*), with greater powers to police its decisions, but whose thirteen-strong membership was predominantly and obviously politically right-wing, a feature which discredited it with public opinion. Government pressure led the CNCL to revoke the contracts awarded by the socialists to the franchise holders of the two new commercial Television channels, and it was widely seen as no coincidence that the CNCL chose government sympathizers as the new directors of the television channels and as holders of the franchises for the commercial channels, in particular the right-wing press baron, Robert Hersant. Finally, as part of their wider view of the media, the CNCL's regulatory powers were extended beyond broadcasting to include the telecommunications sector.

It was no surprise, of course, that in such a climate of politicization of broadcasting, the new socialist government of 1988 should decide to embark on another new media reform (*la loi du 17 janvier 1989*), transforming the regulatory body, its membership and its powers yet again. Now called the CSA (*Conseil supérieur de l'audiovisuel*), it is composed of nine members, nominated for six years by the same method as used for the *Haute autorité*. Its responsibilities include appointing (and sacking) the directors of the public service broadcasting channels, advising government on the *cahiers des charges* (the contractual obligations of the broadcasting franchise holders in both the public and private sectors), overseeing respect of these contracts (e.g. in terms of pluralism and fairness of political expression, of quotas of foreign programmes, of standards of public decency, etc.), attributing commercial radio and TV franchises, licensing cable networks, and applying the advertising code of practice. The CSA has powers of sanction through fines and suspension of franchises.

While the continued existence of the regulatory authority does give greater independence from government in the day-to-day running of the broadcasting media and, seen in the longer-term perspective, there has been a gradual freeing of broadcasting and greater professionalization, the temptation to interfere in broadcasting affairs remains part of French political culture. In 1989 the CSA had the courage, or temerity, to appoint, as head of the public service TV channels, a candidate who was reputedly not the government's favourite, François Guilhaume, who was subsequently systematically undermined by the Ministry for Culture and Communications, for example, in terms of budgetary allocations, until he resigned in 1991. Thereupon the CSA appointed Hervé Bourges, seemingly more acceptable to government. The French media are now run by broadcasting professionals rather than by politicians or civil servants, but government still manages one way or another to influence key appointments so that the professionals are ideologically sympathetic. Interference or self-censorship in programme-making may not be as rife as in the 1960s, but a major television retrospective of ten years of Mitterrand's presidency screened in 1991 could blithely ignore the embarrassing Greenpeace affair. The climate has nonetheless changed: there is no going back on the existence of a broadcasting regulatory body, whose powers have furthermore increased with each reform, and the idea has been definitely established that a buffer authority has to exist between government and the media and that ministers are not solely responsible for decision-making on behalf of the state. The next step may be to enshrine the existence of the broadcasting authority within the constitution.

With a new regulatory body in place, what sort of regulation was considered necessary as commercial competition intensified? Controlled deregulation was the watchword at first, but controls on licensing, on quotas, and on advertising were gradually relaxed through the 1980s, as technological change and internationalization of markets eroded government's capacity to regulate in national terms (as will be seen).

Radio networks

Chronologically, the first beneficiary of the freeing of the air-waves was radio broadcasting. The traditional pattern of radio broadcasting was that local radio was practically non-existent, and that the state maintained a near-monopoly of national radio. Before 1981, five 'generalist' radios, each with a similar diet of programmes, shared the national audience. Four commercial radios called *périphériques* (since, although they had studios in Paris, they transmitted from outside France) had the lion's share of listeners on long-wave. They were RTL (Luxembourg) and Europe 1 (near Saarbrücken, Germany), especially dominant in the north and east, RMC (Monte-Carlo) in the south-east, and the small Sud-Radio (Andorra) in the south-west. Radio France's equivalent public service radio station, France-Inter, with no brand advertising, basically devoted its programmes to what was seen as a homogeneous national audience, albeit with different needs at different times of the day.

The only other radio stations of note were Radio-France's two low-audience, high-culture stations: France-Culture with its programmed music and drama and much high level discussion, and France-Musique which concentrated on classical music and discussion of same. Local radio was limited to a few minutes per day of *décrochage* from the national network by the fifteen regional stations of Radio-France. There was little real choice of programme therefore, and a limited choice of programme supplier: state control of broadcasting was not really challenged by the existence of the *périphériques*, since the latter were indirectly controlled through state-dominated holding companies like the SOFIRAD and Havas.

In the 1980s political change and technological innovations resulted in a radical shift, bringing increased competition. Radio broadcasting was opened up to the private sector; the centre of gravity of radio output was displaced to the FM-wave band (offering in principle higher sound quality); the supply of programmes was increased and the listening audience was segmented through '*radio thématique*' formats. In addition, round-the-clock broadcasting was introduced and radio listening was transformed into an individualized activity on personal stereos or the car radio where everyone has their own receiver and is able to listen to their chosen station.

Indeed, the challenge to the state broadcasting monopoly came most noticeably in radio. Since about 1973, a growing number of illegal pirate radio stations on the FM-wave band had been jammed and raided by the state authorities. Many were run by broadcasting fanatics who simply wanted to exercise their freedom of expression over the air-waves. Some set up pirate stations for political reasons or to publicize causes. Others wished to break the state monopoly in order to set up commercial radio stations.

In 1981, faced by an explosion of *radios libres*, the socialist government proceeded to legalize and regulate the situation on the FM band. To avoid political or commercial monopolies, the new *radios locales privées* (RLP) were very tightly regulated. They had to operate as non-profit-making associations, could not therefore take paid advertising, could not set up networks of transmitters, and could not be run by town councils. Anarchy nonetheless continued to reign, as the licensing authority took an inordinately long time to draw up its list of authorized stations since there were far more applications than frequencies available on the FM band. Some stations cynically ignored the agreed transmission strength or allocated frequency. Others, finding the *fonds de soutien à l'expression radiophonique* inadequate, resorted to more or less open advertising or sponsorship. Pressure and confusion built up and the *Haute autorité*'s jurisdiction was undermined, until Mitterrand gave the go-ahead in 1984 for radios to operate as private companies and take advertising income. The deregulation of radio was extended when the state gave up its interest in the *périphériques*, Europe 1 being sold off to Hachette in 1986.

Inexpensive FM broadcasting technology had changed radio broadcasting out of all recognition. The RLP audience grew rapidly (to 4.3 million in 1984, and over a third of the listening public by 1988). Even the *périphériques* had to start broadcasting on FM. Another technological development was to complete the change. The launch, mainly for business and military communications purposes, of French low-power telecommunications satellites, allowed the RLP to set up national FM networks – groups of radios transmitting the same programme in different towns, using a satellite relay. Originally networks were banned, but gradually local stations were either bought up or given the franchise to broadcast programmes produced by a central programme provider, and the state was unable to resist this evolution. Since the 1986 law, half a dozen major networks have established themselves.

Public service radio meanwhile has attempted to halt the drop in audience figures in this climate of increased compititon. Long-term planning at Radio-France has not been helped by frequent (often politically motivated) changes of Director General (five during the 1980s). They too have opted as much as possible for FM frequencies and have opened forty-seven local stations, covering 50 per cent of France. Seeing the potential for thematic stations with the success of Radio-Bleue for the over fifties, Radio-France also established the increasingly successful twenty-four-hour rolling-news station, France-Info. Another innovation is the experiment of two up-market cultural and music programmes broadcast to a European-wide audience in digital stereo sound on the TDF1 satellite.

However, the audience for its national flagship station France-Inter has fluctuated from 13.5 per cent of total radio audience in 1983 to 17.3 per cent by the end of 1986 (which, for the first time in many years, put them ahead of Europe 1), to a worrying 10.9 per cent at the beginning of 1990, a figure partly compensated for by France-Info (whose listening figures shot up during the Gulf war of 1991). If it tots up listening figures across all its stations, Radio-France can still claim in the early 1990s to be '*le premier réseau de France*'.

After a decade of rapid change, the position in French radio in the 1990s is that, of the 1,800 or so independent radio stations in France, some 1,000 are attached to networks and about 300 are non-commercial or community radios. The 1980s saw the gradual triumph of market forces and fragmentation of the audience. In programming terms this means the triumph of formating, i.e. targeting a particular segment of the total listening public for the sale of advertising, and offering a very specific type of programme. The format dominating the networks is 'music-and-news', with NRJ and Skyrock aiming at the fifteen to twenty-five year olds, RFM and Europe 2 at the twenty-five to forty-five year olds, and Nostalgie mainly at the over-forties.

Market forces have also favoured concentration of owner-ship, whether in the form of wholly-owned networks, affiliated stations, franchising of programmes, or advertising networks. The new regulatory framework is nonetheless providing some protection to local commercial independent radios (*radios de proximité*) and non-commercial *radios associatives*. However, the range of community radio in Paris (Radio Notre Dame, Fréquence protestante, Radio Shalom, Fréquence gaie, Radio Beur, Radio Orient, etc) is in no way mirrored in the prov-inces, where the networks dominate.

A further way in which market forces have had an impact is that the *périphériques*, whose dominance over the commercial radio scene was threatened in the mid-1980s, have found ways of using their massive financial resources to recapture the younger end of the market for their basket of audiences to sell to advertisers. Whether, like RMC and RTL, by taking over FM networks, or, like Europe 1, by acting (through Europe 2) as programme-supplier to independent local radios, they are again achieving a strong position. The only newcomers to challenge them are J.-P. Baudecroux's NRJ (with 5 million listeners, over a hundred stations, a 200 million franc annual turnover, and a 63 million franc profit in 1988) and, for a time, RFM, with the backing of the British independent radio giant, Crown Communication.

The pattern of French radio broadcasting in the 1990s seems set: the 1980–1 changes have shaken themselves out. Radio listening as a whole has stabilized too (at about 75 per cent of the population), after the shock of increased TV competition in the mid-1980s. However the loss of a million radio listeners (2.8 per cent of the total) between 1989 and 1990, particularly in the fifteen- to twenty-four-year-old bracket, has reminded investors that FM radio is not a licence to print money. Advertising revenue tightened in 1991. One or two networks failed, like Kiss FM, and others merged (Métropolys and Maxximum), leading to somewhat increased concentration of ownership – but not necessarily at the expense of diversity of programmes. However, under the emerging authority of the CSA, a more stable situation seems likely to impose itself unless major technological innovations again disrupt the status quo.

Television channels and programming

The public service channels (*la télévision publique*)

Since the privatization of TF1 and the creation of new commercial channels in 1985, the diminished state sector has become the poor relation in France's television service. Suddenly confronted with intense private competition, public service television is trying to come to terms with its new role and identity. The key media debate, which used to be on television's relation to government, is, in the 1990s, on the issue of whether, and how, public sector television should differentiate itself from commercial television, in its financing and its programming policy. As a first step, the remaining two public service off-air national TV channels, Antenne 2 and FR3, were given a single Director General in 1989, as a preliminary to more complementarity and harmonization of programming and shared central services, leading perhaps to a merger into a single organization along the lines of BBC Television. The French public service model of broadcasting, however, lacks the prestige of its British counterpart, because of its long association with the exercise of state power, so it remains an open question as to whether the public service channels should strive for excellence in programmes which the private channels are reluctant to produce, or whether it should pursue a mass audience and the ratings and therefore programme a lot of light entertainment.

France 2 (formerly Antenne 2)
Originally the second channel, born in 1964, and becoming Antenne 2 in 1974, it remains a general public channel, '*une chaîne populaire de qualité*', catering for a mass audience, so

far in direct competititon with its main commercial rival TF1. Its best-known and long-lasting programmes over the years have included *Les Dossiers de l'écran* (serious treatment of issues) and *Des chiffres et des lettres* (game show), *Apostrophes* (the literary discussion programme with Bernard Pivot), *Le Grand échiquier* (with Jacques Chancel, variety), *Champs-Élysées* (a variety show with Michel Drucker), and its news and current affairs programmes. In the 1970s, these came under the direction of Jean Lefèvre and Jean-Pierre Elkabbach and, in the 1980s, they were presented by household names, PPDA (Patrick Poivre d'Arvor) and '*la reine Christine*' (Ockrent).

France 3 (formerly FR3)

The third channel, as FR3, began in 1972 with a regional vocation but most of its programming (including national news) is networked to the nation from its headquarters in Paris, with twice-daily local news programmes in each region. Its relationship to France 2 in terms of differentiated programming has still to be fully worked out, as '*une télévision de découverte et de différence*', to quote H. Bourges. Originally its local news bulletins were used by the Gaullist regime to put across a version of local news more politically acceptable than that offered by the regional newspapers. Its news coverage is now much more highly respected. The networked progammes were, and many still are, of a rather high cultural model, with a good reputation for documentary magazines: *Thalassa, La Marche du siècle*, and *Océaniques*). Mornings see *Continentales* (foreign news bulletins and *Monty Python* for language learning), and evenings a cinema film, but it has its own game shows and, until its relation to France 2 is redefined, it seems to be aiming at a general public audience.

Arte and la SEPT

The *Société européenne de programmes de télévision*, the seventh channel, was founded in 1986 with entirely public sector capital, with a vocation to become an up-market European-wide 'cultural channel'. La SEPT provides programmes for Arte, which took over the fifth channel, evenings only, in 1992. As a Franco-German cultural channel, Arte aims to provide high quality, cultural programmes, and eventually to incorporate other European countries into its organisation, symbolically based in Strasbourg. German-produced programmes are subtitled in French.

RFO
Having split from Radio-France in 1982, RFO manages public service broadcasting to French overseas territories.

The commercial channels (*les télévisions privées*)

TF1
TF1, the continuation of France's oldest television channel, inaugurated in 1935, was privatized in 1987, and bought by a consortium headed by the industrialist Francis Bouygues. It quickly used its new financial muscle to attract many stars from Antenne 2 (Anne Sinclair, Christine Ockrent, Michèle Cotta, Patrick Poivre d'Arvor) in a ratings war with the other channels. Ockrent went back to Antenne 2 after a year or so, complaining of '*la dictature de l'Audimat*' at TF1, i.e. a programming policy too dependent on audience figures.

Popular progammes have included: the documentary programme *Cinq colonnes à la une*, major political interview or discussion programmes called over the years *Face à face*, *À armes égales*, *Droit de réponse*, and *7 sur 7* (with Anne Sinclair), the indescribable *Intervilles* (a domestic French version of *Jeux sans frontières* with Guy Lux and Léon Zitrone), children's programmes like *Le Manège enchanté* and *L'Ile aux enfants*, the midday news programme *Midi première* (synonymous with Yves Mourousi), its evening *Journal télévisé* (consistently the highest in audience ratings), American soaps like *Dallas*, a series of American-style game shows such as *La Roue de la fortune*, and its highly popular *Bébête Show* (a political satire, with puppets similar to *Spitting Image* and *The Muppets*). Since privatization it has a *Télé-Shopping* programme.

Canal Plus
France's first subscription television channel, Canal Plus, began broadcasting in 1984 under the direction of André Rousselet of Havas, a personal friend of President Mitterrand. It is now wholly private, with Havas, the *Compagnie générale des eaux*, l'Oréal, and Granada Television among the shareholders. After a hesitant start, it benefited from various

concessions, even being allowed to carry advertising. Now financially the most dynamic of the private channels, it has set up its own production company, and is seeking to expand with channels on French cable networks, and pay-TV channels in other European countries, notably Spain and Germany. It specializes in recently released cinema films (one film new to television per day, with several repeats), early evening humour and sports coverage.

La Cinq

La Cinq went bankrupt and ceased broadcasting in 1991. The original franchise of the fifth channel was given to Seydoux and Berlusconi; it was re-attributed to Hersant and Berlusconi in 1986, before Hachette bought the major share in 1990, with Hersant keeping only a minority holding. It aimed at a mass general audience, broadcasting twenty-four hours a day. Unable to achieve financial stability, it experimented with various programming policies, bringing it into conflict with the regulatory bodies, which sanctioned la Cinq for over-programming of American television films, for not respecting European production quotas, and for showing soft-porn material too early in the evening. Abandoning Hersant's stress on news coverage, Hachette tried to turn la Cinq into a family channel, but was unable to increase audiences and advertising revenue sufficiently quickly to avoid going into voluntary liquidation at the end of 1991. The channel was re-allocated to the public service channel Arte in 1992.

M6

The sixth channel was originally dedicated to programmes for young people as a mainly music channel, but under the name M6, its new franchise holders (led by the CLT and *Lyonnaise des eaux*), while retaining a lot of music videos (*Boulevard des clips*) and aiming some programmes at the fifteen to twenty-five year olds, have pretensions to being a general audience channel, albeit a low budget one.

On the national *généralistes* channels, drama series and films make up the biggest single category of programmes (nearly 30 per cent), with quiz and game shows, *variétés* and the evening news programme being important prime-time shows. The programming schedules are more tightly regulated in France under the *cahiers des charges* than European Community rules demand. One justification is the protection of the French cinema industry. Examples of the type of regulation are that, excluding Canal Plus, the main channels cannot show more than 192 cinema films per year, of which no more than 104 may be in evening prime time. The films must be at least eighteen months old, 50 per cent must be French productions, and 60 per cent European. There are also regulations on the proportion of French-made programmes, and on the maximum amount of advertising per hour (twelve minutes, with a daily average of no more than six minutes for TF1 and France 2). There has even been a debate, on aesthetic and moral grounds, on whether films should be interrupted by advertising: TF1 is allowed one advertising break, France 2 none. A major rationale behind these restrictions is the defence of French culture and identity in the face of importations of American programmes.

Production of programmes

The introduction of market forces into television has had the effect of more clearly demarcating the roles of programme producer and programme provider. Programme production has long been a weakness in French television. Alongside the traditional state programming monopoly, there had also been, until 1986, a production monopoly. Channels (programme providers) had been obliged to use the SFP (*Société française de production*) for all their French-made documentary, entertainment and drama productions. As an attempt to stimulate French programme production, channels may now have recourse to independent programme-makers, and, with constant deficits the future of the SFP, never in a very healthy financial position since it became autonomous in 1974, seems in doubt. As in other countries, since a crucial part of their schedules are films, the French networks are increasingly financing co-productions with European partners, both cinema films and films specifically for television. However, the language and cultural problems of producing for a market wider than the national one conflict with the defence of French cultural identity, as enshrined in the programming quotas relating to '*œuvres françaises*'.

The audience and the economics of broadcasting

A mass television audience emerged only in the 1970s in France. From only 6 million sets in 1965, the number grew to nearly 16 million by 1980, by which time 90 per cent of homes had sets. In the 1990s most French people can receive at least five off-air channels, (the fifth and sixth channels are spreading their geographical coverage) and viewers watch on average at least three hours per day. The availability, free at point of consumption, of five off-air channels, plus an off-air subscription channel, has satisfied most viewers, who feel less need to invest in either a cable link (600 francs for the installation and 150 francs or so for the monthly subscription) or a DBS receiving dish plus decoder.

The emergence of a commercial sector has changed the media culture and changed the relationship with this mass audience. The viewer is seen as a consumer and programmes as commodities. Channels are placing enormous faith in the measurement of audience figures, e.g. via the dreaded *Audimat*, in order to sell advertising space. The consequences are a '*chasse aux vedettes*' and consequent public criticism of inflated salaries for star presenters, a suspicion of standardization of programme formats as programmers seek the lowest common denominator, and a reliance on tried-and-tested and often cheap American serials or Japanese-made cartoons. A constant danger is the blurring of the line between programmes and advertising: TF1 was fined over 2 million francs by the CSA in 1991 for a flagrant violation of the rules on sponsorship: a brand of coffee had been mentioned fifty-four times during the programme *Sacrée soirée*, whereas regulations allow for one mention of a sponsor's name at the beginning and one at the end of the programme.

Before privatization, TF1 and Antenne 2 had similar numbers of viewers. In the 1990s TF1 has become the clear

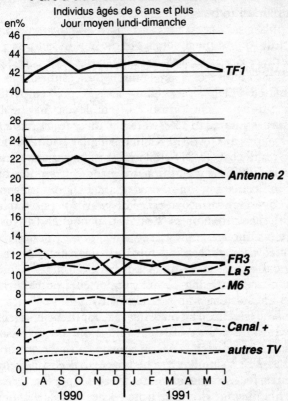

Part d'audience des chaînes

Individus âgés de 6 ans et plus
Jour moyen lundi-dimanche

From *Le Monde*, 16 July 1991.

market leader in terms of audience share, over 40 per cent, followed by France 2 coming back to 24–5 per cent, and France 3 on 14–15 per cent. Before its demise la Cinq had risen to 11 per cent, and M6 now has about 10 per cent. TF1 is therefore able to demand a higher price for its advertising space, especially in evening prime time (8 p.m. to 10.30 p.m.), with the consequence that it has managed to operate at a profit. Canal Plus, with its main source of income from subscriptions, is also financially sound at 4 per cent, whereas M6 was still not making a profit in the early 1990s. La Cinq's bankruptcy confirmed the predictions of those saying too many channels were fishing in too small a pool of advertising demand for all to be able to survive.

The public service sector is not spared in the new competitive culture: one of the first tasks of the new director of France 2 and France 3 was to seek to balance the books. In 1991 he received a promise of a one billion franc subsidy to cover accumulated deficits, in exchange for a 20 per cent reduction of staff numbers. The number of employees in the public sector was estimated in 1990 as two to three times higher than that in the private sector. FR3 in particular had traditionally had high staff costs (3,244 staff across its twenty-two regional centres in 1990). In addition to income from the annual television licence free (*la redevance*), state channels have been taking advertising since 1968. This was not popular at the time with the written press (heavily dependent on advertising revenue), although now some of the larger newspapers companies have diversified into broadcasting. Other more ideological objections to paid advertising on public service television are surfacing again, supported ironically by the commercial stations who see their salvation in reserving the whole of the television advertising cake for themselves. France 3 receives 80 per cent of its income from licence fees, but France 2, if its mission is to continue to compete on the same ground as TF1, is unlikely to be happy to see its dependence on licence fee income increase from 40 per cent, and its advertising income decrease from 54 per cent (1990 figures).

The television audience is in the process of being fragmented and the economics of broadcasting redefined not only through the creation of commercial television, but also as a result of the introduction of new broadcasting technologies in the 1980s, the implications of which, certainly as regards television, are still being worked through in the 1990s.

New broadcasting technologies and the communications revolution

The communications revolution of the 1980s and 1990s combines changes in computing, telecommunications and broadcasting, which converge in the new communications media. Technological innovations in micro-electronics and telecommunications (broadband cable and satellite) have radically improved the transmission of information in the form of data, graphics, sound and vision, so that the same communications system may carry, for instance, telephone, FAX, videotex, remote computer links, as well as broadcasting signals. Modernizing national communications systems using telematics (a combination of telecommunications and micro-computer technology) offered advanced economies like France in the 1980s an opportunity to modernize broadcasting and to plan for what has been called the wired or interactive society. Such projects seemed all the more essential since communications policy has become of strategic importance in a European Community haunted by the prospect of growing American and Japanese domination of European information technology sectors. Telecommunications in particular is a sector where EC countries are best placed to retain a competitive position. In this context, France-Télécom had amitions to retain France's technological lead by developing its own series of telecommunications satellites and by providing a national broadband cable, Integrated Services Digital Network (ISDN), to cater for all such data, voice and image transmission in the same digital form along the same cables, just as in the 1970s it had made its considerable reputation, as the *Direction générale des télécommunications* (DGT), by developing (and exporting) French telephone systems technology.

In the 1980s French governments were acutely aware of threats to national sovereignty coming from two sides of the cultural industries sector. Firstly, America and Japan had not only established an unassailable lead in computing hardware and software, but by the mid-1980s Japan had also acquired a dominant world position in the field of audiovisual equipment (TV sets, video recorders, hi-fi) and seemed about to attack the market for satellite reception equipment and high definition television (HDTV). Secondly, the USA had the world's most powerful programme production industry, and was seeking overseas markets for programmes (like *Dallas*) which had achieved profitability on the home market and therefore could undercut European products.

French broadcasting policy was made therefore in the context of these industrial and cultural challenges to national independence. The problem was how to reconcile, on the one hand, the promotion of French industrial competitiveness in terms of equipping the nation with the most modern broadcasting infrastructure (thereby creating a large market for programmes) with, on the other, the aim of protecting French cultural identity by preventing foreign programmes flooding onto French screens. The task was not made easier by the growing adoption of economic liberalism in the world economy, which eventually seduced Mitterrand's socialists almost as much as the French right.

Initial developments in deregulating and expanding the supply of television in France, however, relied on traditional off-air or terrestrial broadcasting technology. The fourth, fifth and sixth channels were transmitted like the first three channels by Télédiffusion de France (TDF), the state-owned transmission company, as *chaînes herziennes* (ground-based transmitters, Hertzian wave signals, and individual receiving aerials). This expansion of the supply of television programmes seemed bound to slow down consumer investment in new cable and satellite broadcasting technologies. The one technological novelty was Canal Plus's mode of financing as subscription or pay TV. It relies on encryption (scrambling) of the signal, requiring a special decoder to view the picture. The renting of the decoder allows the collection of the subscription fee. Pursuing encrypted TV technology was seen in a small way as developing an export market for a French hi-tech product. Subscription television is also the clearest indication of a new philosophy of broadcasting, and takes it into the marketplace. It is claimed that by creating a direct contractual link between viewer and broadcaster, viewers have an ability to express their preference for the type of programmes they want in a way that, in a competitive environment, programme providers will act upon. It creates a 'market for programmes'.

Cable

A second new technology used to create a market for TV programmes was in local cable television networks. With the exceptions of a nationally funded experiment in cabling in Biarritz, and networks in five or six frontier towns where far-sighted mayors like Jean-Marie Rausch in Metz had invested, cable television was almost unknown in France in 1982 (0.6 per cent of homes cabled with 1970 copper coaxial cable technology). Belgium, on the other hand, had cabled as many as 90 per cent of homes. In the 1980s new fibre-optic cable technology, capable of sending a choice of up to 100 different programmes to a user, in conjunction with micro-computer technology, was also able to offer interactivity, two-way communications, an exciting prospect to the new socialist government. In the framework of the strategic industrial aims mentioned above, an ambitious national cable plan was consequently set up in 1982, with the objective of cabling six million homes (nearly one third of all households) by 1992.

It was a strategy which had industrial, cultural and political attractions. It was ideologically attractive, since it offered not just a passive reception of television programmes, but allowed more choice and active involvement ('*convivialité*') for the citizen. It was given added legitimacy through the socialists' emphasis on decentralization, political, administrative and economic, intended to be 'la grande affaire du septennat': setting up of cabling systems was to be dependent on unique co-operation between the DGT and local authorities, newly empowered to decide their own local economic and political futures by the *loi Defferre*.

Economically, cable television was intended to be the incentive to set up the DGT's modern national communications system which would be made financially viable by a host of other interactive personal and commercial electronic data interchange services, such as tele-banking and tele-shopping, the electronic office, consultation of remote data bases, the videophone and so on. In terms of economic and industrial strategy, demand for new French hi-tech products at home and abroad (France had a lead in fibre-optic technology) was intended to counter American and Japanese competition,

open up new markets for French electronics and telecommunications industries and therefore safeguard jobs.

The ambitious cable plan did not prove as attractive to
local authorities as central government had hoped. Despite
government spending of 18 billion francs in the first seven
years of the project, the cabling of towns was three years
behind schedule in 1990, by which time the demand for cable
subscriptions had reached only a quarter of a million. The
plan had suffered from the economic downturn of 1983,
incoherence of policy by the socialists, changes of government, and personal rivalries.

First of all, in pursuing at the same time the *Minitel* videotex
(viewdata) system, developed by the DGT using existing
telephone lines, French governments have separated the telematics market from the cable television market. *Minitel*, not a
market-led project, but imposed by state planning, has
become much more than a computerized telephone book, and
has successfully created and satisfied a market for interactive
information and communication services, with 5.6 million
terminals in use in 1990.

As regards broadcasting policy, successive decisions
seemed alternately to favour either cable or satellite technology, or, over-ambitiously, to try to promote both. Government policy was initially complicated by rivalry between two
technical arms of the *administration*, the DGT and TDF. This
conflict is prolonged in the 1990s by rivalries between France-
Télécom and *Lyonnaise des Eaux* (pro-cable, relayed by low-
power telecommunications satellites) on the one hand and
Canal Plus and the users of the direct-broadcast satellite
TDF1 on the other. Political rivalries overlap because the
head of Canal Plus, Rousselet, is close to Mitterrand and the
socialists, whereas the head of Lyonnaise, Jérôme Monod, a
former Secretary General of the Gaullist Party, is close to
Chirac.

The cable plan was further undermined in 1984–85 by
Mitterrand's decision to offer viewers three new off-air
stations, two of which were free at point of consumption,
which inevitably satisfied much of the demand for a wider
choice of television. This decision owed less to consistent
policy-making and more to narrow political considerations.

Mitterrand needed to regain the political initiative in terms of '*un nouvel espace de liberté*' after retreating from a disastrous attempt in 1984 to amalgamate the state and private schools into a single system. With elections looming, there were also fears that the right, if elected, would privatize one or two channels, and have them run by enemies of the left like Hersant. The creation of two new private stations by Mitterrand was regarded as a pre-emptive strike.

Domestic programme production has not met the cultural challenge of cable. Encouraged by the Minister of Culture, Jack Lang, the *Mission TV câble* attempted to assemble 2,000 hours of French programmes for transmission. But potential cable operators demanded foreign stations on their networks to help the financial attractiveness of cable. So conflict emerged between supporters of a more liberal regulatory regime and those putting cultural imperatives first: the protection of cultural sovereignty through import quotas on foreign programmes and banning foreign stations.

Further erosion of the initial strategy came in 1984 when, for reasons of commercial viability, government allowed new cable systems the option of using a mix of the cheaper coaxial technology with fibre-optic cable, therefore ruling out interactivity. Chirac went further along the deregulation route by handing over responsibility to private enterprise, stopping France-Télécom's installation monopoly, and allowing private firms such as *Lyonnaise des Eaux* not only to construct city cable networks, but also to act as cable operators and even programme providers.

A number of cities have, of course, invested in such market-led cable television networks and, by 1992, demand was rapidly picking up: 123 networks were in service, covering a potential 4 million homes, with about a million actual subscribers. The largest new system, in Paris, offers nineteen channels including five foreign stations, the six national off-air channels, plus Canal-J(eunesse) (produced by Europe 1-Hachette and Lyonnaise communications), two local channels (including Paris première, owned by Lyonnaise communications), Music TV, TV5, Ciné-Cinémas, Euro-Sport and TV-Sport. The major difference between the type of programme offered via the new media and those on conventional television is the number of thematically focused channels (sport, music, children's TV, a news channel or a film channel). This serving of specialized audiences is sometimes called 'narrowcasting'.

Local television

A related development is the birth of local off-air commercial stations broadcasting for a few hours a day: Télé-Toulouse (from 1988), Canal 8 Mont-Blanc in the Haute-Savoie (and Swiss) skiing areas (1989), Télé Lyon métropole (1989) and Aqui-TV in the Périgord (1991). Some sixteen other local channels (including Paris première) were being broadcast on city cable networks in 1991. Limited local advertising revenue will, however, severely restrict such developments, whereas nation-wide audiences for focused channels catering for special interest groups seem more promising. One such is Canal Santé, broadcasting professional material by satellite to 4,700 of the 58,000 French GPs since 1990.

Satellite

The other major new area of competition to terrestrial television, and indeed to cable, is direct broadcasting by satellite (DBS television). Since the satellite footprint spills over national frontiers, national control of broadcasting is eroded, not to say destroyed, by foreign satellites. The state monopoly over television could not be pursued into the era of DBS. At best, regulation can be negotiated at European level. Its limitation for the viewer is that a fixed receiving dish can take in programmes usually from only one satellite. However, satellite broadcasting may be seen as complementary to cable, since cable systems can be and are used to distribute broadcasts emanating from several different satellites.

An early and successful attempt to use satellite broadcasting to promote the French language and culture in the world is TV5. Since 1985, this state-subsidized channel has been broadcasting from the European EUTELSAT satellite, mainly in Europe, North America and North Africa, as an international collaborative project showing repeats from

French, Belgian, Swiss and Quebec television. Its prime purpose is cultural rather than commercial: an arm of French cultural defences against the threat of American television programmes broadcast from 'Coca-Cola satellites' (to quote a minister). It carries no advertising, and is mainly aimed at cable systems, but may be received as DBS.

However, TV5 is carried on a European satellite, not a French one. Maintaining a national satellite construction, launching and management capacity is not only of industrial importance, but is also an element of national sovereignty, both for military purposes and because satellite technology is crucial to the strategic sector of telecommunications. Consequently, satellite television has been used by France in a context wider than broadcasting, not only, as TV5, for cultural policy or for industrial reasons, but also as part of European policy and to cement Franco-German relations.

Once France had been allocated a satellite position to cover western Europe by an international telecommunications agreement in 1977, TDF was given the go-ahead for a DBS project, in collaboration with West Germany (reconfirmed in 1982). A five-channel French satellite (TDF1) and a German satellite were to be launched by the European rocket Ariane. The project was linked to the European cultural channel now called Arte. A complication was potential competition (economic and cultural) from a proposed American-built and Luxembourg-owned satellite, Astra, suspected of wishing to sell channels to American companies, which France unsuccessfully tried to stop by offering two TDF1 channels to the CLT.

Another strategic European aspect of the project was the adoption of the European D2 MAC wide-screen transmission standard as a transitional stage towards high-definition television (HDTV), which France and the European Community saw as a way of maintaining a competitive European presence in producing for the home-electronics market in face of Japanese and American competition. A further attraction, in the light of concerns about the defence of the French language, was the French technology's ability to allow several sound channels for every picture channel, therefore allowing multilingual broadcasting.

The typically French state-led grand technological project was to suffer setbacks, some reminiscent of the cable plan: multiplying terrestrial television stations in 1985 reduced the potential market for DBS; failure of the Ariane launch in 1985 put the project well behind schedule (TDF1 was eventually launched in October 1988); early doubts were expressed by the DGT about obsolescent technology (the DGT favoured their own low-powered Telecom satellites); the franchises for the satellite channels were allocated and reallocated twice as governments came and went before broadcasting began in 1989; and international competition increased: potential operators are more attracted to the private Luxembourg satellite Astra, launched in 1988, with sixteen channels and lighter regulation. There were forty-nine satellite television channels broadcasting to western Europe in 1989, with a satellite capability for up to 160 channels in 1992. The Astra system alone promised to have capacity for forty-eight channels accessible through a single receiving dish by 1993.

In 1991 serious technical failures reduced the satellite's transmission capacity and TDF1 was broadcasting only four channels: Canal Plus, la SEPT, Antenne 2, and, temporarily, Euromusique. Doubts about TDF1's commercial and technological viability have caused other channels to pull out in favour of cable or other satellites. Even Canal Plus has decided to hedge its bets by buying into the three major cable operators. A further problem, which the French government (and the European Commission) may be rashly ignoring, is that recent American advances in HDTV broadcasting using digital data compression may make the European MAC HDTV standard obsolete before the end of the decade.

Since the French project has been more technology-led than demand-led, even if the technology has a viable future, there are still unresolved problems regarding programmes and audience. Will an audience be prepared to invest for what is on offer? Whereas in Britain the number of DBS dishes had reached 1.5 million by 1991 (still not enough to ensure a profit for an operation based on advertising revenue such as BSkyB Television), the number of DBS receivers in France was estimated at no more than 10,000 in 1990. Will a French DBS audience be attracted to Astra by its proposed French-language entertainment channel RTL2, and therefore not to TDF1? Do French DBS channels need extra outlets? Will the cable operators (in competition for viewers with DBS) agree to put them on their networks? If so, should they be on the D2 MAC standard (requiring expensive receiving equipment) or in SECAM, or both? Will Arte retain its terrestrial channel under a right-wing government? Should a French music channel be supported to defend the French music industry, and thereby French culture? If so, should it be given access to as wide a potential audience as possible, on the seventh channel and/or the satellite, or rely solely on cable? Will additional terrestrial channels again slow the development of cable television? The various actors involved, in particular the Ministry of Culture and the CSA, are at odds on these questions. They need to be resolved quickly and coherently to counter the charge that French broadcasting policy is again being made in a hand-to-mouth way.

Video

Video cassettes are a further means of programme distribution. The home video market has not developed in France as quickly as in Great Britain. Development was deliberately slowed down in the early 1980s when a special tax on video recorders was introduced, partly because the home manufacturers were not ready to compete with imported Japanese machines, and secondly to protect the other new French television media from competition. Chirac ended the tax in 1986 as another step in the direction of letting market forces prevail. By the beginning of the 1990s, although estimates vary, it was thought that video recorders were to be found in about one-third of French homes, compared with over half of British.

Conclusion

New technologies, deregulation, market forces, international-ization, sovereignty, and cultural identity, are key words in the media policy sector in France in the 1980s and 1990s. The multiplication of television channels and radio stations seems to herald a new age of consumer choice in broadcasting, although commercial pressures are for a standardized mass market product in terms of programme. Into what was traditionally a state and public service monopoly until the 1980s have come major commercial firms and intensified competition for audiences and for advertising revenue. There has been a consequent erosion of the boundaries between broadcasting and such sectors as press and publishing, electronics, and advertising: for example, publishing giants Maxwell, Hersant and Hachette have held interests in French radio and television; the French electronics firm Thomson is exploiting new, potentially lucrative, but high-risk markets tied to the development of new products such as HDTV sets or optic-fibre cabling; important income for Aérospatiale and Arianespace derives from the launching of telecommunications satellites used for broadcasting; and the advertising firm, Havas, has developed multimedia interests. Neither the French state nor private enterprise can any longer consider broadcasting policy as an autonomous sector of decision-making and investment. If a strength of French media policy has been their attempt to conceive it in a wider economic and technological context, it can only be hoped that its implementation in the 1990s will be more coherent than in the 1980s.

Broadcasting is not only enmeshed into broader economic and industrial issues, it has also developed an irrevocably cross-national and European dimension. Media groups like Canal Plus are investing across the European Community, influential French media planning companies buying and selling advertising space, like Carat Espace, are seeking foreign partners, and, in their turn, foreign firms are buying into the French broadcasting market (Berlusconi, CLT, Crown Communication).

In an era of global telecommunications, the new broadcasting media erode national cultural and economic sovereignty. As a reaction, concerns have arisen in France to protect French language and culture and therefore the national programme-making industry. National multimedia groups have been built up in order to resist perceived threats from international (usually 'anglo-saxon') media conglomerates. The French state has helped Canal Plus's cross-national development and Hachette's growth into a multimedia company of international proportions in publishing, radio, and television. In the context of broadcasting's links with strategic issues of industrial and technological independence, France, as in other areas of policy, has seen its salvation, more enthusiastically than Britain, as lying in European co-operation. Successive governments have supported the European Commission's desire to harmonize technical norms in order to compete against Japanese and American competition in the electronics industry, as well as the programme-making industry, hence the nationalized consumer electronics firm Thomson's involvement with Philips in the European HDTV standard in the Eureka programme, and support for the MEDIA 92 programme to help European TV and cinema production.

In the Fifth Republic, as political communications from de Gaulle to Mitterrand have accorded a privileged role to the medium of television, the French political class has traditionally been very sensitive to the media as a policy area. Under the impact of recent technological change, and related economic, cultural and political issues, broadcasting is increasing in commercial and political significance, at the same time as the ability of the French state and its masters to control it has been diminishing, as a result of technological change, but also through adoption, for ideological reasons, of greater deregulation and a free market approach – '*la logique radio-télé-fric*'. In the light of these political, industrial, technological, and cultural implications for French national identity, broadcasting is unlikely to fade as a controversial issue in France.

Bibliography

General

Chauveau, A. and Hare, G., *Media Studies in France: a guide to sources of information.* Kingston-upon-Thames, the APEX Centre, Kingston Polytechnic, 1991. Covers official organizations, documentation and research centres, periodicals, and books on the media published in France since 1980.

Important specialist periodicals are *Dossiers de l'audiovisuel, La Lettre du CSA,* and, particularly, *Médiaspouvoirs.* Articles also appear in *French Cultural Studies* and *Modern and Contemporary France.*

A well-stocked specialist bookshop in Paris is La Librairie Tekhne, 7 rue des Carmes, 75005 Paris, tel. (1) 43.54.70.84.

General works on radio and television in France

Albert, P., *Les Médias dans le monde 1990–1991.* La Garenne-Colombes, Editions Européennes ERASME (coll. Documents pédagogiques), 1990. An excellent introduction, especially on France, covering press agencies, media in the industrialized world, the written press, radio, and TV.

Albert, P. and Tudesq, A.-J., *Histoire de la radio et de la télévision.* Paris, PUF (Que sais-je?, 1904), 2ᵉ édition remise à jour, 1986. Excellent introduction, putting French experience in world perspective.

Cayrol, R., *Les médias: presse écrite, radio, télévision.* Paris, PUF (Thémis, science politique), 1991. Excellent up-to-date study and source book.

Cazenave, F., *Les Radios libres: des radios pirates aux radios locales privées.* Paris, PUF (Que sais-je?, 1867), 1984. Useful introduction to changes in French radio in late 1970s and early 1980s.

Cojean, A. and Eskenazi, F., *FM, la folle histoire des radios libres.* Paris, Grasset, 1986. Two specialist journalists, from *Le Monde* and *Libération,* trace a lively history of early independent (and pirate) radio from 1977 to 1985.

Harrison, M., 'The Politics of Media Reform', in Hall, P. A.,

Hayward, J., and Machin, H., *Developments in French Politics*. London, Macmillan, 1990. A careful up-to-date assessment.

Kuhn, R., 'The Modernisation of the Media', in J. Gaffney (ed.), *France and modernisation*. Aldershot, Avebury/Gower, 1988. A study of the socialists' reforms 1981–86.

Works on more specialized topics

Bahu-Leyser, D., Chavenon, H. and Durand, J., *Audiences des médias – guide France-Europe*. Paris, Eyrolles, Collection Communication, 1990. Good on how the audience for different media is measured in Europe.

Cayrol, R., *La Nouvelle Communication politique*. Paris, Larousse, 1986. Excellent synthesis of uses of the media in general in politics.

Chevallier, J., 'Les instances de régulation de l'audiovisuel', in *Regards sur l'actualité*. La Documentation française, no. 149 (Mar. 1989), pp. 39–55. Excellent summary of powers and effectiveness of the different media regulatory bodies HACA, CNCL, and CSA.

Dyson, K. and Humphreys, P., *Broadcasting and New Media Policies in Western Europe*. London, Routledge, 1988. Good analysis of the development of policies to regulate broadcasting in response to new broadcasting technology.

Toussaint-Desmoulins, N., *L'Economie des médias*. Paris, PUF (Que sais-je?, 1701), 2e édition, 1987. Good introduction to the economics of broadcasting.

'Témoignages' and memoirs by media professionals

Bourges, H., *Une chaîne sur les bras*. Paris, Seuil, 1987. Memoirs of his three and a half years as successful PDG of TF1 from July 1983.

Cavada, J.-M., *En toute liberté*. Paris, Grasset, 1986. By former head of News and Current Affairs of TF1 before and after 1981.

Cotta, M., *Les Miroirs de Jupiter*. Paris, Fayard, 1986. Useful account of her time as president of the HACA licensing authority.

Jeanneney, J.-N., *Echec à Panurge: l'audiovisuel public au service de la différence*. Paris, Seuil, 1986. PDG of Radio-France (1982–6) describes his achievement in a vigorous defence of public service broadcasting.

Ockrent, C., *Duel. Comment la télévision façonne un président*. Paris, Hachette, Coll. Le Libelle, 1988. The 'queen of the small screen' analyses the televized duels between presidential election candidates.

Index

Abbas, Sheik, 191
abortion, 15
Abou Daoud affair (1977), 139
Accords de Matignon, 150
Action catholique ouvrière (ACO), 200
Action française, 199
affaire du foulard, 186, 192, 197
Agence nationale pour l'emploi
  (ANPE), 14
agriculture, 3, 6–10
Albert, P, 207
Algeria, 101, 102, 131; Algerian
  immigrants, 191
Amaury, E, 219
anti-semitism, 190
Antony, B, 199
Arte, 250–1
Association de recherche et d'initiatives
  pour l'autogestion et le socialisme,
  57
Auroux, J, 93, 95
autogestion, 22, 64, 94

baccalauréat, 20
baccalauréat professionnel, 162
Balladur, E, 40, 93
Bayard-Presse, 215–16
Bérégovoy, P, 40, 97
Bergeron, A, 86, 90
Berlusconi, 243, 252
Beurs, 99, 113, 117
Beuve-Méry, H, 220
Bokassa, J.-B, 142
Boulez, P, 32
Bourges, H, 244
Bourses du travail, 73
brevet d'études professionnelles (BEP),
  161
Brisson, P, 218

cadres, 3, 17, 19–20, 28
Camp David agreements, 139

Canal Plus, 251–2
Canard enchaîné, 233
Cancun summit (Mexico, 1981),
  143
Capitant, R, 86
Carter, J, 136
Catholic church, 186–9, 193–205;
  and education, 21, 173–7; and
  the press, 223; and trade
  unions, 75
censorship, 21
Centre Beaubourg, 31–2
Centre des démocrates sociaux (CDS),
  59
Centre d'études, de recherche et
  d'éducation socialistes (CERES), 55
Centre d'intelligence de la foi (CIF),
  201
Centre national des indépendants et
  paysans (CNIP), 47
Centre national des jeunes agriculteurs
  (CNJA), 9
Centres dramatiques, 30–1
Cercles ouvriers, 73
Cergy Pontoise, 3
Certificat d'aptitude professionnelle
  (CAP), 161
Ceyrac, F, 87
Chaban-Delmas, J, 86, 241
Chambre des députés, 18
Charter of Amiens, 78
Chevènement, J.-P, 56
Cheysson, C, 144
Chirac, J, x, 36, 37, 51, 55, 56, 61,
  67, 90, 93, 148–9; and
  television, 261
Cinq, la, 252
code de la famille, 2
code de la nationalité, 113
cohabitation, 38
collèges d'enseignement général
  (CEG), 169

collèges d'enseignement secondaire (CES), 169–70
Comité chrétienté-solidarité, 198
Comité interministériel à l'Intégration, 119
Commissariat au Plan, 104
commission de sages, 113, 114
Communauté, 102
Communism, the collapse of, 150
Communist Party, see Parti communiste français
Compagnie Lyonnaise des Eaux, 239, 260, 261
Confédération française de l'encadrement (CFE-CGC), 75
Confédération française et démocratique du travail (CFDT), 22, 75, 80–1, 82, 83, 86, 87, 88, 89, 91, 94
Confédération française des travailleurs chrétiens (CFTC), 74–5, 80–1, 96–7
Confédération générale des cadres (CGC), 83
Confédération générale du travail (CGT), 22, 73–4, 75, 78–9, 80, 82, 83, 84, 85, 86, 87, 88, 89, 90, 91, 94, 96
Confédération générale du travail–force ouvrière (CGT-FO), 74–5, 80, 82, 89
Confédération générale du travail unitaire (CGTU), 79
Confédération nationale du patronat français (CNPF), 95
conscription, 24
Conseil de réfléxion sur l'Islam en France (CORIF), 191
Conseil national de la communication et des libertés (CNCL), 243
Conseils régionaux, 1, 31
Conseil supérieur de l'audiovisuel (CSA), 243–4
Cot, J.-P, 144
Cotta, M, 242
Couve de Murville, 127
Cresson, E, 5, 37, 72, 108
Croix, la, 223

Debatisse, M, 9
Debray law, the, 176
decentralization, 2, 11–12, 24, 29–33; of broadcasting, 240–4; of education, 165–8, 183
Declaration of the Rights of Man, 101
Decourtray, A, 202
de Gaulle, General C, 21, 58, 64, 80, 85, 199; and foreign policy, 126–8; and television, 240
Delors, J, 204
de Saint-Germain, P, 202
Deuil, G, 95
divorce, 2, 16
Dreyfus affair, 106
Ducaud-Bourget, abbé, 194, 195
Dumas, R, x, 146, 150
Dupont, J.M, 207
Duval, J, 201–2
Duverger, M, 47

Ecole cathédrale (Notre Dame) institut catholique, 201
école libre, 186
ecology, 10
Editions Amaury, 215
Editions Mondiales, 215
education, 1, 14, 20, 21–2, 156–84; demonstrations (1968, 1986 and 1990), 179–82; and immigration, 119–20, 177–9
European Community (EC), 8, 71, 130, 138, 141, 146–7, 151–2; European Assembly, 138; European Council of Ministers, 146; European Monetary System (EMS), 71, 138, 146; European Single Market, 38; European Union, 152; and immigration, 124
Evénement (du jeudi), L', 232
évêque parle, Un, 194
Evian agreement, 102
Exchange rate mechanism (ERM), 71
Express, L', 230, 231

Fabius, L, 54, 67
family, the, 1, 23
farming, 6–10
Fédération de l'éducation nationale (FEN), 75, 83, 96
Fédération nationale des musulmans de France (FNMF), 191
Fédération nationale des syndicats, 73
Fédération nationale des syndicats d'éxploitants agricoles (FNSEA), 9
Fifth Republic, 21, 56, 58, 59, 62, 63, 64, 67, 92, 133
Figaro, Le, 218
First World War, 128
Fiterman, C, 57
Fonds d'action sociale (FAS), 119–20
Fonds régionaux d'art contemporain (FRAC), 30
Fontaine, A, 220
Force ouvrière (FO), 83–4, 86, 87, 88, 89, 90–1
Fouchet, C, 170
Fourth Republic, 74, 101
France 2 (formerly Antenne 2), 249–50
France 3 (formerly FR3), 250
France Dimanche, 230
France Soir, 221–2
Francoscope, 209
Fraternité sacerdotale de Saint-Pie X, 194
Front islamique du Salut, 121
Front national (FN), 36, 39, 54, 56, 100, 108, 111, 115, 199

Gaddafi, Colonel, 145
Gaillot, J, 202
Gattaz, Y, 95
Génération écologie, 40, 58
Germany, 151–2; and unification, 150
Giesbert, O, 218
Girod, R, 191
Giscard d'Estaing, V, 36, 37, 39, 47, 53, 59, 62, 66, 67, 73; and broadcasting, 241–2; foreign policy, 132–43
Goldman, A, 192

Goldsmith, Sir J, 231
Golias, 202
Gorbachev, M, 148
grandes écoles, 11, 18, 162–3
Green Party, *see Verts, les*
Grenelle agreements, 85, 86
Groupe Filipacchi, 215
Groupe Hersant, 214–15
Groupe Le Monde, 216
Groupes de presse communistes, 216
Guilhaume, F, 244
Gulf War, 153–4, 204

Habitations à loyer modéré (HLM), 120
Hachette-Presse, 214
Haut Comité de la Population, 109
Haut Conseil à l'Intégration, 119
Haute autorité, la, 240
Haute autorité de la communication audiovisuelle, 242
Héberlé, J.-C, 242
Helsinki conference (1973), 129
Henri, A, 92
Hersant, R, 243
Humanité, L', 222–3

immigration, 2, 5–6, 99–124; and the armed forces, 120–1
income, 17–18
Institut français d'opinion publique (IFOP), 27
Institut national de la statistique et des études économiques (INSEE), 17
Institut national d'études démographiques (INED), 23
Institut universitaire Saint-Pie X, 198
Iran-Iraq War, 139–40
IRCAM, 32
Islam, 117

Jeunes Chrétiens Service, 202
Jeunesse agricole chrétienne (JAC), 9
Jeunesse catholique ouvrière (JCO), 200
Jews in French community, 190
Jobert, M, 129

John-Paul II, Pope, 203
Jospin, L, x, 67, 178
Jouhaux, L, 78–9
Journal du Dimanche, Le, 230
Joxe, P, 191
July, S, 222
Juppé, A, 56
Juquin, P, 57

Kaspar, J, 88
Kohl, H, 147
Krasucki, H, 88

Lacrampe, Bishop A, 201
Laguérie, P, 197
Lang, J, ix, 31, 32, 261
Lazareff, P, 221
Lefebvre, M, 193–9, 203
Legrande report, 171
Léotard, F, 67
Le Pen, J.-M, 40, 62–3, 100, 108, 116, 199
Libération, 222
Lire, 235
loi Defferre, 259
loi d'orientation (1989), 167
loi Gayssot, 119
loi Joxe, 114, 119
loi le Chapelier, 73
loi Pasqua, 112
Lomé convention, 142
Lustiger, J, 192, 195, 199, 202, 203–4
lycées, 20, 22
lycées professionnels, 161

Maastricht treaty, 40, 152
Maire, E, 81, 86, 88, 90
Maison de la culture, 29–30
Maisons des jeunes, 29
Maisons familiales, 27
Malraux, A, 29
marriage, 15, 23
Marty, cardinal, 194–5
Mauroy, P, 93
May Events (1968), 60, 73, 77, 80, 84–7, 95, 179–80, 208; and broadcasting, 241

métropoles d'équilibre, 12
military service, 1
Milli Gorus, 191
Ministère à la Ville, 119
Ministère de la Culture, 25
Ministère du Temps Libre, 25
Minister for women's rights, 16
minitel, 260
Minute, 116, 233
Mission de France, 200
Mitterrand, F, 31, 36–7, 55, 56, 60, 65, 66, 67, 114, 133, 141; and broadcasting, 242; and the EC, 146–7; and education, 174; and foreign policy, 143–54; and television, 260–1
Mollet, G, 55
Monde, Le, 219–21
Moslems in French community, 121–3, 190–3
Mouvement des radicaux de gauche (MRG), 56, 60
Mouvement républicain populaire (MRP), 58

Napoleon, 9
National Assembly, 36, 37
NATO, 127, 129, 148
New Towns, 3
Nouveau parti socialiste, 45
Nouvel Observateur, Le, 230, 231–2
nuclear arms, 127, 129, 134–5, 147

Office national de l'immigration, 109
oil, 131, 139–40
Organization for Economic Co-operation and Development (OECD), 18
Organization of African Unity (OAU), 141
Ouest-France, 208, 215, 225, 226

Palestine Liberation Organization (PLO), 139
Paul VI, Pope, 194
Paris, 3, 10–13
Paris Commune, 46, 76

Parisien (libéré), Le, 219
Paris-Match, 232
Parti communiste français (PCF), 17, 18, 37, 48, 52, 53, 55, 57–8, 60, 61, 63, 75, 79, 85, 87, 88, 89, 92–3, 96, 222
Parti radical, 47, 56, 60
Parti républicain (PR), 47
Parti socialiste (PS), 21, 36, 37–8, 39–40, 45, 47, 53, 54, 55–6, 57, 60, 61, 63, 67, 87, 91
Pasqua, C, ix, 56
Pétain, Marshal P, 199
Peyrefitte, A, 241
Pinochet, 199
Planchon, R, 30–1
Polisario front, 141
Pompidou, G, 32, 66, 128–32; and broadcasting, 240
Popular Front, 25, 79
population, 11–12
Présent, 199
press, the, 207–37; and advertising, 212–14; and the arts, 235–6; and the catholic church, 233; economic and financial, 234–5; and news agencies, 216–17; Parisian dailies, 217–18; periodical press, 229–36; and political parties, 232–4; regional dailies, 224–9; women's weeklies, 234
Prisma Presse, 215
Promouvoir la fraternité, 204
Protestants, 189

Quotidien de Paris, Le, 223

Radical Party, *see Parti radical*
radio, 245–9; networks, 245; *périphériques*, 245, 248; pirate, 246; public service, 247
Radio-France, 247
Radios locales privées (RLP), 246
Radio télévision française (RTF), 241
Rassemblement pour la République (RPR), 36, 53, 54, 55, 56, 61, 62

Reagan, R, 147
refugees, 106–8
Républicains indépendants (RI), 47, 133
Rerum Novarum, 74
Resistance, 74, 79
retirement, 2, 15
revolutionary syndicalism, 78
RFO, 251
Rigout, M, 57
rioting, 5–6
Rocard, M, ix, x, 37, 39, 44, 55, 108, 149–50, 192
Roland, M, 92
RPR-UDF, 39, 40, 48, 62
Rushdie, S, ix, 192
Russian Revolution, 79

Salaire minimum interprofessionnel de croissance (SMIC), 17, 85
SALT 2, 135
Sarcelles, 3
Savary, A, 93, 171, 175
Schengen Agreement, 114
Schmidberger, F, 198
Schmidt, H, 138
Scrutin uninominal majoritaire à deux tours, 42
Second Vatican Council, 193, 198
Second World War, 2, 24, 74, 79, 100
Section française de l'internationale communiste, 45
Section française de l'internationale ouvrière (SFIO), 45, 47, 55, 60, 74, 80
Seguin, P, ix, 56, 93
Séguy, G, 85, 88
Seydoux, J, 243, 252
Single European Act (SEA), 147, 212
Siri, cardinal, 203
social classes, 16–20, 28
Socialisme et république, 56
Socialisme maintenu, 56
Socialist Party, *see Parti socialiste*
Société européenne de programmes de télévision, (la SEPT), 250

Société française d'enquêtes par sondages (SOFRES), 94
Société française de production, 253
standard of living, 16–17
Stoléru, L, 100
suburbs, 2–3, 11
Sudreau Report, 73, 81
Syndicat national de la petite et moyenne industrie (SNPMI), 95

teachers, 19
Tedjini Haddam, Sheik, 192
television, 49, 203, 249–54; and advertising, 212–14, 253, 254–6; audience figures, 254; cable, 259–62; commercial channels, 251–3; local television, 262; and the press, 234; public service channels, 249–51; satellite, 260, 262–5; subscription television, 251, 258; and video, 265
TF1, 251, 254–5
Théâtre de Villeurbanne, 30
Théâtre national populaire, 30
Third Republic, 46, 63, 210
Third World, 132, 142
tourism, 10
trade unions, 9, 21, 29, 71–97
tronc commun, 20

unemployment, 2, 5, 14, 71; amongst immigrants, 105; youth unemployment, 157

Union de la gauche, 60, 61
Union des sénateurs non-inscrits, 41
Union du rassemblement et du centre (URC), 39
Union française, 101
Union pour la démocratie française (UDF), 36, 53, 61
Union pour la France (UPF), 46
Union républicaine et démocrate–Parti réformiste, 44
United Nations (UN), 135
USA, 127, 129, 130, 132, 133, 136, 137, 141, 144, 148
USSR, 126, 129, 130, 136, 137, 148

Vacances-Loisirs-Familles, 27
Verts, les, 40, 44, 49, 58
Viannet, L, 90
Vichy regime, 210
Vilar, J, 30
Villages-Vacances-Familles, 27
Ville, M, 187
Voix du nord, La, 225

Warcholak, S, 95
women: in employment, 2, 6, 10, 23; social position of, 15–16; unemployment among, 14

Yamgnane, K, 119
Yeltsin, B, 151
Yugoslavia, 151
Youssof Leclercq, D, 191